Kubany and Ralston have developed a systematic approach to the treatment of PTSD in battered women that is firmly grounded in empirically-supported principles of cognitive behavioral therapy. This approach is tested in research and comprehensively described in this clear, session-by-session procedural guide, which is complete with client handouts and homework forms. This manual is a crucial resource for anyone treating women traumatized by intimate-partner violence and abuse.

> —Josef I. Ruzek, Ph.D., acting director of the Education Division of the National Center for PTSD located in the Veterans Administration Palo Alto Health Care System in Menlo Park, CA

Finally, a manual that describes a highly effective cognitive-behavioral treatment for PTSD in formerly battered women—boasting a 90 percent recovery rate—with such detail that even helpers with no prior psychotherapy training have used it successfully. Experienced therapists treating PTSD in any population will also find this volume of value for its brilliant integration and sequencing of interventions that prepare real world clients for success with the difficult but essential exposure components of PTSD treatment. Highly recommended for every clinician who treats trauma, and essential reading for therapists who treat battered women.

> —Irene G. Powch, Ph.D., psychologist on the PTSD Clinical Team at the Portland Veterans Administration Medical Center, and faculty in the Division of Psychology, Department of Psychiatry at Oregon Health and Science University

At last! A book that addresses the unique struggles of battered women in their battle to reclaim their dignity and personal power. Kubany and Ralston have done a masterful job applying the proven principles of cognitive behavioral therapy to the specific issues that plague abused women. This concise, well organized guide is a must-read for anyone in the field of domestic violence.

> —Aphrodite Matsakis, Ph.D., practicing psychologist with more than thirty years of experience working with trauma survivors, including abused women, and author of twelve books on trauma-related subjects

Kubany and Ralston have produced a superb clinical guide that clearly describes and richly illustrates their state-of-the-art, empirically supported cognitive-behavioral treatment of PTSD in formerly battered women. The book offers a masterful synthesis of science and clinical wisdom that guides therapists through the complexities of treating PTSD in survivors of domestic violence. The volume is essential reading for anyone who works with survivors of spousal abuse.

—Steven Taylor, Ph.D., ABPP, professor of psychiatry in the Faculty of Medicine at the University of British Columbia, and author of *Clinician's Guide to PTSD: A Cognitive-Behavioral Approach*

Written by clinical scientists, this volume is an excellent resource for clinicians from all disciplines who are interested in learning specific strategies for addressing problems associated with surviving domestic violence. In addition to providing specific guidelines for treating PTSD symptoms, the authors deal with related problems, including mistrust of others and managing contact with abusers. The chapters on guilt and negative self-talk present best-practice procedures for psychological interventions with these clinical problems, which are commonly associated with surviving a battering relationship. The authors include data on the efficacy of this approach, providing yet another reason to consider this volume as an outstanding source of information on treatment in this area. Guidelines for modules provide objectives for sessions, homework assignments, and handouts that can be photocopied for clients. While the treatment of battered women has been of clinical interest for many years, this text is one of the first to present treatment strategies based on empirical findings. This important text will definitely be an asset to practitioners who are new to this area, as well as experienced providers in the field.

—Victoria M. Follette, Ph.D., chair of psychology and professor of clinical psychology at the University of Nevada, Reno, and clinical scientist specializing in the treatment of trauma in women

Treating PTSD *in* Battered Women

A Step-by-Step Manual
for Therapists & Counselors

EDWARD S. KUBANY, PH.D., ABPP
TYLER C. RALSTON, PSY.D.

New Harbinger Publications, Inc.

Distributed in Canada by Raincoast Books

Copyright © 2008 by Edward S. Kubany and Tyler C. Ralston
New Harbinger Publications, Inc.
5674 Shattuck Avenue
Oakland, CA 94609
www.newharbinger.com

"No Longer 'A Worthless Person'" by Helen Altonn, originally published on September 6, 1999, is reprinted with permission of the Honolulu Star-Bulletin.

"Abused Women to Share in New Therapy Project" by Helen Altonn, originally published on September 6, 1999, is reprinted with permission of the Honolulu Star-Bulletin.

"New Hope for Battered Women" by Seabrook Mow, originally published on August 9, 2000, is reprinted with permission of MidWeek.

Attitudes About Guilt Survey on page [181] and Thinking Errors That Contribute to Guilt on page [191] from Kubany, E. S., & Manke, F. P. (1995). Cognitive therapy for trauma-related guilt: Conceptual bases and treatment outlines. *Cognitive and Behavioral Practice, 2,* 27-61. Reprinted with permission.

Negative Self-Talk Monitoring Form on page [56] from Kubany, E. S., & Watson, S. B. (2002). Cognitive trauma therapy for formerly battered women with PTSD (CTT-BW): Conceptual bases and treatment outlines. *Cognitive and Behavioral Practice, 9,* 111-127. Reprinted with permission.

Final paragraph of relaxation script text on page [78] from Knox, D. (1971). Marriage happiness. Champaign, IL: Research Press. Reprinted with permission.

Clinicians may freely copy and use the handouts in this book in their own practice, but all other rights are reserved.

Printed in the United States of America

Acquired by Catharine Sutker; Cover design by Amy Shoup;

Edited by Jasmine Star; Text design by Tracy Carlson

Library of Congress Cataloging-in-Publication Data on file with publisher

10 09 08
10 9 8 7 6 5 4 3 2 1   First printing

To Belinda and Anamaria

—ESK

To KR, GR, GR, and PW

—TCR

Contents

Introduction

The intervention described in this manual, cognitive trauma therapy (CTT), represents an innovative advance in the study of psychosocial interventions in at least two respects. First, the intervention directly targets and addresses symptoms of post-traumatic stress disorder (PTSD) in battered women. Although some counseling or therapy approaches for battered women have been reported, these accounts are largely descriptive or anecdotal in nature, they haven't generally been aimed directly at PTSD, and few have been subjected to peer review (e.g., Douglas & Strom, 1988; Goodman & Fallon, 1995; Walker, 1994).

A second way in which this intervention is innovative is in how the treatment is described. Cognitive trauma therapy, is highly psychoeducational, and its delivery is described more specifically than any other psychotherapeutic intervention of which we are aware. For example, most procedures are described in such detail that they can literally be read or paraphrased by therapists conducting CTT. Moreover, as you will learn, CTT has proven to be highly efficacious in two treatment-outcome studies.

THE NEED TO TAILOR PTSD TREATMENT FOR BATTERED WOMEN

PTSD became an official psychiatric diagnosis in 1980 (American Psychiatric Association). It is a pernicious and widespread problem affecting an estimated 10.4 percent of U.S. women and 5.4 percent of U.S. men at some point in their lives (Kessler, Sonnega, Bromet, Hughes, & Nelson, 1995). PTSD symptom clusters include (a) *reexperiencing the trauma* (for example, unwanted intrusive memories or distressing trauma-related dreams), (b) *avoidance* (for example, efforts to avoid thinking about the trauma), (c) *emotional numbing* (for example, being emotionally cut off from other people), and (d) *hyperarousal* (for example, insomnia or difficulty concentrating). In addition, trauma-related guilt, anger, and grief, while not considered key features in making a PTSD diagnosis, are commonly associated with PTSD. Depression and many other psychiatric problems often co-occur with PTSD, and PTSD is also a risk factor for serious medical problems (see Kubany, Leisen, Kaplan, & Kelly, 2000, for a brief review). Moreover, PTSD is often a chronic condition. For example, it has been estimated that more than one-third of those diagnosed with PTSD still have the condition five years later (Kessler et al., 1995).

In recent years, a number of treatments for PTSD have been developed and evaluated. Cognitive behavioral interventions, in particular, have yielded promising results (see Blake & Sonnenberg, 1998; Foa & Meadows, 1997). Much of the PTSD treatment-outcome literature has focused on women survivors of sexual abuse or assault. Studies of cognitive processing therapy (CPT) for rape victims (e.g., Resick & Schnicke, 1992) and prolonged exposure (PE) for the treatment of rape-related PTSD (e.g., Foa & Rothbaum, 1998) have achieved reductions or elimination of PTSD in a substantial proportion of clients treated.

Yet, until recently (Kubany, Hill, & Owens, 2003; Kubany, Hill, et al., 2004), there were no published treatment-outcome studies targeting the alleviation of PTSD in battered women or female survivors of domestic violence, who as a group comprise one of the largest traumatized populations in North America (Council on Scientific Affairs, American Medical Association, 1992), if not the world (Heise, Ellsberg, & Gottemoeller, 1999). According to the National Violence Against Women Survey (Tjaden & Thoennes, 2000), almost 25 percent of American women are raped or physically assaulted by a current or former spouse, cohabitating partner, or dating acquaintance at some time in their life. According to the survey, approximately 1.5 million American women are raped or physically assaulted by an intimate partner each year. Rates of PTSD among battered women are much higher than in the population at large (Kubany, Haynes, et al., 2000; Kubany, Leisen, et al., 2000; see Kubany & Watson, 2002). For example, the prevalence of PTSD among women in shelters for battered women has ranged from 45 to 84 percent (see Kubany, Abueg, et al., 1995).

The intervention described in this book is a cognitive behavioral treatment tailored to the needs of women who suffer from PTSD related to abuse by an intimate partner. CTT has been shown to be effective in two randomized controlled research trials (Kubany et al., 2003; Kubany, Hill, et al., 2004). Intended for women who are no longer in an abusive relationship, the treatment includes elements adapted from existing, empirically supported PTSD treatments, such as psychoeducation, stress management, and exposure (e.g., Foa & Rothbaum, 1998; Resick, Nishith, Weaver, Astin, & Feuer, 2002). CTT also addresses other issues especially relevant to battered women, such as self-advocacy strategies, managing stressful contacts with former abusers, avoiding revictimization, and correcting problematic beliefs related to guilt, shame, and anger (e.g., Kubany & Watson, 2002).

Because CTT is a highly structured and primarily educational intervention, paraprofessional counselors with little or no prior training in conducting psychotherapy can learn to conduct CTT. Research comparing use of this approach by professionals versus paraprofessionals or others with little or no formal psychotherapy training suggests that the latter group achieves therapeutic outcomes comparable to those of professional therapists (e.g., Christensen & Jacobson, 1994; Faust & Zlotnick, 1995). More specifically, in the second treatment-outcome study of CTT, positive results were achieved by therapists with no prior psychotherapy training (Kubany, Hill, et al., 2004). For example, two therapists with only baccalaureate degrees were successful in helping 91 percent of their clients overcome PTSD.

These findings may have important public health implications because the majority of victim services providers who counsel and conduct support groups for battered women are paraprofessionals with no formal training in psychological or psychiatric counseling. Such individuals represent a large pool of potential counselors who could be trained to conduct CTT. Dissemination of CTT into the hands of victim services providers may represent an extraordinary, cost-effective way to reach countless thousands of formerly battered women who aren't presently receiving effective treatment for post-traumatic stress.

WHAT THE LITERATURE TELLS US ABOUT PTSD IN BATTERED WOMEN

There is considerable evidence that cognitions or beliefs play an important role in the intractability and chronic nature of post-traumatic stress (e.g., Foa, Ehlers, Clark, Tolin, & Orsillo, 1999; Kubany et al., 1996). Much of this research has focused on survivors' conscious evaluations of their role in their trauma, much of which has to do with experiences of guilt and self-blame (see Kubany, 1998, for a brief review). In fact, guilt is a common problem among women who have been physically or sexually abused.

There is considerable evidence that cognitions or beliefs play an important role in the intractability and chronic nature of post-traumatic stress (e.g., Foa, et al., 1999; Kubany, et al., 1996). Much of this research has focused on survivors' conscious evaluations of their role in their trauma, much of which has to do with experiences of guilt and self-blame (see Kubany, 1998, for a brief review). In fact, guilt is a very common problem among women who have been physically or sexually abused. In a study of 168 women in support groups for battered women, 49 percent had at least moderate guilt related to their abuse. In a study of 212 physically and/or sexually abused women with PTSD based on structured interviews, 75 percent had at least moderate abuse-related guilt (Kubany, 2000).

Higher-order language conditioning may be the mechanism that accounts for the observation that memories of trauma can still evoke emotional pain and symptoms of post-traumatic stress long after the trauma has ended (Kubany & Watson, 2002). Memories of traumatic events can elicit painful guilt- and shame-related appraisals, such as "I should have left sooner. Why did I stay so long? I must be stupid." If emotion-eliciting appraisals like these are chronically paired or associated with memories of trauma, the memories can be expected to continue to elicit emotional pain due to higher-order language conditioning (see Staats, 1972, 1996). In addition, emotionally painful guilt and shame appraisals may provide self-punishment that serves to strengthen or maintain depression (Pitman, et al, 1991). Extinction of emotional responses to memories of trauma may be hindered by insufficient exposure to these memories because of the natural tendency to suppress or avoid memories that evoke emotional pain (Rohrbaugh, Riccio, & Arthur, 1972).

Based on a review of the literature on battered women, Kubany and Watson (2002) identified several issues faced by many battered women that can complicate their treatment and which may be important to address in interventions: guilt and shame issues, prolonged or repeated trauma, ongoing contact with former abusers, and risk of revictimization. First, many battered women have guilt and shame issues that are unique to the population, such as guilt and shame related to a "failed" relationship, to effects of the violence on any children, or to decisions to stay in or leave the relationship. Many battered women may require specialized cognitive interventions that target these complicated cognitive issues.

Second, many battered women who seek treatment have experienced prolonged, repeated trauma. Not only are they likely to have been repeatedly traumatized by intimate partners in multiple ways (for example, threats, stalking, and sexual abuse), many battered women also have histories of exposure to other forms of interpersonal violence, such as physical or sexual abuse in childhood (e.g., Street, Gibson, & Holohan, 2005; see table I.1, derived from Kubany, Hill, et al., 2004). Such repeated abuse in a variety of forms may contribute not only to the severity of PTSD but also to collateral problems, such as tolerating disrespect and not being assertive. Self-advocacy and empowerment issues (e.g., Ozer & Bandura, 1990) may be particularly important to address in treatments for battered women.

Third, the lives of many formerly battered women remain enmeshed with their ex-partners because these men are fathers of their children, and this continuing contact is a frequent source of stress (Shalansky, Ericksen, & Henderson, 1999). Many formerly battered women would benefit from interventions that enable them to effectively manage stressful contacts with former abusers (e.g., Kubany, Hill, et al., 2004).

Fourth, many battered women are at risk for revictimization by subsequent intimate partners. For example, in one study, 51 percent of battered women had been physically hurt by more than one intimate partner (Kubany, Hill, et al., 2004). Learning how to identify potential abusers would be an important element to include in any comprehensive recovery program for battered women, and the approach we present here does include such education.

Table I.1. Partial Trauma Histories of 125 Battered Women (Other Than Partner Abuse)

Type of Trauma	N	%
Sudden or unexpected death of loved one	96	77%
Growing up: witnessed family violence	63	50%
Growing up: physically abused	79	63%
Physically assaulted by acquaintance or stranger	36	29%
Sexually abused: before age 13	69	55%
Sexually abused: ever	105	84%
Miscarriage	44	35%
Abortion	64	51%

OVERVIEW OF COGNITIVE TRAUMA THERAPY (CTT) FOR BATTERED WOMEN

CTT includes several elements adapted from existing cognitive behavioral treatments for PTSD, including psychoeducation about PTSD, stress management (with relaxation training), talking about the trauma, and exposure homework. In addition, CTT includes specialized procedures for reducing negative self-talk and assessing and correcting irrational guilt-related beliefs. CTT also includes interventions addressing issues that can complicate the treatment of battered women. These interventions focus on self-advocacy and empowerment and include education on self-advocacy strategies, building skills in assertive communication, managing stressful contacts with former abusers, and learning how to identify potential perpetrators, thereby enabling women to prevent revictimization.

The course of treatment includes fifteen modules that are used with all clients, five optional modules addressing issues that may be less relevant for some clients, and a closing module that is used with all clients. Most modules require one to two sessions to complete with the exception of the module on guilt, which usually takes four to five sessions. The number of sessions needed to complete each module can vary depending on the client's specific trauma issues. Obviously, it will also vary depending on length of sessions. Fifty minutes is most typical, so table I.2 outlines how the modules are utilized in a fifty-minute session format.

Table 1.2. Conducting CTT in a Fifty-Minute Session Format with a Typical Client

Module	Module Title	Typical # of sessions required	Session(s) in which module is typically conducted
1	Beginning Treatment	1	1
2	Monitoring Negative Self-Talk	.25	2
3	Stress Management I: Education About Stress	2	2-4
4	Stress Management II: Progressive Muscle Relaxation	1	4 or 5
5	Trauma History Other Than Partner Abuse	1	5
6	Education About PTSD	2	6-7
7	Exposure Homework	.5	8
8	Learned Helplessness and How to Overcome It	1.5	9-10
9	Education About Negative Self-Talk	1	11-12
10	Addressing Trauma-Related Guilt	4-5	13-17
11	Challenging Guiding Fictions and "Supposed to" Beliefs	1	17-18
12	Assertiveness Training	1.5	19-20
13	Managing Mistrust	.5	21
14	Identifying Potential Abusers	1.5	21-22
15	Managing Unwanted or Stressful Contacts with Former Abusers	1	23
16	Managing Anger (optional)	1	varies
17	Personality Characteristics of Abusive Partners (optional)	1	varies
18	Countering Ideas of Denial and Codependence (optional)	1	varies
19	Making Important Decisions (optional)	1	varies
20	Implications and Consequences of Remaining in an Abusive Relationship (optional)	1	varies
Last	Self-Advocacy Strategies Revisited	1	varies

Module 1: Beginning Treatment

The main purposes of the first module are to establish rapport, obtain a partner abuse history, provide an overview of the therapeutic approach, and briefly discuss topics to be addressed. In a ninety-minute session format, the first session also includes module 5, the inquiry into other significant traumatic experiences based on responses to the Traumatic Life Events Questionnaire (TLEQ; Kubany, Haynes, et al., 2000), which clients complete prior to the start of the first session. (The TLEQ is available from Western Psychological Services.) In a fifty-minute session format, this inquiry occurs after modules 3 and 4, on stress management. At the end of session 1, clients are given a variety of homework assignments, including a handout asking them to write what they believe about twenty-five self-advocacy strategies. Giving this assignment at the beginning of treatment provides clients with a sense of what they want to accomplish in therapy, highlights issues that will be addressed in subsequent modules, and often has immediate positive effects on optimism and symptom levels. Clients are given the assignment again prior to the last session, when the self-advocacy strategies are revisited and elaborated upon.

Module 2: Monitoring Negative Self-Talk

Starting in session 2, and at the beginning of every subsequent session, clients are asked their reactions to the previous session and what they learned from listening to the recording of the last session, "over and above what you got out of the session itself." Then homework assigned at the previous session is reviewed. Systematic observation or self-monitoring of behavior can facilitate breaking maladaptive habits (Korotitsch & Nelson-Gray, 1999; Frederiksen, 1975). In module 2, clients are introduced to the topic of negative self-talk and instructed on how to monitor it using a self-monitoring form on which they record observations of themselves engaging in four categories of negative self-talk. This ongoing homework assignment is introduced early in therapy because of the important role negative self-talk plays in producing and maintaining negative mood states, and to ensure that clients have sufficient time during the course of therapy to break negative self-talk habits. This module takes only ten to fifteen minutes.

Modules 3 and 4: Stress Management

Module 3 starts with psychoeducation on stress and stress management. The therapist emphasizes the strong relationship between physical stress and mental stress and explains the importance of keeping one's body relaxed. In module 4, clients are first instructed in tensing up and releasing muscles as a means of relaxing and letting go of tension, and then they are instructed in progressive muscle relaxation (PMR) using a scripted exercise. The client is given a homework assignment of doing PMR with a twenty-minute audio-recording twice a day for the duration of therapy. This recording may be made as

PMR is conducted during the session, or a prerecorded PMR exercise may be used. (A PMR recording is available for downloading at www.treatingptsd.com.) Finally, clients are taught how to systematically scan their major muscle groups to identify which muscles tense up in response to stress. They are instructed to do a body scan and relax affected muscles when experiencing stress during the week. These relaxation strategies enable most clients to regulate their moods by lowering their tension levels.

Module 5: Trauma History Other Than Partner Abuse

After the module on stress, the therapist reviews the client's history of exposure to prior trauma other than partner abuse based on the client's responses to the Traumatic Life Events Questionnaire (TLEQ), which clients complete prior to the first session. This review allows clients to vent about traumatic experiences that may continue to have an emotional impact and enables therapists to identify guilt and grief issues about trauma other than partner abuse (for example, childhood sexual abuse), which may be addressed in subsequent sessions.

Module 6: Education About PTSD

In this module, therapists provide psychoeducation about PTSD and the rationale for exposure homework. In the course of this education, the client learns that her symptoms are a normal response to extreme stress, which is reassuring. Clients also learn that asking "why" questions usually leads to guilt and anger, causing symptoms to persist, and that escape and avoidance strategies only provide temporary relief. The primary purpose of this module is to normalize clients' perceptions about PTSD and to increase clients' motivation to do the exposure homework.

Module 7: Exposure Homework

In this module, the therapist negotiates with the client to do a homework assignment of systematically experiencing nondangerous reminders of the abuse and her abuser. A typical exposure assignment is for a client to devote ten minutes a day to looking at pictures of her abusive partner or visualizing him while simultaneously experiencing other reminders that will heighten the reality of the experience (for example, smelling the ex-partner's cologne or cigarette smoke, or listening to music her partner liked). Clients are also asked to watch two movies on domestic violence: *Sleeping with the Enemy* and *Once Were Warriors*.

Module 8: Learned Helplessness and How to Overcome It

In this module, therapists provide psychoeducation on learned helplessness, which fosters passivity and beliefs that problems can't be solved (e.g., Peterson & Seligman, 1983). Therapists emphasize the importance of cultivating a problem-solving attitude and focusing on solutions rather than obstacles. This orientation inspires hope and ultimately helps women achieve better outcomes that are more likely to serve their best interest.

Module 9: Education About Negative Self-Talk

The primary objectives of this module are to maximize clients' motivation to break negative self-talk habits and to ensure their full compliance with the negative self-talk monitoring assignment. Toward these ends, therapists elaborate on reasons that each category of negative self-talk is detrimental to clients' emotional well-being and their ability to think clearly.

Module 10: Addressing Trauma-Related Guilt

This module directly targets trauma-related guilt through a highly structured approach that involves identifying guilt issues, completing the Attitudes About Guilt Survey (AAGS; Kubany & Manke, 1995), a guilt incident debriefing, and psychoeducation about guilt. This is followed by cognitive therapy proper, which involves exercises in logic for correcting thinking errors that lead to faulty conclusions associated with guilt (Kubany & Manke, 1995; Kubany & Ralston, 2006). The thinking errors are addressed in the context of four semistructured exercises in which clients are taught to distinguish what they knew in the past from what they know now: a foreseeability and preventability analysis, a justification analysis, a responsibility analysis, and a wrongdoing analysis.

Module 11: Challenging Guiding Fictions and "Supposed to" Beliefs

In this module, clients learn about some common "supposed to" beliefs that women acquire while growing up. These beliefs keep many women subordinate in relationships with men and often contribute to women's decisions to stay in abusive relationships. The accuracy of these guiding fictions is challenged in an exercise designed to help clients understand why they stayed with an abusive partner as long as they did.

Module 12: Assertiveness Training

The emphasis of the assertiveness module is on the importance of advocating for one's rights and not tolerating disrespect. Clients are taught to identify aggressive or disrespectful speech in others, and modeling and role-playing are employed to provide practice in responding to hostile and disrespectful comments. This module is designed to teach clients to deal more effectively with verbal aggression, to be less intimidated by aggressive people or authority figures, and to increase their sense of self-efficacy.

Module 13: Managing Mistrust

In this module, clients are taught how mistrust develops and explore the idea that battered women often rely on gut feelings as a cue for keeping their distance from men. Clients learn that gut feelings aren't evidence and can't be relied upon to make informed decisions, but that gut feelings may be a signal to look for evidence as to whether someone is trustworthy.

Module 14: Identifying Potential Abusers

This module is directed at increasing the client's ability to identify potential abusers, thereby enabling her to prevent future victimization. In the first part of this module, the therapist describes twenty red flags that suggest someone has the potential to become abusive. In the second part of this module, the client learns what she can do during the early stages of a relationship to elicit behavioral tendencies that indicate someone is likely to become abusive. For clients, developing confidence in their ability to identify potentially abusive men before they become emotionally involved can be very empowering.

Module 15: Managing Unwanted or Stressful Contacts with Former Abusers

Many battered women have at least occasional contact with former abusive partners, and these encounters are often stressful. These interactions arise for a variety of reasons: sometimes about issues related to the children, sometimes about desires to reconcile, and sometimes apparently just by way of harassment. In this module, the therapist emphasizes the importance of keeping these interactions brief and having a plan of what to say and do if a former abusive partner calls or if there is face-to-face contact. Sometimes the therapist and client will practice anticipated interactions using modeling and role-playing.

Module 16 (Optional): Managing Anger

The module on managing anger is conducted if the client's comments during therapy indicate that anger is an issue for her. In this module, clients learn that even if anger is considered legitimate, it usually isn't in a person's best interest, and that anger is often only a source of pain for the angry person—not for the target of the person's anger. The therapist explains that trauma survivors who aren't angry usually have fewer PTSD symptoms than those who hold on to anger, that spending time being angry is usually a very poor use of a person's time, and that letting go of anger involves a conscious decision.

Module 17 (Optional): Personality Characteristics of Abusive Partners

The module on characteristics of abusive partners is conducted with clients who blame themselves for getting involved with an abusive partner or think they have bad judgment in the men they date. Many battered women—and others who judge them negatively—believe they have poor judgment in their choice of men with whom they become involved. In this module, clients learn that in most cases it is the men who are choosing the women, not the other way around. Therapists teach clients that clinical evidence and some research evidence (e.g., Holtzworth-Munroe & Stuart, 1994; Waltz, Babcock, Jacobson, & Gottman, 2000) suggest that many male batterers have psychopathic personalities and that predatory men may know how to identify and seek out women who are vulnerable to being deceived and seduced into an abusive relationship.

Module 18 (Optional): Countering Ideas of Denial and Codependence

The module on denial and codependence is usually conducted if the client or someone else has labeled or referred to her as codependent or in denial—something that's all too common. Clients are taught that these are confusing, poorly defined concepts that are not useful for explaining why battered women remain in abusive relationships.

Module 19 (Optional): Making Important Decisions

The decision-making module is usually conducted if the client is facing an important decision or seems to be very indecisive. In this module, therapists teach clients a method of making decisions that is likely to promote their long-term best interests. Clients are taught to make decisions by intellectually weighing the likely short-term and long-term positive and negative consequences of each course of action under consideration.

Module 20 (Optional): Implications and Consequences of Remaining in an Abusive Relationship

While CTT is primarily directed at women who are safely and permanently out of an abusive relationship, occasionally CT is conducted with clients who are still involved with an abusive partner or are considering reconciliation with an abusive partner. In this module, therapists teach clients about several implications or potential negative consequences of staying in an abusive relationship. For example, if a battered woman is suffering from PTSD related to partner abuse, her PTSD is unlikely to go away if she remains in an abusive relationship—even if she hasn't been abused for a considerable period of time. Other issues include long-term guilt and modeling dysfunctional relationships for any children. The client also learns that it isn't likely that an abusive partner is going to change.

Last Module: Self-Advocacy Strategies Revisited

In this module, therapists review with clients their responses to handout 1.2, Empowering Yourself: Self-Advocacy Strategies, which clients complete for a second time as homework prior to this module. Therapists expand on the implications of using the strategies as guidelines for living one's life and reinforce clients' efforts and progress in self-advocacy.

DOES CTT WORK?

Two studies have been conducted to evaluate how well CTT works (Kubany et al., 2003; Kubany, Hill, et al., 2004). In an initial study, thirty-seven ethnically diverse formerly battered women were randomly assigned to an immediate CTT group or to a delayed CTT group (Kubany et al., 2003). During the waiting period to receive CTT, there were no significant reductions in symptoms among women in the delayed CTT group. Of the thirty-two women who completed CTT (86 percent of participants), all but two overcame their PTSD based on assessment by structured interviews. Compared to pre-therapy assessments, there were also significant reductions in depression, trauma-related guilt, and shame. Self-esteem scores increased a mean 92 percent. All gains were maintained at three-month follow-up assessments.

The second treatment-outcome study was conducted with 125 ethnically diverse formerly battered women using the same design employed in the initial trial. Of the women who completed CTT, 87 percent overcame their PTSD, with large reductions in depression and guilt and substantial increases in self-esteem. All ethnicities of women benefited equally from CTT, and therapeutic gains were maintained at three- and six-month follow-up assessments. These two studies represent the first published studies of a therapeutic approach specifically designed to treat PTSD in battered women.

IMPLEMENTING CTT

To implement CTT effectively, several considerations must be kept in mind, including setting, practitioner qualifications, and suitability of the client. The sections below also address various tools and methods used in this approach, including assessment tools, Socratic questioning, storytelling, homework, and tailoring the approach to the client.

Appropriate Settings

To date, CTT has been conducted almost exclusively in one-on-one individual therapy. Because it is primarily an educational approach, CTT also lends itself to delivery in a group format, but how it would need to be adapted and how effective it would be if delivered in a group setting is yet to be determined. Although the two studies described above indicate it is equally effective with clients from different ethnic backgrounds, we suspect that ethnic differences would be more likely to emerge if CTT were conducted in a group setting because of cultural differences in women's willingness to publicly disclose personally sensitive information.

CTT has not been conducted at shelters for battered women. If it were, it would be important to add a module on safety planning and to conduct module 19, on decision making, and module 20, on the implications of remaining in an abusive relationship, early in the protocol to help these women decide whether to permanently break off ties with an abusive partner. In addition, self-advocacy, which is an important theme throughout CTT, could be problematic, if not dangerous, for women who are in abusive relationships.

Who Is Qualified to Conduct CTT?

Clinicians interested in conducting CTT with battered women need to be well-informed about domestic violence issues (for example, safety issues, safety planning, confidentiality, custody options, and court orders) and would be well-advised to complete at least one of the widely offered multiday training workshops for people interested in working in the domestic violence field.

To become a competent CTT therapist, certain personal qualities are essential, in addition to knowing what content to deliver. These qualities include the ability to establish rapport and trust; the capacity to communicate genuine empathy, positive regard, and warmth; and, above all, a nonjudgmental attitude. Many paraprofessional victim services providers possess these qualities. Effective CTT therapists will also see themselves as advocates and mentors, and take a collaborative approach while using the Socratic method (discussed below) to challenge clients to think. Therapists must be comfortable allowing clients to cry and not be shy about asking personally sensitive questions. These qualities are not necessarily acquired during the process of formal or higher education.

In our experience, two of the most common types of complaints battered women make about previous therapy experiences are that their therapists told them to put the trauma behind them and get on with their lives, and that their therapists judged them negatively for staying in the relationship after the abuse first occurred. Related value judgments with connotations of blaming the victim include references to the women being in denial or codependent.

Who Is and Is Not an Appropriate Client for CTT

CTT is most applicable to women who are no longer in an abusive relationship, who have no intention of reconciling with an abusive partner, and who are for the most part safe. In certain respects, CTT may not be appropriate, or would have to be adapted, for women who are still in an abusive relationship or are considering reconciliation with an abusive partner. As mentioned above, safety concerns and safety planning, which are important topics in support groups for battered women, aren't emphasized in CTT. A module on safety issues and safety planning would be important to include early on if CTT were conducted with women who are currently in an abusive relationship.

Another reason why CTT isn't recommended for women who are currently involved with an abusive partner, also mentioned above, is CTT's focus on self-advocacy. In CTT, we strongly and repeatedly recommend that clients make getting their wants and needs satisfied a top priority. In this regard, we emphasize the importance of standing up for one's rights and not tolerating disrespect. While this kind of self-advocacy poses no risk for women who aren't in an abusive relationship or who are in the early stages of a new relationship, it is potentially dangerous in abusive relationships, where the dominant strategies for "keeping the peace" are for women to place their partners' wants above their own and to avoid conflict. And finally, the approach in this book includes only an optional module on decision making. For women in abusive relationships, decisions about whether to leave or reconcile with an abusive partner can be a critical and time-consuming process.

When someone is referred for CTT, we conduct a telephone screening to briefly get to know the woman and evaluate her appropriateness for the program. This screening includes brief questions to determine her history of partner abuse and how long she's been out of an abusive relationship. We also ask about several PTSD symptoms, including abuse-related guilt. We then give potential clients a brief overview of CTT and some of the issues and problems our approach addresses. If the screening indicates that a woman is likely to be a good candidate for CTT, we schedule an initial appointment. If the screening reveals that she isn't experiencing PTSD symptoms or is currently involved in an abusive relationship, she ordinarily isn't accepted for CTT treatment.

Formal Assessment in CTT

Before starting CTT, clients are administered a broad-spectrum measure of prior trauma exposure and several questionnaires to assess treatment outcomes. The Traumatic Life Events Questionnaire (TLEQ; Kubany, Haynes, et al., 2000; Western Psychological Services, 2003c) assesses exposure to twenty-one different types of potentially traumatic events. For each experienced event, respondents are asked if the event evoked intense fear, helplessness, or horror to determine if the event was a *traumatic* stressor (*DSM-IV-TR* PTSD criterion A2; American Psychiatric Association, 2000, p. 428). During CTT, clients are asked for details about traumatic events reported on the TLEQ to identify trauma issues other than partner abuse that may also need to be addressed, such as childhood sexual abuse, sudden death of a loved one, or abortion. The TLEQ is available commercially from Western Psychological Services (WPS), 12031 Wilshire Boulevard, Los Angeles, California, 90025; (800) 648-8857; fax: (310) 478-7838; e-mail: customerservice@wps publish.com; website: www.wpspublish.com. If you are unable to obtain the TLEQ, you may wish to utilize one of the trauma inquiry questionnaires in the public domain. Short of this, you may simply conduct an unstructured trauma history interview.

Questionnaires assessing PTSD, depression, trauma-related guilt and anger, and self-esteem are administered before and at the end of treatment to assess the effectiveness of CTT. These questionnaires include the PTSD Screening and Diagnostic Scale (PSDS; Kubany, Leisen, et al., 2000; Western Psychological Services, 2003a), the Beck Depression Inventory (BDI; Beck, Steer, & Garbin, 1988), the Trauma-Related Guilt Inventory (TRGI; Kubany et al., 1996; Western Psychological Services, 2003b), the Rosenberg Self-Esteem Scale (RSES; Rosenberg, 1965), and the Trauma-Related Anger Scale (TRAS; Kubany, 2000). The PSDS and TRGI are available from WPS; and the BDI is available from the Psychological Corporation. The RSES and the TRAS are in the public domain and may be duplicated freely, at no charge.

Learning to Conduct CTT

Throughout the manual, suggested actual wording for therapists to use when conducting CTT (hereafter referred to as the "therapist script") is formatted in a **bold font**. General instructions or guidelines for the therapist are in a regular font. Optional scripts are formatted differently, so that therapists can easily see where the optional text begins and ends; these scripts are formatted in a different font. This is not meant to imply that the general instructions and therapist guidelines are less important than the suggested therapist wording. Therapists need to become familiar with the instructions and guidelines before they start to conduct CTT, and may only need to refer back to these sections occasionally. Having the scripts for conducting CTT stand out in a bold font is simply intended to facilitate the smooth delivery of CTT. Occasionally, the scripts include brief bracketed material giving the therapist direction on what to say. These are not intended to be read aloud; rather, they are prompts for the therapist to deliver the information.

Having scripts is not meant to suggest that therapists need to rigidly follow the scripts verbatim. Experienced CTT therapists often paraphrase the scripts or use their own words for making important points. It is always a good idea to personalize the approach to the client's situation. The general instructions point out places where this is particularly important or relevant, such as in discussing the client's responses to a questionnaire. And of course, where the scripts include a question or a request for the client to elaborate on something, the therapist must pause to allow the client to respond.

Learning to conduct CTT fluently or skillfully requires a therapist to first become familiar with the material and ideally to practice using the manual with colleagues or friends who aren't actual clients. Therapists new to CTT tend to do a lot of formal lecturing or literal reading of manual procedures without much attention to increasing clients' active participation in the learning process. Reading aloud from the manual is expected and perfectly okay, and clients aren't put off when therapists do so. With experience, however, therapists can increasingly paraphrase the material, present certain memorized phrases in natural or conversational ways that don't appear memorized, and more easily engage clients by asking questions that stimulate clients to think critically.

Socratic Questioning

Socratic questions challenge the person queried to think critically. These questions typically require a narrative response, rather than calling for a simple yes or no answer. The interactive or Socratic style employed in CTT is somewhat different than that involved in "Beckian" or traditional cognitive behavioral therapy (CBT; e.g., Beck, Rush, Shaw, & Emory, 1979). CTT involves more formal education of the client than traditional CBT, as well as transmission of much more factual information. In traditional CBT for depression, therapists collaboratively involve clients in searching for answers to their dilemmas. They also refrain from imposing their views of the "facts" or giving clients specific answers to questions. In CTT, questioning is directed at getting clients to think critically and challenging them to discover answers that already exist.

Storytelling

An important identifying feature of CTT is the frequent or liberal use of storytelling—providing anecdotes or giving examples that illustrate important points or principles. One characteristic that differentiates experienced CTT therapists from novices is the number and richness of the stories they have at their disposal for illustrating concepts in CTT. With more anecdotes and examples to call upon, experienced CTT therapists are also more able than novices to tell stories that closely match or are directly relevant to specific issues being addressed.

Homework

Cognitive behavioral interventions employ homework as an important treatment component, and there is considerable homework in CTT. Throughout this manual, instructions guide the therapist in assigning homework, which includes listening to audio-recordings of therapy sessions, documenting negative self-talk, completing questionnaires, practicing progressive muscle relaxation, reading articles, and doing exposure exercises. This manual also includes forms and handouts for clients to use in completing homework.

Client Workbook

In 2004, New Harbinger published *Healing the Trauma of Domestic Violence: A Workbook for Women* (Kubany, McCaig, & Laconsay). This workbook for women suffering from PTSD due to partner abuse is written in a self-help format. Modules in this manual roughly correspond to chapters in the workbook, although they've been reorganized a bit. In the homework assignments in this manual, we indicate which workbook chapters correspond with the module. Therapists who plan to conduct CTT using this manual would be well-advised to have their clients purchase and work through *Healing the Trauma of Domestic Violence* while receiving CTT.

Tailoring CTT for Individual Clients

We believe that CTT works because it's tailored to meet the needs of the great majority of women for whom it is intended. As discussed above, it has proven successful in helping a wide variety of women overcome PTSD, regardless of their ethnicity or level of education. CTT modules addressing stress, PTSD education, negative self-talk, exposure to trauma reminders, alleviation of guilt, assertiveness, and managing contacts with former abusers are highly relevant for almost all formerly battered women with PTSD. And as a bonus, CTT's emphasis on self-advocacy addresses problems or concerns faced by many women in our male-dominated society, in which the needs and rights of women are often considered subordinate to the wants and rights of men.

The most common way that CTT is further tailored to individual clients is in the pacing of modules. There is some variability in the number of sessions it takes to complete the CTT protocol with different clients, due primarily to individual differences in client engagement or the number of traumas or guilt issues that need to be addressed.

The core modules are usually conducted in the sequence described in this manual. However, in some circumstances it may be advisable to conduct later modules earlier in the therapy. For example, a therapist may conduct the decision-making module out of sequence if the client is facing an imminent decision, such as whether to have an abortion, to move, or to file a restraining order. Or the therapist may conduct the module on dealing with unwanted contacts early on if the client is faced with current or ongoing harassment by anyone, including a former partner. It may be advisable to conduct the module on identifying potential abusers sooner if the client has recently started dating someone new, or the module on characteristics of abusive partners if the client is contemplating reconciliation with an abusive ex-partner.

HOW THIS BOOK IS ORGANIZED

After a brief introduction, each module presents lists of objectives, materials needed for that module, and homework assignments. Next is a checklist of module procedures, followed by detailed descriptions of module procedures, including therapist scripts. As therapists become familiar with the detailed procedures, they may choose to use the procedural checklists instead of relying on the detailed descriptions and scripts. One important note in regard to optional modules: If you decide any of these are appropriate for a client, read ahead to determine what homework to assign in the session prior to conducting any optional module.

Sequence in Which Modules Are Ordinarily Conducted

We will elaborate briefly on our rationale for conducting CTT modules in the sequence described in this manual. Our clinical experience has shown that it is a good idea for clients to start talking about traumatic experiences at the very first session. This initiates the process of overcoming trauma survivors' tendencies to avoid reminders of traumatic experiences. Also, we believe that talking about traumatic experiences in a nonjudgmental interpersonal atmosphere is therapeutic. Clients often cry when disclosing events that were highly distressing, and they typically feel better after they have cried. We believe that crying facilitates grieving, and clients are explicitly encouraged to cry, both in and out of session (for example, "I have plenty of tissue. Please don't try to hold back the tears").

In the second session, the therapist shifts the focus by addressing negative self-talk and stress. The therapist assigns homework for monitoring and breaking negative self-talk habits (module 2) and then focuses on managing stress (modules 3 and 4) to provide clients with some practical coping skills for regulating their levels of tension or emotional arousal. Having these skills will help clients cope with talking about traumatic experiences, and help them tolerate the exposure homework assigned a bit later in the course of CTT. Module 5, in which the therapist inquires about trauma history other than partner abuse, serves to identify other trauma issues that may need to be addressed and gives clients additional opportunities to discuss or disclose other emotionally charged memories or issues.

PTSD psychoeducation (module 6) sets the stage for the exposure homework by giving clients a strong rationale for the often difficult work of experiencing abuser- and abuse-related reminders. We assign exposure homework (module 7) early enough in therapy to be confident that clients will have sufficient time to overcome abuse- or abuser-related avoidance issues before the end of CTT. Module 8, on learned helplessness and how to overcome it, is an extension of the PTSD education module in which clients learn why PTSD may not diminish with the passage of time.

Module 9, which provides psychoeducation about negative self-talk, is particularly important for clients whose negative self-talk is still at a high level after eight modules. When negative self-talk remains high, PTSD symptoms almost always remain at relatively high levels too. With heightened motivation to break negative self-talk habits, most clients are able to reduce negative self-talk to an insignificant level by the end of therapy.

The guilt intervention (module 10) also addresses exposure and avoidance issues. For example, the guilt incident debriefings often require clients to revisit experiences of abuse, and here too, clients often cry while discussing and disclosing painful events from the past. The module on challenging "supposed to" beliefs or guiding fictions (module 11) is usually conducted directly after the guilt work because one of this module's goals is to put to rest any residual guilt about not having left an abusive partner sooner—an extremely common guilt issue among formerly battered women.

Building assertiveness skills (module 12) provides clients with practical self-advocacy skills for dealing with interpersonal conflict and getting their needs met in relationships. Of course, an important aspect of this is to avoid getting involved in abusive relationships in the future. To that end, module 13, on managing mistrust, teaches clients about some clues that are likely to indicate someone can't be trusted. Module 14 builds on this by teaching clients additional ways to tell whether someone is likely to become abusive. Module 15, on managing contacts with former abusers, builds directly on the assertiveness skills developed in modules 12 and 13.

The order in which the optional modules are conducted—most of which focus on some aspect of self-advocacy or self-empowerment—is somewhat arbitrary. The final module (Self-Advocacy Strategies Revisited) is in some respects a review or compilation of everything covered in earlier modules. The self-advocacy exercise in this module is typically uplifting for clients, as it heightens their awareness of how much they have overcome, learned, changed, and grown psychologically as a result of their experiences with CTT.

Sessions vs. Modules and Numerical Formatting of Manual

Since there is some variability in the number of sessions it takes to complete CTT with different clients, we decided to organize the manual by modules rather than by sessions. As stated earlier, the majority of modules take one to two fifty-minute sessions to complete. Because module durations don't correspond perfectly with session durations, modules often conclude and begin midsession. This hasn't been problematic for most clients, and therapists can note where sessions end by utilizing the numerical formatting system in the manual, which separates module sections or subtopics into numerical segments: 10.1, 10.2, 10.3, and so on. The number before the decimal point signifies the module number; the numbers after the decimal point signify the section and correspond to the numbers in the procedures checklist near the beginning of the chapter. In many cases, sessions may be ended at meaningful junctures by concluding at the end of a section and writing down the numerical marker for where to resume at the next session (for example, "Resume at 10.14").

When CTT is conducted in a fifty-minute session format, which is most common, it usually takes about twenty-five sessions to complete the protocol. Table I.2 shows how many fifty-minute sessions are typically required to complete each module and the session numbers in which modules are conducted with a typical client.

PROCEDURES FOR BEGINNING AND ENDING SESSIONS

There are several therapist instructions and scripts that aren't module specific, relating instead to topics addressed at the beginning and end of most sessions after the first session. Because sessions can break at various points in a module, and because this manual is organized by module not by session, this seemed to be the most logical place for these therapist instructions and scripts. As you're learning to conduct CTT, you may find that copying the sections below on procedures for beginning and ending sessions and placing the copy on top in the client's file will cue you to remember to follow these therapist instructions and scripts until they become habits.

Procedures for Beginning Sessions

At the beginning of every session, turn on the audio-recorder. **What were your reactions to our last session? How did you apply what you learned in the last session? What did you learn from listening to the recording of the session, over and above what you got out of the session itself?** If the client didn't listen to the recording, emphasize its importance and secure her commitment to listen to the recording of the previous session and the current session by the next meeting by asking, **Will you make a point of listening to the recording of the last session and this session by our next appointment?** Say something similar for all other incomplete homework assignments.

Because modules and sessions don't necessarily coincide, we aren't able to provide reminders about asking the client about her homework at an appropriate point in the script. Whenever assigning homework, it would be a good idea to place a note in the client's file as a reminder to ask about the homework at the start of the next session. Because some homework assignments are ongoing, we've provided scripts for asking the client about them.

At the beginning of every session **after module 2**, in which homework on monitoring negative self-talk is assigned, ask, **How is the self-talk monitoring going?** Always ask to see the client's self-monitoring form and review it with her.

At the beginning of every session **after module 4**, on progressive muscle relaxation, ask, **How is the progressive muscle relaxation going?**

After going over any homework, therapists may wish to summarize the agenda for the current session. This can help keep the session on track and help the client understand why side issues aren't explored.

Procedures for Ending Sessions

When closing sessions, always ask the client what she got out of the session: **We're going to wrap up now. What did you learn today? Is there anything else you got out of today's session?** At the end of every session, label the audio-recording with the date and the client's initials and give it to her for listening homework.

Therapist Planning and Client Progress Notes

To assist you in documenting clients' progress and planning for future sessions, we have included a template for session 1 in the materials for module 1. A similar template, included in the materials for module 2, may be used for session 2 and all subsequent sessions.

CONCLUDING REMARKS

As with most major endeavors, cognitive trauma therapy for battered women is a work in progress. Although it is highly effective in its current form, refinements and improvements are continually being made. We encourage you to check our website, www.treatingptsd .com, for updates, additional handouts, and further documentation of results obtained with this approach.

We wish you great success in conducting CTT and hope you find this therapy as rewarding as we have. If you have been accustomed to conducting therapy in an unstructured way or are uncomfortable conducting therapy in a highly structured and prescribed fashion, please be patient. After you have conducted CTT with a few clients, we believe you will be impressed with the outcomes and will become comfortable with the CTT style of delivery.

Beginning Treatment

As this is the beginning of treatment, emphasis is placed on developing the therapeutic relationship. Subsequent modules focus on assisting the client in learning and understanding the content of each module. Developing a healthy therapeutic relationship is key to a strong foundation for CTT. This is accomplished in module 1 by developing good rapport with the client, allowing her to come to trust you as the therapist, and engendering hope and an eagerness to learn more. At the end of the session, most clients are eager for the next session and are already feeling more hopeful.

OBJECTIVES

■ To develop rapport and engender the client's trust

■ For the client to get used to talking about experiences of abuse in an atmosphere of nonjudgmental acceptance

■ To engender hope in the client

■ To get the client to look forward to subsequent sessions and be enthusiastic about coming to therapy

MATERIALS

■ Audio-recorder (needed for all sessions)

■ Overview of Topics in Cognitive Trauma Therapy (handout 1.1)

- Empowering Yourself: Self-Advocacy Strategies (handout 1.2)

- Is Anger Worth the Hangover? Strategies for Letting Go (handout 1.3)

- Symptoms of Post-traumatic Stress (handout 1.4)

- *MidWeek* article: "New Hope for Battered Women" (handout 1.5)

- CTT Homework Assignments checklist (handout 1.6)

- Therapist Planning and Client Progress Notes for session 1

HOMEWORK

- Listen to the audio-recording of this session (continuing assignment).

- Complete the questionnaire Empowering Yourself: Self-Advocacy Strategies (handout 1.2).

- Complete the questionnaire Is Anger Worth the Hangover? Strategies for Letting Go (handout 1.3).

- Study the PTSD symptoms list (handout 1.4).

- Read the *MidWeek* article "New Hope for Battered Women" (handout 1.5).

PROCEDURES CHECKLIST

1. _____ Obtaining permission to audio-record the session

2. _____ Introduction

3. _____ Five to ten minutes of small talk

4. _____ Inquiry into prior or current other therapy and domestic violence counseling

5. _____ Inquiry into problems that have brought the client to therapy

6. _____ Inquiry into the history of the client's relationship with her abusive partner(s) and the abuse (saving the last twenty to thirty minutes of the session for items 8 and 9 no matter how far you get in partner abuse history exploration)

7. ____ Inquiry about the client's history of trauma other than partner abuse (only in ninety-minute session format)

8. ____ Explanation of CTT's theoretical orientation and the therapy process

9. ____ General guidelines for the therapy process

10. ____ Overview of topics that will be covered in therapy (handout 1.1)

   ▪ Stress and relaxation

   ▪ Exploration of trauma history other than partner abuse

   ▪ PTSD education

   ▪ Education on why negative self-talk is detrimental

   ▪ Guilt—the good news and the bad news

   ▪ Assertiveness

   ▪ How to manage stressful or unwanted contacts with former abusers

   ▪ How to identify potential abusers

   ▪ Self-advocacy strategies

11. ____ Assigning homework

   ▪ Empowering Yourself: Self-Advocacy Strategies (handout 1.2)

   ▪ Is Anger Worth the Hangover? Strategies for Letting Go (handout 1.3)

   ▪ Symptoms of Post-traumatic Stress Disorder (handout 1.4)

   ▪ *MidWeek* article: "New Hope for Battered Women" (handout 1.5)

   ▪ Give the client handout 1.6 (homework assignments checklist), to help her keep track of homework assignments

12. ____ Asking the client what she got out of the session

DETAILED PROCEDURES FOR MODULE 1

1.1. Obtaining Permission to Audio-Record the Session

We routinely audio-record therapy sessions and ask clients to listen to the recordings as homework. You must obtain permission from the client to record the sessions.

Before we get started formally, I'd like to talk about audio-recording our sessions together. One advantage of having the recording would be for you to be able to experience the therapy from a different perspective than you do as a client. You'd be able to listen to it from the perspective of an outsider or third person, listening to a therapist and a client interacting. A second advantage of having the recordings is that it would remove the pressure of having to absorb everything during the session itself. And because there's so much education in this therapy, remembering everything that happens during our session based solely on your memory of the session would be difficult at best. You could listen to the recordings at your leisure and even take notes, which many clients do. I'll give you the recordings at the end of each session. They are for you to keep. Many women listen to the recordings more than once. **May I have permission to record our sessions?** Clients almost always give permission to record the sessions. If a client refuses, proceed without recording the sessions.

1.2. Introduction

The purpose of our first session is for me to get to know you, for you to get to know me, and for you to tell me about the problems you're having that brought you to therapy. During the second half of our session today—no matter how far we get in talking about issues you're trying to deal with—I'll give you a brief overview of the theoretical approach in this form of therapy and of the topics we'll cover in subsequent sessions.

1.3. Small Talk

Spend about five to ten minutes on small talk. The main purposes of the small talk are to establish rapport by showing interest in the client as a person, to get to know a little bit about her generally, and to put her at ease by discussing topics that are easy to talk about and not overly personal or threatening.

Here's an example: **Are you originally from [this city or town]?** If not: **How long have you lived here? What brought you here? Do you like living here? Do you have any brothers or sisters? Are you close? How far did you get in school? Where did you go to school? Are you employed?** If yes: **How long have you done this kind of work? Do you like it? Do you have children?** If yes: **Where do your children go to school?** Please note: Here, and in all subsequent scripts, the therapist must pause between questions, and sometimes after statements, to allow the client to respond.

1.4. Prior Therapy and Domestic Violence Counseling

The main purposes of this inquiry are to learn a little about the client's history and her evaluation of any prior counseling experiences, to find out whether she has sought domestic violence services, and to help her further warm up to talking about the personal problems that are the main reasons she's seeking therapy at the present time.

Have you ever had psychotherapy or counseling? If yes: **Tell me about that.** If the client has seen more than one therapist or counselor, ask her to give a brief summary of whom she saw and when. For each therapist seen, ask, **What kinds of problems was that therapist helping you with? Did it help? Have you ever received services from an agency that serves battered women?** If yes: **What agency? What kinds of services did you receive? Were you in a support group? Did you finish the program? Have you ever gone to a shelter for battered women?** Why?

1.5. Problems That Brought the Client to Therapy

Now I'd like you to tell me about problems you're having that are reasons for coming to therapy ... Have you been abused by more than one intimate partner? Who abused you? If the client has been abused by more than one partner: **Who were these people? What were their first names and when were you involved with them?**

1.6. History of the Client's Relationships with Abusive Partners and the Abuse

Tell me how you met [the abusive partner] ... What did you like about him? How did the relationship change over time? When did he first hurt you? What did he do? Please briefly describe two of the worst or most distressing incidents of abuse ... How did the relationship end? If the client has had more than one abusive partner, repeat the above questions for each partner, starting with the first one.

1.7. Other Traumatic Experiences Inquiry

When CTT is conducted in a ninety-minute session format, the inquiry about trauma history other than partner abuse is conducted now. In the more typical fifty-minute session format, this inquiry is conducted immediately after completion of the stress management modules (3 and 4). Therapist procedures for conducting the inquiry into other trauma history appear in module 5.

1.8. Theoretical Orientation and Approach to Therapy in CTT

During the last twenty to twenty-five minutes of the session, give the client an overview of CTT's theoretical orientation and what will be covered in subsequent sessions. If the partner abuse history has not been completed, which is rare, tell the client you will complete it later, after the stress management module, and make a note reminding you to do this.

Now I'll share a little bit about the theoretical orientation of the form of therapy we'll be using. This approach is based on the view that therapy is a learning or educational process rather than a medical treatment. PTSD isn't a sickness, like the flu. Rather, PTSD can be understood in terms of unhealthy thoughts, emotions, and behaviors that you've learned, often through subtle but pervasive social conditioning, or socialization. This is why I refer to the people I see as clients rather than patients. In fact, there is so much education in this program that I could just as easily refer to you as a student and myself as a teacher.

Another important part of this approach is that problems of depression and anxiety are seen more as thinking problems than as emotional disorders. How we think affects how we feel. If we change our thinking, we'll feel better. Similarly, in PTSD, the meaning that trauma has for the survivor has everything to do with the degree to which the person can recover from the effects of the trauma. There's some good news and some bad news. The bad news is that we can't change or undo what happened. I wish we could, but we can't. *Optional humor:* If I could change what happened, I would definitely raise my fees. However, the good news is that we may be able to change your interpretation of what happened.

1.9. General Guidelines for the Therapy Process

I'm going to give you lots of education—lots of information. I'll give you tools—thinking tools and behavioral tools—that will empower you and enable you to take control of your life and determine your own future happiness. I encourage you to take notes. You may want to bring a notebook.

If the client agreed to recording her sessions: As you know, I'm recording our sessions, and I'll give you the recordings to listen to for homework. This will help you remember what you learned here and help you to process the material. I'm also going to give you lots of homework to reinforce the learning that takes place during therapy sessions.

At the end of every session, I'll ask you, "What did you learn today? What did you get out of today's session?" This will help bring to the forefront of your mind some of the most important things you learned during the session. Asking you what you learned also holds me accountable. Very few therapists ask this question, and many wouldn't want to know the answer. If I ask you what you learned today and you say "nothing," then I'm not doing my job.

At the beginning of each session, I'll ask you, "What were your reactions to the last session? How did you apply what you learned in the last session?" I'll have an agenda for each session and will try to stick to that agenda. Related to sticking to the agenda, I see myself as your advocate. As such, I'll always try to act in your best interest, and I'll encourage you to act in your best interest too. As part of being your advocate, I want us to make the best possible use of our time together. For everything we talk about, there are many other things we can't talk about. So if I notice you getting off the subject, talking about something that may be interesting but not as important as something else, I'll interrupt and steer you back to our agenda. This isn't because I'm not interested; it's because we need to make the best possible use of our time.

Another way of thinking about our relationship is as a partnership—a collaboration or team effort, very much like a coach and an athlete. To be successful, both must do their share. In fact, what you do between sessions is just as important as what goes on during sessions—sometimes even more important. Between our sessions, it's very important that you give a lot of thought to what went on in therapy and try to apply what you learned. In this regard, it's also very important that you do the homework.

This form of therapy is called cognitive trauma therapy, or CTT. It's very goal-oriented and structured, with very clear objectives that we're trying to accomplish during every session. The therapy will be primarily focused on issues related to the traumas you've experienced and your PTSD. Other issues and concerns, such as employment, problems with the children, housing, and finances, won't be addressed.

1.10. Overview of Topics Covered in CTT

Now I'll give you an overview of the topics we'll cover in the course of your therapy. Give the client handout 1.1, Overview of Topics in Cognitive Trauma Therapy. The next two sentences require modification if session duration is other than fifty minutes. We'll have about twenty-five fifty-minute sessions, give or take a few, and we'll meet once a week.

For the next three sessions, I'll teach you about stress and how to manage it. We'll talk about how controlling or reducing physical tension results in less mental stress and can improve your mood. I'll talk to you about seven different reasons you want to keep tension in your body at a low level. For example, if your muscles are relaxed, you're much more likely to be in a good mood than if your muscles are tense. I'm also going to teach you how to relax and how to practice relaxing. By relaxing your body, you'll be able to relax your mind. I'll teach you a method of relaxation called progressive muscle relaxation, which involves sequences of tensing and relaxing your muscles. I'll give you a recording of that relaxation exercise, which I want you to use at least twice a day.

After our sessions on stress management, I'll ask you about other traumatic events you may have experienced in addition to partner abuse. If you've experienced other traumas, it may be necessary for you to address them to fully overcome your PTSD.

Next, I'll teach you about PTSD. I'll help you understand why trauma produces the same kinds of symptoms and reactions in everyone, and you'll learn that your memories and other reminders of traumatic experiences aren't dangerous. I'll also explain why avoiding memories and other reminders of your trauma only gives you temporary relief, and how this temporary relief is causing your PTSD symptoms to persist. Relief-seeking behavior is the major reason that people come to therapy, because temporary relief maintains all kinds of bad habits and unhealthy behaviors that aren't in a person's best interest. I'll have much more to say about this later.

After the PTSD education, I'll ask you to confront some things you've probably been avoiding as a result of your history of abuse. For example, I'll ask you to engage in activities that remind you of your abusive partner. This may not make sense to you now, but it will later.

Next, I'll teach you about learned helplessness, which has been widely used to explain depression. As a result of their history of abuse, many battered women come to believe that they have very little power and that they aren't good at solving their problems. Many battered women continue to have this attitude even after they're safely out of an abusive relationship. We'll discuss the importance of developing a problem-solving attitude, which focuses on finding solutions, to replace an attitude that focuses on obstacles and reasons why problems can't be solved.

The next topic will be reasons why certain ways that you may be talking to yourself, both in your speech and in your thoughts, aren't in your best interest. The purpose of this is to maximize your motivation to stop using certain words and phrases, such as "should have," "could have," and asking why, in your speech and in your thoughts. Using these words and phrases is just a habit, and you will be able to break it.

Following this, we'll address your guilt and I'll teach you how to feel less guilty. There's some good news and some bad news about guilt. The bad news is that guilt is a very common and severe problem among trauma survivors. For example, in a study of 168 women in support groups for battered women, only 6 of the women had no guilt related to their abuse (Kubany et al., 1996). The good news is that trauma survivors tend to exaggerate the importance of their roles in the trauma and tend to experience guilt that has no rational or logical basis. This means you can change the degree to which you experience guilt by correcting this faulty thinking.

When we reduce your guilt, any shame you're experiencing will go away, your self-esteem will improve, your depression will lift, and your PTSD symptoms will diminish. To address your guilt, I'll engage you in an exercise in logic in which you'll learn to develop an objective and realistic appraisal of your role in your trauma. This may involve working on more than one guilt issue.

After working on guilt, we'll take a look at a related topic: "supposed to" beliefs, which can be heavily involved in guilt. These are beliefs about things you think you're supposed to do or ways you think you should behave. All of us learn these beliefs from an early age, often in subtle ways. Some of the common beliefs about how women are supposed to behave definitely aren't in your best interest, so we'll refer to them as "guiding fictions." We'll take a close look at how these guiding fictions may have influenced you to stay in an abusive relationship as long as you did.

The next topic we'll look at is assertiveness and how to be more effective and promote your best interest in your communication with other people. I'll teach you how to identify disrespectful or aggressive speech in others, then I'll teach you how to handle aggressive speech by responding to the style of the message rather than the content. This will increase your confidence and help you to deal effectively with aggressive people. It may also help you be less intimidated by aggressive people or authority figures. We'll practice these skills using modeling and role-playing.

The next two topics are related: trust and how to identify potentially abusive men. You'll learn that feeling safe or unsafe isn't a solid basis on which to make decisions about trust, although your feelings may be a signal to look for objective evidence as to whether a person is trustworthy. Then I'll teach you how to distinguish men who are likely to treat you with respect from those who won't. I'll do this in two ways. First I'll teach you about a number of red flags that will help you identify people who are likely to become abusive. Then I'll teach you what you can do early in the relationship, when things are just wonderful, to bring out signs that indicate a person has the potential to become abusive.

One of our final topics will be how to deal with unwanted or stressful contacts with your former partner; for example, what to say if you run into him or if he calls you on the phone. We may role-play what you could say. The assertiveness skills I'll be teaching you will come in handy here.

During the later sessions, we may work on some additional topics, depending on their relevance for you. The first optional topic is how to manage and let go of anger. The second optional topic will help you understand the personality characteristics of abusive partners and show you that these men are often predatory. The third optional topic addresses the concepts of denial and codependency, including why these concepts are neither accurate nor helpful. The fourth optional topic involves how to make important decisions you may be facing and how to figure out what course of action is likely to promote your long-term best interest. The fifth optional topic explores implications and consequences of staying with an abusive partner.

You and I will decide together which of these optional topics are the most important and relevant for you, and we'll work on them in the order in which they are priorities or important concerns for you. We may not be able to get through them all, but we'll try to cover those that are high priorities.

In our last session, we'll look at self-advocacy—ways of thinking and acting that will help you manage stress, take control of your life, and help you overcome PTSD. Self-advocacy and its importance are themes that are addressed throughout CTT, and concluding with self-advocacy strategies will tie together much of the material covered throughout our sessions together.

1.11. Homework

As part of your homework before our next session, I'd like you to complete this questionnaire on self-advocacy strategies. Give the client handout 1.2, Empowering Yourself: Self-Advocacy Strategies. Following each set of statements, I'd like you to write down what you believe about that strategy. Then I'd like you to write down how important it would be for you to adopt that strategy as a guideline for living your life. When women first come to therapy, most of them haven't been living their lives according to these statements.

For example, look at item 1: "Getting my wants and needs satisfied is more important than satisfying the needs of someone else." Most of my clients have spent a large part of their lives taking care of other people and trying to avoid disapproval. When they put themselves first, they think they're being selfish and rude, which often leads to guilt. But if you don't put yourself first, who will? It's very important that you become your own strongest advocate, because this will empower you.

We won't spend much time in our next session talking about your responses to the self-advocacy strategies questionnaire. But this exercise may provide you with a road map of what you'd like to accomplish in therapy. Most women really like these strategies. I'll have you complete this assignment a second time before our last session, when we'll take a closer look at these strategies. You may be very surprised at how much your answers change by the last session. Strategies that may at first seem foreign to you will probably start to feel comfortable and fit, just like a new hairstyle or pair of shoes that you become accustomed to over time.

Give the client handout 1.3, Is Anger Worth the Hangover? Strategies for Letting Go. Before our next session, I'd also like you to read and complete this questionnaire on letting go of anger. It will provide you with some food for thought and may help you start to let go of anger if that's an issue for you.

Give the client handout 1.4, Symptoms of Post-traumatic Stress Disorder. I'd also like you to read this handout on symptoms of post-traumatic stress disorder. Please examine this list before our next session, when I'll ask you what you think about these symptoms as they relate to you.

Give the client handout 1.5, the *MidWeek* article "New Hope for Battered Women." I'd also like you to read this short article about CTT, "New Hope for Battered Women." I'll ask you what you got out of reading this article at our next session.

Give the client handout 1.6, the CTT Homework Assignments checklist. Here's a to-do list. I'll fill in today's date next to all the homework assignments I've given you today. To-do lists are for reminding you to do important things, and doing the homework is important because it will contribute to your ability to overcome post-traumatic stress. The homework checklist contains most of the homework assigned through the course of CTT. It's especially useful for the first session, where the client receives a number of homework assignments. Using this template for future homework is a matter of therapist preference.

1.12. Closing the Session

Even though the major purpose of today's session was for me to hear from you and find out what kinds of problems you've been having, I'm going to end this session the way we'll end all of our sessions. What is something you've learned today? What have you gotten out of this session? Anything else?

CONCLUDING REMARKS

Clients typically have a positive response to the first session. Responses we look for and often hear are that the first session has engendered hope, that clients are enthusiastic about or look forward to future sessions, that the topics mentioned are seen as relevant, or that the program described is seen as doable. Very rarely, clients are at a loss for words about what they learned (sometimes because of evaluation anxiety or perceived pressure to respond), or they may say that they don't know what they learned. If a client doesn't come up with a response to the closing questions, you may suggest that she take notes while listening to the recording of the session and report back about what she learned at the beginning of the next session.

Handout 1.1: Overview of Topics in Cognitive Trauma Therapy

Education about stress

Progressive muscle relaxation

Exploration of trauma history other than partner abuse

Education about PTSD and exposure assignments

Learned helplessness and how to overcome it

Education about the harmful effects of negative self-talk

Assessment and treatment of trauma-related guilt

Challenging guiding fictions or "supposed to" beliefs

Training in assertive communication skills

Managing mistrust

How to identify potential abusers

Managing unwanted or stressful contacts with former abusers

Managing anger (optional)

Personality characteristics of abusive partners (optional)

Addressing concepts of denial and codependence (optional)

Making important decisions (optional)

Implications and consequences of staying with an abusive partner (optional)

Self-advocacy strategies revisited

Handout 1.2: Empowering Yourself: Self-Advocacy Strategies

Client Initials: _____   Date: _____

To recover fully from the effects of trauma, it is in your best interest to become your own strongest advocate. This handout lists twenty-five self-advocacy strategies that will promote your best interest and empower you. If you embrace and come to live by these statements, your recovery from trauma will go forward at a rapid pace.

After each set of statements, please write down what you believe about that set of statements. Also indicate how important or relevant each self-advocacy strategy is for you (that is, how important it is for the ideas expressed to become true for you, or how important it would be for you to adopt that strategy as a guideline for living your life).

1. Getting my wants and needs satisfied is more important than satisfying the needs of someone else. It is in my best interest to advocate for my needs and wants as a top priority. Advocating for my best interest means doing things and making decisions that promote long-term happiness and quality of life for me (and my children).

    _____

    _____

    _____

2. Getting my wants and needs satisfied belongs at the top of my daily to-do list. If I don't put myself first, who will? If I get my needs satisfied, I will have more energy to satisfy the wants and needs of others.

    _____

    _____

    _____

3. It does not promote my long-term happiness to think or talk about things I cannot change, such as dwelling on the unfairness of the system or past injustices. The time I spend on such things is time I can't spend working on things I can control, change, or do something about. In business, they call this an opportunity cost. Time spent doing things of little value costs us the opportunity of spending that time doing something more worthwhile. In other words, spending time on things I can't change does not belong on my daily to-do list!

    _____

    _____

    _____

4. To get my needs met, it is in my best interest to tell people how I feel (for example, "I'm upset" or "My feelings are hurt") and what I want (for example, "I would appreciate it if …"). Other people can't read my mind and won't know how I feel or what I want unless I tell them.

_____

_____

_____

5. It is in my best interest to stand up for my rights and not allow myself to be taken advantage of. I not only deserve respect, I must demand respect. To demand respect means not tolerating disrespect.

_____

_____

_____

6. It's a good idea to make decisions based on what is in my best interest (and my children's best interest). It is in my best interest to stop doing things because I think I should. The question to ask myself when trying to decide what to do is "What course of action is most likely to promote my long-term happiness or quality of life?"

_____

_____

_____

7. When I do something or make a decision in order to get immediate relief from painful feelings, chances are good that I'm not acting in my best interest.

_____

_____

_____

8. If a decision will lead to either guilt or resentment, go with guilt! (Because this means it's more likely I will be acting in my best interest rather than someone else's.)

_____

_____

_____

9. Strong feelings associated with thoughts or ideas are not evidence that those ideas are correct (or incorrect). It is not in my best interest to make important decisions based on how I feel about things; important decisions should be made on the basis of the evidence and an intellectual analysis of what is in my best interest.

_____

_____

_____

10. If I'm in a high state of distress (anxiety, worry, dread, depression, and so on) about an important decision I think I have to make, any course of action that will give me immediate relief from this distress is not likely to be in my best interest. It has been said that "when anxiety goes up, IQ goes down." If I achieve a state of calm before making important decisions, I will be more objective and think more clearly.

_____

_____

_____

11. Just because somebody says that I have negative qualities does not mean it's true. However, I do not have control over the words that come out of other people's mouths. It is in my best interest to remember that words are just sound waves (not fists or baseball bats).

_____

_____

_____

12. Just because someone blames or blamed me does not mean it was my fault.

_____

_____

_____

13. Just because someone apologizes to me for some wrongdoing does not mean I am obligated to do what that person wants or to go back to the way things were, whether or not I forgive the person.

_____

_____

_____

14. If I never say "could have" or "should have" again, I will be a happier person.

_____

_____

_____

15. Tearing myself down with put-downs, such as "I'm worthless (stupid, never going to be happy, and so on)," makes me feel depressed and want to give up or go away. It is in my best interest to treat myself with the same respect that I would like to get, and deserve to get, from others.

_____

_____

_____

16. When talking about things I don't like about myself, it's much better to say "This is the way I have been (or have done things) in the past," rather than "This is the way I am (or what I always do)." The second wording implies that this is the way I am always going to be; the first implies that I can do things differently in the future.

_____

_____

_____

17. Just because I think a thought or have an idea does not mean the thought or idea is true. It is in my best interest to stop automatically believing everything that comes into my mind. Some thoughts may just be superstitious habits. It is in my best interest to evaluate the evidence for some of the "weird" or "crazy" ideas that pop into my mind.

_____

_____

_____

18. It is in my best interest to stop saying "I feel" with words that aren't emotions (for example, stuck, obligated, overwhelmed, and so on). Instead, ask myself what the evidence is for *thinking* that I'm stuck, obligated, overwhelmed, and so on. If I evaluate the evidence for these negative ideas, I may realize I'm not really stuck, obligated, overwhelmed, or whatever.

_____

_____

_____

19. It is in my best interest to stop asking why. Knowing why will not change what happened, and it keeps me stuck in the past.

_____

_____

_____

20. I may have been helpless and out of control when I was abused by my partner or as a child, but I am not powerless or out of control now!

_____

_____

_____

21. If I focus on possible solutions to my problems, I may solve them. If I focus on reasons why my problems can't be solved, my problems will only be solved if I get lucky.

_____

_____

_____

22. I am an innocent survivor and am likable and lovable. I also deserve to be happy!

_____

_____

_____

23. When a woman says "I feel sorry for him," she is making the other person's problem _her_ problem. If I "feel sorry" for my abuser, I may believe that I'm supposed to do something about it—something he would like me to do, such as go back to him or stay in the relationship. This is faulty thinking! If I do something he wants because I "feel sorry" for him, I may be putting his wants above my own (and my children's) best interest. It's important to act in my best interest whether or not I "feel sorry" for him.

_____

_____

_____

24. When a woman says "I had to," it usually means she chose to. Ordinarily, only children, slaves, prisoners, and people threatened with violence have to comply. In most cases, when I do something that I think somebody expects when I don't want to, I *choose* to do it, rather than have to do it. This distinction is important because when I have choices, I have power and am in control. When I perceive myself as not having choices, I think I'm powerless and out of control. For example, when I say someone is taking advantage of me, it usually means that I'm allowing that person to take advantage of me. This latter way of looking at the situation implies that I can do something to stop the "unfair treatment" and prevent it from happening in the future.

_____

_____

_____

25. When I get out of bed tomorrow, who is going to decide whether or not I'm going to have a good day? Me? Or someone else? Of course, I *want* to be the one who decides. However, I may put others in control by hoping that they won't ruin my day by treating me in a certain way or by saying something I don't want to hear. In that scenario, someone else is deciding whether or not I have a good day. If I'm worried that someone might ruin my day by acting in a certain way, I'm only going to have a good day if I get lucky. This is like being in a rudderless boat and hoping or praying that a friendly wind will blow me ashore rather than out to sea. On the other hand, if I know I'm going to have a good day no matter what somebody else says or does, I am in control of my well-being.

_____

_____

_____

Overall comments on how these self-advocacy strategies can have a positive effect on my recovery or quality of life:

_____

_____

_____

_____

_____

_____

Handout 1.3: Is Anger Worth the Hangover? Strategies for Letting Go

Client Initials: _____   Date: _____

1.   If I get angry about what someone else did (or continues to do), that person is still controlling my feelings; that is, they are still able to make me feel bad.
       Do I want this person to be able to control how I feel?

       _____

       _____

2.   Anger and resentment do more damage to the "container" in which they are stored than to the "object" on which they are poured.
       What do I believe about this statement and how is it relevant for me?

       _____

       _____

       _____

3.   In some ways, getting angry or resenting someone is like taking poison and waiting for the other person to die.
       What do I believe about this statement and how is it relevant for me?

       _____

       _____

       _____

4.   To forgive means "to pardon." To pardon means "to release from punishment." If I pardon a guilty person, it does not excuse the person's crimes or suggest that they did not occur. It only means that continued punishment is not worth the energy and cost it would require.
       Would I want to spend the rest of my life as my ex-partner's jailer or warden? What kind of life would that be?

       _____

       _____

       _____

5.   What am I going to do tomorrow? Read the newspaper. Go to work. Clean the house. Go shopping. Have a little fun. And spend ten minutes being angry at someone? Would this be a good use of my time? Would I put "spending time being angry" on my daily to-do list? Will getting angry improve my day or my future? If it's only

going to make me feel worse, I need to take it off of my to-do list. If getting angry isn't going to improve my day, getting angry is not in my best interest.

What do I believe about this statement and how is it relevant for me?

_____

_____

_____

6. Letting go of anger isn't some kind of mystical process; actually, it's quite straightforward. Letting go of anger simply involves a decision. Anger requires rumination. It requires a memory or thought about unfair treatment, often accompanied by thoughts of wanting to hurt someone or see them suffer. In other words, anger is a choice. And because it's a choice, anger is controllable. I can choose to stop being angry. If I make a decision to stop ruminating or obsessing about unfairness, I will start breaking the anger habit. Change the subject! It doesn't belong in my head.

What do I believe about this statement and how is it relevant for me?

_____

_____

_____

7. "Why would anyone be so cruel?" "Why is the system so unfair?" "Why me?" Immediately after asking why I or a loved one has been treated unfairly, it's important to quickly ask myself a second question—a "what" question: "What am I going to do about it?" If the answer is "nothing" (to improve the situation), I'm wasting my time. Make a decision to change the subject and stop ruminating or obsessing in a way that just makes *me* feel bad. Anyway, there is only one good answer to those kinds of "why" questions. Damn bad luck! What happened may have been tragic, but I didn't deserve it. Now that I know why, I can stop asking why.

What do I believe about this statement and how is it relevant for me?

_____

_____

_____

8. "There's no justice! It's not fair. I was set up—deceived! How dare he (she, they)! How could anyone be so cruel? Why would someone do something like that? Senseless! It never should have happened! Pig. Scum. Low-life bastard! I hate his guts. I hope he rots in hell!" Feel better now? Not likely. Using emotionally charged words that convey anger and hostility only makes me feel bad and doesn't solve anything. When thinking about a perpetrator or some injustice, I will feel less bad if I use neutral or descriptive words rather than evaluative or judgmental words—if I talk about it like it's on the front page rather than the editorial page.

What do I believe about this statement and how is it relevant for me?

_____

_____

_____

9. Do I want some past perpetrator or abuser to control how I feel? Of course not! On the other hand, if I get angry when I think about him or what he did, that person is still controlling how I feel. If he were watching me, he would be laughing and thinking, "See? I can still get a rise out of her. I can still jerk her around and push her buttons!" If he can no longer get a rise out of me, I have taken my power back. My goal may be something like this: Let's say that the person I've been mad at walks right between me and my therapist. My therapist asks, "Who was that?" and I answer, "Who was who?"

    What do I believe about this statement and how is it relevant for me?

_____

_____

_____

10. Directing anger at others antagonizes them, alienates them, makes them angry too, and escalates conflict. It increases the chances they will say something hostile in return and decreases the chances that they'll do what I want them to do. If my goal in communicating is to piss people off or make them upset, by all means, I should get angry. On the other hand, if my goal is to get someone to do what I want them to do, I may want to express my unpleasant feelings as distress, rather than as anger. For example, I can say "I'm frustrated," "I'm upset," or "My feelings are hurt." Expressing negative feelings as distress is much more likely to elicit empathy and compassion and not anger. It's always worthwhile to think about what I want to accomplish in my communication before I express anger.

    What do I believe about this statement and how is it relevant for me?

_____

_____

_____

Overall comments on how these strategies for letting go of anger can have a positive effect on my future happiness or quality of life:

_____

_____

_____

Handout 1.4: Symptoms of Post-traumatic Stress Disorder

The following symptoms (American Psychiatric Association, 1994) are normal and common reactions to highly stressful or traumatic events—events that often evoke intense fear, helplessness, or horror.

1. Unwanted thoughts about the event when nothing has happened to remind you

2. Distressing dreams or nightmares about the event

3. Suddenly reliving the event, experiencing flashbacks of the event, or acting or feeling like it was actually happening again

4. Distress when reminded of the event

5. Physical reactions when reminded of the event, such as sweaty palms, rapid breathing, pounding heart, dry mouth, nervous stomach, or tense muscles

6. Efforts to avoid thoughts or feelings that remind you of the event

7. Efforts to avoid activities, people, or places that remind you of the event

8. Inability to recall important parts of what happened

9. Loss of interest in important activities, such as your job, hobbies, sports, or social activities

10. Feeling detached or cut off from others around you

11. Feeling emotionally numb—unable to feel tenderness, loving feelings, or joyful feelings, or unable to cry

12. Thinking your future will be cut short in some way; for example, no expectation of a career, a serious relationship, or children, or expectations of a premature death

13. Trouble falling asleep or staying asleep

14. Irritability or outbursts of anger

15. Difficulty concentrating

16. Being alert, watchful, or on guard; for example, looking around you, checking out noises, or checking to see if windows and doors are locked

17. Being jumpy or startled by sudden sounds or movements

18. Feeling guilt related to the event or feeling upset because you think you should have thought, felt, or acted differently

19. Feeling anger related to the event or feeling upset because you think *someone else* should have thought, felt, or acted differently

20. Grief, sorrow, or feelings of loss in regard to loved ones, belongings, identity, self-worth, faith in God or human nature, optimism, loss of control, loss of innocence, or loss of time

Handout 1.5: New Hope for Battered Women

by Seabrook Mow

You know the term—post-traumatic stress disorder—and when you hear it, you think of war victims. But you may not think of domestic violence victims.

Dr. Edward S. Kubany is helping to change that.

More importantly, he is changing the way that medical professionals deal with women who suffer from posttraumatic stress disorder because of violence suffered at the hands of men they loved.

"PTSD is actually a normal reaction to extreme stress," says Dr. Kubany. "It's when a certain type of event creates that extreme fear or stress."

According to Kubany, the rate of PTSD among battered women is much higher than in the population at large. In samples of battered women in shelters, 45 to 84 percent suffered from PTSD.

Go with the higher number. In two Hawaii studies of battered women seeking shelter, approximately 84 percent experienced PTSD.

Julie Owens knows all about it from firsthand experience. Nine years ago, she survived a kidnapping and two stab wounds—one to her stomach and another to her neck—by her ex-husband.

Today, Owens is helping other abused women as a co-investigator and therapist with the Cognitive Trauma Therapy for Battered Women project (CTT-BW).

Kubany, a research psychologist with the Pacific Islands Division of the Department of Veterans Affairs, is co-principal investigator and developer of CTT-BW and creator of a cognitive trauma therapy for battered women.

Together, Owens and Kubany are working to find a better treatment for battered women who suffer from PTSD.

This $300,000, three-year, federally funded project is intended to evaluate the effectiveness of cognitive trauma therapy for battered women by sampling 120 formerly battered women.

The project is awarded to Lt. Col. Elizabeth Hill, principal investigator and a nurse at Tripler Army Medical Center. The project represents a collaboration endeavor between Veterans Affairs and the Department of Defense.

"This study is the first PTSD treatment outcome study ever conducted with battered women," Owens says.

Domestic abuse affects nearly one out of three American women.

According to the Bureau of Justice statistics, 900,000 American women were victimized by their intimate partners in 1994. Of women who seek emergency care, 22 to 35 percent involve domestic violence.

"It's OK and it's necessary to make yourself important," says Owens. "In fact, women should start advocating for themselves."

Easier said than done. Although her ex-husband was found guilty and served time, she continued to be tormented by his violence. That is PTSD.

"I was very confused, afraid and full of mixed emotions that I didn't understand," Owens says.

PTSD is caused by life-threatening experiences which cause a person to suffer intense fear, helplessness and horror. PTSD victims experience four core symptoms: re-experiencing the trauma, avoidance, emotional numbing and hyperarousal. But Kubany believes there are additional symptoms that should be addressed: trauma-related guilt, anger, and grief, sorrow or feelings of loss.

What's so exciting about the new treatment is that it has been eliminating PTSD in just nine to 10 sessions. The 90-minute sessions, usually one-on-one, are held twice a week.

Kubany has developed an effective therapy that is more "educational" compared to other types of treatments. "It's like a college course, where participants are actively engaged and learn a lot," Kubany says. Said another way, clients are given the guidelines and answers to overcoming PTSD.

Kubany emphasizes that women who suffer from PTSD should be treated as clients or students instead of patients. "PTSD is not a disease, it's a learned problem," Kubany says.

He says that, unfortunately, many battered women automatically assume that it's their fault, so they feel guilty about it. They've thus created a no-win situation for themselves, but he assures them it's not.

"How could they have foreseen it or feel responsible for it?" says Kubany. "The guys (abusers) are real charmers and smooth talkers. It's like, does an injured zebra attract a lion, or do lions know to spot an injured zebra?"

From the start, clients are taught to confront their fears and empower themselves, taking back the power that was taken from them.

For example, Owens recalls how a former client was afraid of going to the beach, because she had been assaulted on the beach. Owens reassured her that if she didn't visit the beach, then she was actually reinforcing her PTSD symptoms with short-term "relief," a very powerful reward that is temporary. Owens reminded her that the beach didn't assault her, but that she related the beach to the assault.

"It's changing their interpretation of what they thought was harmful," Kubany says.

Once the client went to the beach and got over her fear, she realized that the beach wasn't dangerous and it was enjoyable again.

"What we try to do is show them that what they believe is dangerous is not actually that harmful after all," Kubany says.

Another method Kubany applies is "higher-order language conditioning," where clients are taught not to "recharge" their PTSD by using negative words like "I should have" or "I was stupid." Those images and words rekindle the connection between the client and the abuse.

When a client reaches her goal of eliminating PTSD, Kubany and Owens agree the client does a complete 180. Owens said that "most times the client couldn't believe she acted that way before coming to the sessions."

"What I tell them is, I don't know how you felt, but I know how I felt," Owens says. "I was terrified and all those feelings are normal. This (treatment) will help you."

This article appeared in the August 9, 2000, issue of *MidWeek* and is reprinted with the permission of *MidWeek* editor Don Chapman.

Handout 1.6: Cognitive Trauma Therapy Homework Assignments

Client Initials: _____   Date: _____

1. _____ Listen to the audio-recording of each session before the next session.

2. _____ Complete handout 1.2, Empowering Yourself: Self-Advocacy Strategies.

3. _____ Complete handout 1.3, Is Anger Worth the Hangover? Strategies for Letting Go.

4. _____ Study handout 1.4, Symptoms of Post-traumatic Stress Disorder.

5. _____ Read handout 1.5, *MidWeek* article: "New Hope for Battered Women."

6. _____ Monitor and record negative self-talk using handout 2.1, Negative Self-Talk Monitoring Form, which you've agreed to carry with you at all times.

7. _____ Practice PMR while listening to the recorded instructions, twice each day.

8. _____ Do a body scan and over-tense and relax affected muscles after experiencing stress.

9. _____ Complete handout 6.3, Identifying Harmless Reminders Survey.

10. _____ Read handout 6.4, *Honolulu Star-Bulletin* article: "Abused Women to Share in New Therapy Project."

11. _____ Do agreed-upon exposure exercises (documented in handout 7.1, Escape and Avoidance Busting Exposure Homework Agreement).

    _____ Look at pictures

    _____ Visualize (with other reminder cues also present)

    _____ Watch *Sleeping with the Enemy* and *Once Were Warriors*

    _____ Engage in activities and go to places that are reminders of the abuse

    _____ Other exposure exercises

12. _____ Read handout 10.4, the article "Thinking Errors, Faulty Conclusions, and Cognitive Therapy for Trauma-Related Guilt."

13. _____ Complete handout 17.1, Characteristics of Abusive Partners questionnaire.

14. _____ Use handout 19.2, Worksheet for Making Important Decisions, to analyze a current decision.

15. _____ Other: _____

16. _____ Other: _____

17. _____ Other: _____

Therapist Planning and Client Progress Notes (Module/Session 1)

The therapist can use this form for making progress notes for module/session 1.

Session 1/Module 1: Day: _____ Date: _____ Time: _____

Guilt issues identified:

1. _____

2. _____

3. _____

Other issues identified to be addressed later:

1. _____

2. _____

3. _____

Homework assigned:

1. _____ Listen to audio-recording of session.

2. _____ Complete the self-advocacy strategies questionnaire.

3. _____ Complete the questionnaire on letting go of anger.

4. _____ Read the *MidWeek* article.

5. _____ Study the PTSD symptoms list.

6. _____

Agenda for session 2:

_____

_____

Summary appraisal of session 1 and important issues raised:

_____

_____

_____

Significant others:

Husband(s), boyfriend(s), or other partner(s)

_____

_____

Names and ages of children

_____

_____

_____

_____

Other(s)

_____

_____

Monitoring Negative Self-Talk

Because module 1 corresponds with session 1, module 2 is always started (and completed) during the second session. The assignment to keep track of negative self-talk is very important. We have found that when negative self-talk remains high, PTSD symptoms almost always also remain at a high or relatively high level. Conversely, reduction in negative self-talk is almost always associated with a reduction in the severity of PTSD symptoms.

OBJECTIVES

■ To briefly educate the client about the impact of negative self-talk

■ To increase the client's motivation to become aware of and eliminate negative self-talk

■ To provide the client with a tool for increasing awareness of her negative self-talk as an essential step in breaking habits of negative self-talk

MATERIALS

■ Negative Self-Talk Monitoring Form (handout 2.1)

■ Therapist Planning and Client Progress Notes for session 2 and beyond

HOMEWORK

- Listen to session audio-recordings.

- Record occurrences of negative self-talk using the Negative Self-Talk Monitoring Form (handout 2.1; continuing assignment).

- Read and complete chapter 4 in *Healing the Trauma of Domestic Violence* (optional).

PROCEDURES CHECKLIST

1. _____ Homework review

2. _____ Brief explanation of negative self-talk and why it's important to become aware of it

3. _____ Explanation of the Negative Self-Talk Monitoring Form (handout 2.1)

DETAILED PROCEDURES FOR MODULE 2

2.1. Homework Review

Did you complete the self-advocacy strategies questionnaire? What did you get out of this exercise? Have the client turn in this questionnaire, and keep it in her chart for review at the final session, when self-advocacy strategies are revisited. Clients almost always like this exercise; the strategies make sense to them and often buoy them with optimism. Adopting these strategies as guidelines for living one's life is seen as a worthwhile objective. Occasionally the first two strategies, which emphasize the importance of getting personal wants and needs satisfied, are initially viewed as selfish or rude—as strategies that might make the client feel guilty. Typically, clients have not been living their lives in accordance with these strategies. They may say something like "They sound good, but how do you do it?"

Did you complete the questionnaire on letting go of anger? What did you get out of this assignment? Have the client turn in this questionnaire, and keep it in her chart for review during the managing anger module. Having the clients complete this assignment typically helps them realize that they are the ones who suffer the most when they get angry, and that they would be better off without anger.

Did you read the *MidWeek* article about CTT? What did you get out of reading that article? Clients almost always say they liked this article and were impressed by the description of CTT.

Did you study the list of PTSD symptoms? What did you think about these symptoms, as they relate to you? All of my clients relate to at least some of these symptoms—and sometimes to most or all of them. Sometimes when clients look at these symptoms, they think, "How does my therapist already know so much about me?" One way to handle this is to use statements along these lines, using symptoms the client indicated on her initial PTSD questionnaire: **I bet you get upset when you're reminded of the trauma. You probably don't like to think about what happened and would rather avoid activities that remind you of it. It wouldn't be unusual if you feel detached from others and have lost interest in activities you used to enjoy—or if you have trouble sleeping and trouble concentrating. I bet you feel guilty about what happened.**

The fact is, when I first met you, I didn't know anything about you. I didn't know anything about your character, or spirituality, or determination. But I knew something about what happened to you. These are the kinds of symptoms or problems that people have after experiencing really bad things. It doesn't have anything to do with you; it has to do with what happened to you. If someone else had the same trauma history that you have, she would probably be having problems similar to those you're having. I'll have more to say about this later.

Are there any problems you're having that would be important for me to know about that didn't come up in our first session?

2.2. Brief Explanation of Negative Self-Talk

In this module, clients are taught to increase their awareness of negative self-talk and instructed on how to monitor it as a means of breaking habits of negative self-talk. At this time, only minimal rationale is provided as to why negative self-talk is harmful. In module 9, the therapist elaborates on reasons why the various categories of negative self-talk are harmful to one's well-being in order to heighten the client's motivation to break these habits.

The way you talk to yourself—the specific words you use when you think and speak—have a great deal to do with how fast you're going to overcome the negative effects of your experiences of abuse. There are certain words and phrases that interfere with survivors' ability to overcome their PTSD. The developers of CTT have identified four problematic categories of thoughts and speech. If you never use them again as long as you live, you'll be a happier person. Negative self-talk is a habit that isn't good for you. If you stop talking to yourself with negative words, it will improve your emotional well-being. If I could, I'd send you to a laser surgeon to make it impossible for you to say or think these words! The bottom line is that it's in your best interest to treat yourself the same way you want and expect other people to treat you.

2.3. Explanation of the Negative Self-Talk Monitoring Form

I'm going to teach you how to keep track of four categories of negative self-talk—in your thoughts and speech—to help you break this destructive habit. I'll give you a homework assignment to keep track of the way you talk to yourself. Give the client several copies of the Negative Self-Talk Monitoring Form (handout 2.1).

The developers of cognitive trauma therapy have identified four categories of negative self-talk, which are shown at the top of this form. Category 1 includes the word "should," the phrases "should have" and "could have," and "why" questions. Category 2 includes put-downs of your entire personality, character, or intelligence—words and phrases like stupid, dummy, wimp, selfish, there's something wrong with me, or I have bad judgment.

Category 3 is the most subtle and the most difficult to get a handle on. It includes the use of the phrase "I feel" in sentences that end with words or conclusions that aren't emotions, like "I feel obligated," "I feel overwhelmed," "I feel sorry for…," or "I feel responsible." The problem is that the feelings associated with these conclusions aren't evidence for the conclusions. However, the feelings give the conclusions a false ring of truth. For example, "responsible" is not an emotion, and how you feel about your perceived responsibility isn't evidence of whether you are or are not responsible for causing something to happen. Using the phrase "I feel" with words that aren't about emotions impairs your ability to think clearly.

Category 4 reflects something that many women with PTSD do. Do you apologize very much? Later, I'll explain to you why many women with PTSD apologize and say "I'm sorry" a lot—even when there's nothing to apologize for.

On the monitoring form, days are broken into blocks. The first time each day that you say or even think a category 1 word or phrase, write the number 1 in the block for that day and time. The first time you say or think a category 2 phrase, write the number 2 in that time block. The same holds for the first time you say or think a category 3 or category 4 statement.

You only write each number once in each time block. It means that the category of negative self-talk occurred at least once in that block. We can't tell whether it occurred only once or many times. So the maximum amount of numbers or symbols you can write in any block is four—a 1, a 2, a 3, and a 4. This method of recording is simpler and tends to be more helpful than recording every single occurrence of negative self-talk, which is hard to do accurately.

The first time each day that you use a category 1, 2, or 3 phrase, at the bottom of the form write down exactly what you said or thought. For example, if you say, "I should have been stronger," write that phrase down in the space next to the day of the week. Category 4, apologies, are almost always expressed as "I'm sorry," so there's no need to write them down.

It's very important that you carry this form around with you at all times and record your negative self-talk immediately after it happens. If you wait until later, it defeats the purpose of the exercise. Writing down the numbers may be an inconvenience or a hassle and is mildly self-punishing, but it's supposed to be. It's in your best interest to punish this kind of behavior. On the other hand, if you don't engage in any negative self-talk, you don't have to write anything down.

Down below, on the right-hand side, there are spaces for you to estimate your level of muscle tension when you write down what you said or thought to yourself. A score of 0 represents the most relaxed you have ever been, and a score of 100 represents the worst feeling you have ever had—a feeling of intense fear, terror, or horror. So your tension score is always somewhere between 0 and 100.

Are you willing to carry this form around with you at all times and to record instances of self-talk immediately—when they occur? The immediate goal of this exercise is to increase your awareness of using these statements—not to decrease how often you use them. Later, as you become more aware, you'll start to recognize when you're about to say these words and phrases. When you get to this stage, you may be able to start using different words to express what you want to say.

One last thing about negative self-talk. Would you want to see a therapist who treated you with disrespect? Would you like it if I said things to you like "Wow, you were stupid," "You should have seen it coming," or "You've got bad judgment"? Of course you wouldn't. But if I'm treating you with respect and you're treating yourself with disrespect, we're working against each other. We're canceling each other out. Illustrate by bringing your hands together in an arcing or banging-together motion. It is in your best interest for us to be working together, as a team. Therefore, if I hear you using negative self-talk that you seem to be unaware of, I'll bring it to your attention.

CONCLUDING REMARKS

Education about negative self-talk will be covered in depth in module 9. However, it's important to begin changing these ingrained habits as early as possible.

Handout 2.1: Negative Self-Talk Monitoring Form

Client Initials: _____   Date: _____

Phrases of Concern

Category 1 = "should," "should have," "could have," "why?"

Category 2 = put-downs of your entire personality or character ("I'm stupid [inadequate, a wimp, and so on]")

Category 3 = "I feel . . ." in statements ending with conclusions that aren't emotions ("I feel obligated [overwhelmed, responsible, and so on]")

Category 4 = apologies ("I'm sorry")

When writing down phrases, score your tension level on a scale of 0 to 100, where 0 is no tension and 100 is the most tension possible.

Date							
	Mon.	**Tues.**	**Wed.**	**Thurs.**	**Fri.**	**Sat.**	**Sun.**
8 a.m. to 12 p.m.							
12 p.m. to 4 p.m.							
4 p.m. to 8 p.m.							
8 p.m. to 12 a.m.							
12 a.m. to 8 a.m.							

Monday phrases:	1: _____ Tension score: _____
	2: _____ Tension score: _____
	3: _____ Tension score: _____

Tuesday phrases:	1: _____ Tension score: _____
	2: _____ Tension score: _____
	3: _____ Tension score: _____

Wednesday phrases:	1: _____ Tension score: _____
	2: _____ Tension score: _____
	3: _____ Tension score: _____

Thursday phrases:	1: _____ Tension score: _____
	2: _____ Tension score: _____
	3: _____ Tension score: _____
Friday phrases:	1: _____ Tension score: _____
	2: _____ Tension score: _____
	3: _____ Tension score: _____
Saturday phrases:	1: _____ Tension score: _____
	2: _____ Tension score: _____
	3: _____ Tension score: _____
Sunday phrases:	1: _____ Tension score: _____
	2: _____ Tension score: _____
	3: _____ Tension score: _____

Therapist Planning and Client Progress Notes (Continuing Modules)

The therapist can use this form as a basis for making progress notes for sessions 2 and beyond.

Session #: _____ Module #(s): _____ Day: _____ Date: _____ Time: _____

Material covered:

1. _____

2. _____

3. _____

Appraisal and comments:

_____

_____

_____

Homework assigned:

1. ____ Monitoring negative self-talk

2. ____ Relaxation exercises

3. _____

4. _____

5. _____

Agenda for next session:

_____

_____

Stress Management I: Education About Stress

Because PTSD is a stress disorder, it is very important for clients to learn to master stress management. To get the most out of the stress management tools they will learn in CTT, it is important that clients first gain an understanding of how stress works and how it affects them. This module provides that understanding and offers stress education, which will prepare clients to get the most benefit from the stress management tools they'll learn in the next module.

OBJECTIVES

■ For the client to acquire an understanding that she can learn to regulate her mood and think more clearly by reducing tension in her muscles

MATERIALS

■ Diagrams on Stress (handout 3.1)

HOMEWORK

■ Listen to session audio-recordings.

■ Continue to monitor and record negative self-talk.

- Read and complete chapter 6 in *Healing the Trauma of Domestic Violence* (optional).

PROCEDURES CHECKLIST

1. ____ Defining stress: external stimulus, internal response, and the brain's interpretation of external stimulus (handout 3.1, diagram 1)

2. ____ Change as stress

3. ____ The tendency for stress to be cumulative (handout 3.1, diagram 2)

4. ____ The relationship between mental stress and physical stress

5. ____ Estimating level of tension using the "tension thermometer"

6. ____ Seven reasons to keep muscles relaxed

7. ____ Reason 1: It's easier to identify which muscles tense up in response to a stressful event

8. ____ Reason 2: It's easier to bring your tension down

9. ____ Reason 3: It's easier to stay in control of your emotions when exposed to stressful events (handout 3.1, diagram 3)

10. ____ Reason 4: High levels of tension impair your ability to think clearly and make decisions that are in your best interest (handout 3.1, diagram 4)

11. ____ Reason 5: When your muscles are tense, you're more likely to engage in negative self-talk and other bad habits

12. ____ Reason 6: Chronic hyperarousal and associated muscle tension can contribute to medical problems and poor physical health (handout 3.1, diagram 5)

13. ____ Reason 7: If your muscles are relaxed, you're much more likely to be in a good mood than if your muscles are tense

14. ____ Two ways of regulating stress over the long run

15. ____ Thinking of progress in reducing stress in terms of a trend

16. ____ Summary of the seven reasons for keeping muscles relaxed

DETAILED PROCEDURES FOR MODULE 3

3.1. Defining Stress

Give the client handout 3.1, Diagrams on Stress. **What is stress? What does stress mean to you?** Clients most commonly describe some internal reaction, such as tension, worry, or anxiety; sometimes an external event, such as demands or deadlines; occasionally an interpretation of some external event, for example, something overwhelming or more than they can handle; and once in a while a combination of these three types (external event, interpretation, and internal reaction), such as "something happens that is overwhelming and freaks me out."

Stress has an external aspect, from the environment—an external stimulus or trigger—and an internal reaction in response to the external stimulus. Read aloud what is in the circle on the left in diagram 1. ("External Stimulus: for example, traffic, deadlines, interpersonal conflict, trauma.")

Now read aloud what is in the circle on the far right. ("Internal Response: for example, muscle tension, increased blood pressure, worry, anxiety.")

But stress often involves more than an external event and an internal reaction to the external event. Read aloud what is in the circle in the center. ("Cognitive Filter: the brain's interpretation of the external stimulus. Affects the magnitude of the internal response.")

How the external event is interpreted can influence the internal reaction you experience. The brain's interpretation of the external event can have a big impact on the magnitude of your internal reaction. For example, if you have thoughts like "I'm feeling overwhelmed," "This is more than I can handle," or "I'm spread too thin," you may experience a stronger reaction. Your brain acts as a filter that gives the event meaning. This helps explain why something that is a big deal to you may be no big thing to someone else.

Research on assertiveness has shown that assertive women tend to interpret socially stressful situations as challenging, whereas unassertive women tend to interpret the same situations as threatening. As a consequence, socially stressful situations give rise to more anxiety and negative physical reactions in unassertive women than in assertive women.

Because of their history of abuse, battered women with PTSD tend to interpret disagreements and raised voices much more negatively than women who don't have a history of abuse. As a result, arguments and disagreements are much more stressful for battered women than for women who have never been abused.

Stress is the negative psychological, emotional, and physical reaction you have in response to events you perceive as negative. Many people think of stress in terms of mental stress or psychological pressure in response to the hecticness of life in the twenty-first century. However, when scientists first started studying stress, they examined the effects of actual *physical* stressors on internal reactions—things like blood pressure, water pressure, or placing enough pressure on a person's arm to cause a bruise.

3.2. Change as Stress

Another way of looking at stress is in terms of change. Any change or negative life event produces an interruption in the flow of life—which requires some adaptation or adjustment. Change tends to be stressful. Examples include losing a job, having to move, getting divorced, getting sick, a loved one getting cancer, or experiencing a traumatic event. Some research has shown that the number of major life changes a person has experienced in the past year is associated with the amount of recent illness the person has had.

Another way of looking at change as stress is in terms of the mini changes that occur for everyone every day. Here's an example: The alarm doesn't go off, then you find you're out of milk and one of your children is crying or your kids are arguing with one another. Already late, you can't find something, you get stuck in traffic, and you realize you forgot something at home. Once you get to work, a coworker is complaining, and then you get a phone call from your ex-partner. What are some of the mini stressors you experienced today? Try to elicit at least three examples. Go back to yesterday if today was not stressful at all.

3.3. The Tendency for Stress to Be Cumulative

Read the title of diagram 2. ("Stress Is Usually Cumulative.") The important point that this diagram illustrates—something many people are unaware of—is that stress tends to be cumulative. After a stressful event is over your tension goes down, but it doesn't go all the way back down to the level it was at before the stressful event occurred. Stress leads to an increase in tension.

For example, you wake up late. This script is written using the examples provided above, but try to use examples the client provided. Point to the upward trend line in diagram 2. Your tension goes up, and then it goes back down—but not all the way down. Next, you discover you're out of milk. Your tension goes up, and then it goes back down—but not all the way. Then you're stuck on the freeway. Your tension goes up, and then it goes back down—but not all the way. You realize you forgot something at home. Your tension goes up, and then it goes down—but not all the way.

Can you see how a day can start out great, but by four o'clock in the afternoon you're a nervous wreck? We all have days like this, but people with PTSD have more days like this than people who don't have PTSD.

3.4. The Relationship Between Mental Stress and Physical Stress

When you are stressed mentally, your body reacts in a variety of ways, including increases in heart rate, blood pressure, sweat gland activity, muscle tension, and secretions of hormones. If someone says that her stress is all in her mind, she isn't aware of how her body is reacting. For example, if a person says she's psychologically upset but physically relaxed, she isn't aware of the physical changes occurring in her body. There is an extremely strong correlation between mental activity and physical activity, between the mind and the body, and between mental stress and physical stress. There are a variety of ways that people experience stress, but stress is always associated with increases in physical arousal. Anxiety, fear, panic, bad moods, and depression are all associated with elevations in tension or physical arousal.

3.5. Estimating Level of Tension Using the "Tension Thermometer"

From time to time, I'll want to know how tense or relaxed you are. For this purpose, CTT therapists use a scale called the tension thermometer, where a score of 0 is the calmest you have ever been—awake and alert, but so relaxed that it would be difficult to move a single muscle in your entire body. A score of 100 is the worst feeling you've ever had—terrified, horrified, or like a volcano ready to erupt. So your tension score is always somewhere between these two endpoints of 0 and 100. This is the same scale I mentioned to you when I assigned the negative self-talk monitoring homework.

What is your tension score right now? Where in your body do you experience the most tension when you experience stress? (Alternatively, you can ask, "What muscles in your body usually tense up when you experience stress?")

3.6. Seven Reasons to Keep Muscles Relaxed

For at least seven reasons, it's important to keep muscle tension in your body at a low level. Let's take a quick look at each of these reasons.

3.7. Reason 1: It's Easier to Identify Which Muscles Are Tense

The first reason it's important to keep your muscles relaxed is that it's easier to identify increases in tension and stress when your muscles are relaxed. For example, imagine yourself in a dark auditorium. You could easily detect the source of light if one match was burning. But, what if a thousand matches were burning, and someone were to light one more? Would you be able to tell where the light from the last match was coming from?

Or imagine a battered woman waiting for her support group to start. Her two-year-old daughter is with her and will get child care once the group starts. The woman is preoccupied with her thoughts at a high level of tension, so even though her child is being whiny and clingy, the woman isn't even aware that her daughter is "driving her crazy."

3.8. Reason 2: It's Easier to Bring Your Tension Down

The second reason it's important to keep your muscles relaxed is that it's easier to bring your tension down if it's at a relatively low level than if it's high. For example, it's easier to bring your tension level down 10 points from 30 to 20 than to bring it down 10 points from 70 to 60.

3.9. Reason 3: It's Easier to Stay in Control of Your Emotions

The third reason is that you're more likely to stay in control of your emotions if your muscles are relaxed. If your muscles are tense, you're more vulnerable to losing control in response to a stressful event than if your tension level is low.

Look at diagram 3, "Staying in Control and Losing It." This diagram illustrates that everyone has a point where they will lose control—a point at which they'll panic, lose their temper, or break down and cry. The "losing it" threshold is different for different people, but everyone has one—even North Sea divers who go down deep into cold water in scuba gear to fix oil rigs. How long do you think a diver has to be out of air before panic sets in? [rhetorical question] Not very long.

We can use this diagram to explain how people blow up, panic, or lose control over seemingly little things. Let's say your threshold for losing it is a tension score of 80. If you're having a really bad day and hovering around 70 or so, it's not going to take much to push you over the top.

Many battered women feel guilty about losing it with their children over really minor things, like clinging to them or poking them and calling, "Mommy, Mommy, Mommy ..." People may say, "Why did you lose it over such a little thing?" Well, if you're already near your threshold, it's not going to take much.

Now let's say you're just having a bad day—not a terrible day, just a bad day—and your tension level is about 50. If something major happens and your score goes up 30 points, that will push you over the top. However, if you're at 20 and something stressful happens that increases your tension level 30 points up to 50, you'll be upset, but you'll still be in control.

3.10. Reason 4: It's Easier to Think Clearly

Look at diagram 4, "Level of Arousal and Performance." This diagram illustrates two additional reasons for keeping your muscles relaxed. It shows that as a person's level of arousal or activation increases, her level of functioning will also increase—up to a point or some optimal level. It's similar to how some people seem to need a cup of coffee in the morning before they can start getting anything done. The caffeine is a stimulant that heightens arousal. With no energy, a person may not even want to get out of bed, like someone suffering from major depression.

Once arousal increases past a certain point, however, performance or level of functioning starts to decline. This is a problem for many people who have PTSD. Do you see the horizontal line just past the top of the curve? This is where people with PTSD are most of the time. It's like they've already had ten cups of coffee when they get up in the morning. They are overaroused, and as a result, it isn't surprising that most people with PTSD have problems with concentration. And the more aroused they get, the more poorly they function.

When women are trapped in an actively abusive relationship, they may be so aroused as to be paralyzed with fear, and their ability to think clearly may be severely impaired. Everything seems like a booming, buzzing confusion, and they have difficulty sorting things out or making rational decisions.

I'll give you an example. A very bright woman with an advanced degree in mental health thought she should have left her abusive boyfriend sooner. When asked to describe exactly when she thinks she should have left, she described her boyfriend as extremely controlling. For example, if he wanted to go to bed, he would insist that she go to bed too. At first she resisted, saying that she wasn't tired. But if she continued to resist, he would harass her relentlessly. On at least one occasion, he even kept her awake almost all night. Eventually, she would decide that it wasn't worth the hassle to resist and she would just give in to her boyfriend's demands. She would lie awake in bed until he fell asleep, and then she would get up and go into the living room, where she would lie down on the floor, get into a fetal position, and just rock. Do you think this woman was in any frame of mind to logically weigh the pros and cons about whether it was a good idea to stay or leave the relationship?

This diagram suggests a fourth reason why you want to keep your muscle tension at a low level: High levels of tension impair your ability to think clearly. In particular, the ability to make important decisions that are in your best interest is impaired when your tension level is high. As I sometimes say to clients, "As tension or anxiety goes up, IQ goes down."

3.11. Reason 5: Tension Activates Bad Habits

The fifth reason you want to keep your tension level low is that bad habits are more likely to be activated when your tension level is high. For example, when you're stressed, you're more likely to engage in negative self-talk than when you're relaxed or calm. At times when it would be important for you to be your own strongest advocate, you may actually be acting as your own worst enemy.

Consider a tennis player who has a bad serving habit. He goes to a tennis pro who helps him correct or break the habit. Afterward, he practices what he learned and plays much better. But then he goes to a tournament where there are hundreds of spectators. Can you see how his bad habit might reemerge under the stress of playing in front of a big crowd?

3.12. Reason 6: It's Better for Your Health

The sixth reason you want to keep your tension level low is that chronically high tension can weaken a person physically. It can heighten a person's vulnerability to disease and contribute to poor health.

One way I can illustrate this point is with a brief description of what studies have shown about how people with high blood pressure differ from people with normal or low blood pressure in the way that they deal with stress. Look at diagram 5. Laboratory studies of stress typically have three phases: an initial resting phase in which subjects are asked to relax, a second phase in which stress is introduced (for example, subjects may be asked to put their hands into cold water), and a third phase—the recovery phase in which subjects are allowed to relax again.

People with high blood pressure differ from people with normal blood pressure primarily in only one of the phases. Which phase do you think it is? Right. The third phase, or recovery phase. People with high blood pressure are slower to recover from the effects of stressful events. For example, it may take longer for their heart rate to return to normal after stressful events.

You can see how this may put a person with high blood pressure at risk for heart disease. Parts wear out with overuse. Here's an analogy: Let's say you're driving around town, and when you return home, you park your car but don't turn off the ignition. You leave your car running until you want to use it again. Do you think your car will last as long if you don't turn the engine off whenever you aren't using it? In a similar way, your body may be wearing out more quickly if it's in a chronic state of high tension or hyperarousal. This is a very important reason why it's in your best interest to keep your body relaxed even when you aren't actually dealing with stressful situations.

3.13. Reason 7: It Promotes a Good Mood

A seventh reason it's in your best interest to keep your tension level low is that if your muscles are relaxed, you're far more likely to be in a good mood than if your muscles are tense.

3.14. Two Ways of Regulating Stress over the Long Run

There are two general ways of lowering tension and regulating stress over the long run. The first way is to get less and less bothered or stressed-out when exposed to the same kinds of stressors—to get to the point where certain kinds of stressors bother you less. For example, you might get to the point of letting traffic on the freeway bother you less and less.

The second general way of regulating stress is to recover more and more quickly when the stressor is removed. How can you keep recurring stressful events from ruining your day—things like deadlines or hassles at work, your kids misbehaving, or phone calls from your abuser?

Recognition of the two general ways of reducing overall levels of stress can provide you with two kinds of goals that you can work toward to reduce your general levels of tension or stress: The first goal is to become increasingly less bothered by habitual stressful events in your life. The second is to get your tension back to a low level increasingly quickly after stressful events have ended.

3.15. Thinking of Progress in Lowering Stress as a Trend

It's important that you think of your progress in reducing your general level of stress in terms of a trend. How can you make this week better than last week? How can you make this month better than last month and this year better than last year? Remember, a lapse is not a relapse. For example, a bad day does not signify a bad month. Think in terms of the big picture.

3.16. Summary of the Seven Reasons for Keeping Muscles Relaxed

I'm going to briefly summarize the seven reasons why it's important to keep your muscle tension at a low level. First, it's easier to identify increases in tension at low levels than at high levels. If you don't know which muscles tense up when you experience stress, you can't do anything about it. If you do know which muscles tense up, you can learn to relax them and improve your mood. Body awareness is knowledge, and knowledge is power.

Second, it's easier to relax or bring your level of tension down when your tension is relatively low than when it's high. Third, you're more vulnerable to losing control—panicking, losing your temper, or crying—in response to a stressful event if your tension level is high than if it's low. Fourth, high levels of tension impair your ability to think clearly. Your ability to think clearly and make decisions that are in your best interest is far greater at low levels of arousal than at high levels. Fifth, you're more likely to engage in bad habits when your tension level is high. For example, when you're tense, you're more likely to engage in negative self-talk than when you're relaxed or calm. Sixth, chronically high levels of tension can contribute to medical problems and poor health. And seventh, if your muscles are relaxed, you're much more likely to be in a good mood than if your muscles are tense.

Has this discussion of stress been useful?

CONCLUDING REMARKS

Clients are surprised to learn how much stress affects their physical health, in addition to their psychological well-being. Because this module offers psychoeducational content in a Socratic manner, clients are almost always very engaged and challenged as they learn about stress.

Handout 3.1: Diagrams on Stress

Diagram 1

Stress Is Usually Cumulative

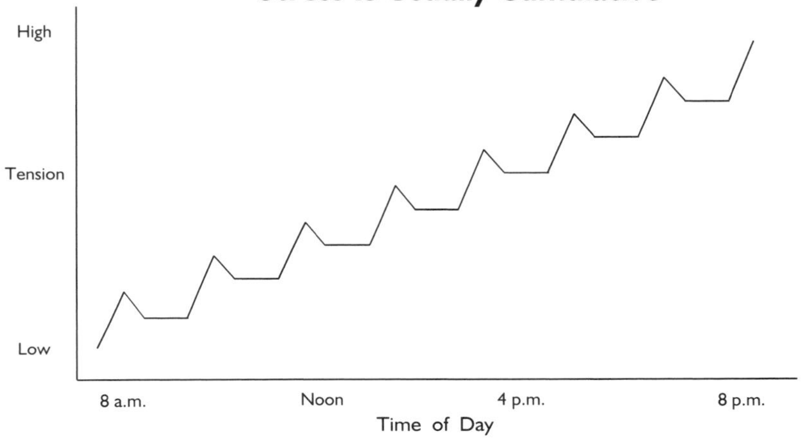

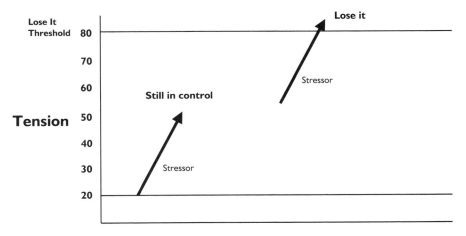

Diagram 2

Staying in Control and Losing It

**Why the Same Stressful Event Can Have Different Effects
Depending on Level of Tension When It Occurs**

Diagram 3

Level of Arousal and Performance

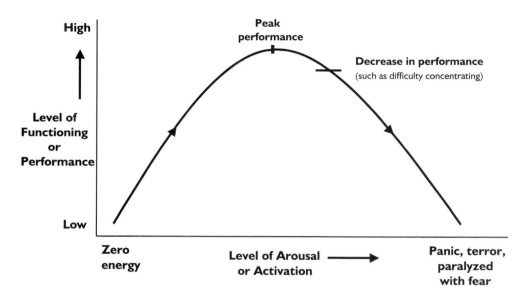

Diagram 4

How People with High and Low Blood Pressure Recover from Stress Differently

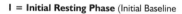

1 = **Initial Resting Phase** (Initial Baseline
2 = **Stressor Phase**
3 = **Recovery Phase** (Return to Baseline)

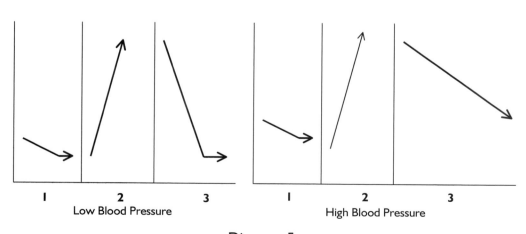

Diagram 5

Stress Management II: Progressive Muscle Relaxation

Clients really enjoy this module. The skills taught here are especially important for people with PTSD, as they typically suffer from chronic muscular tension. The progressive muscle relaxation (PMR) exercise enables most clients to achieve a deep state of physical relaxation, which is also associated with a mental state of calm or tranquility.

OBJECTIVES

- For the client to achieve a state of deep muscular relaxation

- To give the client a tool for achieving a state of relaxation on her own

- For the client to develop an increased awareness of the physical sensations associated with muscle tension and relaxation

MATERIALS

- Prerecorded audio-recording of instructions for progressive muscle relaxation, available for download from www.treatingptsd.com (unless you plan to record the instructions for the client during the PMR portion of this session)

HOMEWORK

- Listen to session audio-recordings.

- Continue to monitor and record negative self-talk.

- Practice PMR while listening to the PMR recording, twice a day (ongoing assignment).

- Do a body scan and over-tense and relax muscles after experiencing stress (ongoing assignment).

PROCEDURES CHECKLIST

1. _____ Introduction to progressive muscle relaxation

2. _____ Instruction in over-tensing and then relaxing muscles

3. _____ Relaxation—one of the few things you can't do better by trying harder

4. _____ Explaining that in strong emotions muscles are always tense

5. _____ Teaching PMR

6. _____ Conducting and (optionally) audio-recording PMR with the client

7. _____ Assigning PMR homework (twice a day for the duration of CTT)

8. _____ Instruction on how and when to do a body scan

DETAILED PROCEDURES FOR MODULE 4

4.1. Introduction to PMR

Let's continue our discussion about the importance of muscle relaxation in controlling stress, mood, and anxiety. I'm going to teach you how to relax using a technique called progressive muscle relaxation, or PMR. It was developed by a psychologist named Edmund Jacobson, who lived well into his nineties. Some people think he lived for so long because he learned to relax so deeply and didn't stress his body.

Originally, Dr. Jacobson thought it would take a long time for a person to learn how to relax completely—something like learning yoga or Transcendental Meditation. But he found that most people can learn how to relax in a relatively short period of time, and that, with practice, people can relax increasingly quickly.

4.2. Instruction in Over-Tensing and Then Relaxing Muscles

PMR involves a sequence of over-tensing and then relaxing various muscles in your body. Let's take a look at how it works. Clench your right fist. As you tense, point with your left hand to where you feel the tension. Certainly in your forearm, and in your fist. You probably even experience tension in your biceps. Touch your biceps to see if there is any tension there.

Now let go. Keep letting go … Do you feel a sensation of letting go? When you tensed up, you became more tense than you were initially. But as you relax and keep letting go, you become more relaxed than you were initially. Letting go involves an uncontracting of muscle fibers, some of which may never relax completely under ordinary circumstances. This letting go sensation is the relaxation response PMR will help you get better at.

4.3. Relaxation—One of the Few Things You Can't Do Better by Trying Harder

However, relaxation is one of the few skills that you don't get better at by trying harder. In that regard, it's similar to falling asleep or sexual arousal. Can you imagine having a race to fall asleep? You'll get better at relaxing by simply focusing on what relaxation or letting go feels like and then trying to reproduce these sensations.

4.4. Explaining That in Strong Emotions Muscles Are Always Tense

Muscle tension by itself isn't the same as anger, anxiety, or fear. You can have tense muscles and still be very relaxed emotionally or mentally. Demonstrate by tensing your biceps and showing that you're still calm and relaxed.

However, when you're in a state of fear, anger, or depression, your muscles are always tense. Have you ever seen a cat who was angry or frightened but had relaxed muscles? It's impossible to imagine, isn't it? But, interestingly, when you relax your muscles, other physical reactions associated with fear, anger, frustration, or depression also diminish. For example, as your muscles relax, your heart rate goes down, your blood pressure goes down, you perspire less, and you secrete fewer hormones.

If your muscles are relaxed, your heart can't be racing and you can't be hyperventilating. It's physiologically impossible. In fact, complete relaxation is associated with a positive sense of well-being. In other words, by controlling the tension in your muscles, you can control your mood and your mind.

4.5. Teaching PMR

Before we get into the specific technique of PMR, let's go through some of the major muscle groups involved in progressive muscle relaxation. I'll explain and demonstrate, and I want you to tense these same muscle groups when I do. We'll do this much more quickly now than when we actually do progressive muscle relaxation. Tense the following muscle groups in sequence, as the client copies what you do. Pause for about five seconds at each ellipses. In our experience, clients typically have much more tension in their upper body than in their lower body; thus, this script and the PMR instructions don't devote as much time to the lower body.

Clench your fists and feel the tension in your forearms and fists ... and relax ... Bend your elbows and tense your biceps ... and relax ... Straighten your arms, reach across the room, and tense your triceps (along the backs of your upper arms) ... and relax ...

Raise up your eyebrows and wrinkle your forehead ... and now relax and smooth out your forehead ... Frown, creasing your eyebrows ... and relax, smoothing out your forehead once more. Close your eyes really tight ... and now relax your eyes ... Grin broadly from ear to ear ... and relax ... Push the tip of your tongue hard against the roof of your mouth ... and relax ... Press your lips together ... and now relax your lips ... Clench your jaw ... and relax your jaw, letting your lips part slightly ...

Push your head back against the chair and feel the tension in your neck. Roll your head to the left ... and now to the right ... Now straighten your head and bring your chin forward against your chest ... and relax ... Shrug your shoulders up ... Now bring your shoulders back so you feel the tension in your shoulders and upper back ... and relax ...

Take a deep breath and hold your breath ... relax; just breathe freely and easily. Tense your stomach by pressing out ... and relax ... Tense your stomach by pulling in ... and relax ... Arch your back and feel the tension along your spine ... and relax your lower back ...

With your legs straight, point your toes away from your face ... and relax ... With your legs straight, bring your toes up toward your face ... and relax ...

These are the major muscle groups that we're going to focus on. As we do these exercises together, all I will want you to do is to concentrate on what it feels like when you tense up and, even more importantly, on what it feels like when you relax.

If the client is sitting in a recliner, ask her to recline. Turn off the audio-recorder at this point. If you plan to give the client a prerecorded PMR exercise for homework, leave the recorder off until after PMR. If you plan to record the PMR instructions for the client's homework at this time, make a recording separate from the session recording for the client's convenience. Start recording when you start the relaxation instructions.

Read the relaxation instructions slowly, pausing at the ellipses. During each of the muscle tensing phases, have the client hold the tension for five to seven seconds.

4.6. Guiding the Client Through Progressive Muscle Relaxation

All right now, please close your eyes and settle back as comfortably as you can ... Take a couple of long, slow, deep breaths ... That's fine ... Now let yourself relax to the best of your ability ... And as you relax, clench your right fist. Just clench your right fist tighter and tighter, and study the tension as you do so. Keep it clenched and feel the tension in your right fist, hand, and forearm ... and now relax. Let the fingers of your right hand become loose and observe the contrast in your feeling ... Let yourself go, and try to become more relaxed all over ... Once more, clench your right fist really tight ... hold it ... and notice the tension again ... Now let go ... Relax. As your fingers straighten out, notice the difference once more ... Repeat that with your left fist. Clench your left fist while the rest of your body relaxes. Clench that fist tighter and feel the tension ... and now relax. Again, enjoy the contrast ... Repeat that once more. Clench your left fist ... tight and tense ... Now do the opposite of tension—relax and feel the difference ... Continue relaxing like that for a while ...

Clench both fists ... tighter and tighter; both fists tense, both forearms tense. Study the sensations ... and relax. Straighten out your fingers and feel the relaxation. Continue relaxing your hands and forearms ... more and more ...

Now bend your elbows and tense your biceps. Tense them harder and study the tension feelings ... All right, straighten your arms. Let them relax and feel that difference again. Let the relaxation develop ... Once more, tense your biceps, hold the tension, and observe it carefully ... and relax. Just relax to the best of your ability ... Each time, pay close attention to your feelings as you tense up and when you relax—as you're doing now.

Straighten your arms in front of you. Reach across the room so that you feel the most tension in your triceps muscles, along the backs of your upper arms. Stretch your arms and feel the tension ... and relax. Get your arms back into a comfortable position and let the relaxation proceed on its own. Your arms feel comfortably heavy as you allow them to relax ... more and more ... Straighten your arms again so that you feel the tension in your triceps muscles. Straighten them and feel the tension ... and relax. Now let's concentrate on pure relaxation in your arms without any tension. Get your arms comfortable and let them relax further ... and further ... Continue relaxing your arms even further ... and even when your arms seem fully relaxed, try to go that extra bit further. Try to achieve deeper and deeper levels of relaxation.

Now let all of your muscles go loose and heavy. Just settle back quietly and comfortably.

Now, keeping your eyes closed, raise up your eyebrows and wrinkle your forehead. Wrinkle it tighter ... Now stop wrinkling your forehead. Relax and smooth it out. Picture your entire forehead and scalp becoming smoother as the relaxation increases ... and the tension drains away ... drains away ...

Now frown. Crease your brows and study the tension ... Let go of the tension again. Smooth out your forehead once more ... Close your eyes really tight. Feel the tension in, around, and behind your eyes … Relax your eyes. Keeping your eyes closed, gently, comfortably, notice the relaxation … Now grin as broadly as you can, from ear to ear. Feel the tension around the corners of your mouth … and relax. Just feel the tension draining out of your cheeks … draining out of your face … draining out … and draining away … draining away …

Now press your tongue hard against the roof of your mouth. Look for the tension … All right, let your tongue return to a comfortable and relaxed position … Press your lips together … tighter and tighter … Relax your lips. And notice the contrast between tension and relaxation. Now clench your jaws. Bite your teeth together and study the tension throughout your jaws … and relax your jaws. Let your lips part slightly … and appreciate the relaxation. Feel the relaxation all over your face, all over your forehead and scalp, eyes, jaws, lips, tongue, and throat. The relaxation progresses further and further …

Now attend to your neck muscles. Press your head back as far as it can go and feel the tension in your neck … Now roll your head to the right and feel the tension shift … And now roll it to the left … Now straighten your head and bring it forward, pressing your chin against your chest … And now let your head return to a comfortable and relaxed position, and study the relaxation … Let the relaxation develop …

Shrug your shoulders up tightly … And now bring your shoulders back so that you feel the tension in your shoulders and upper back … Drop your shoulders and relax … Shrug your shoulders up again … and then bring them back so you feel the tension in your shoulders and upper back … Relax once more … Let the relaxation spread deep into your shoulders, right into your upper back muscles. Relax your neck and your throat, your jaws, and the rest of your face … as the pure relaxation takes over and grows … deeper … and deeper … and ever deeper …

Relax your entire body to the best of your ability. Feel the comfortable heaviness that accompanies relaxation. Breathing easily and freely … in … and out. Notice how the relaxation increases as you exhale … As you breathe out, just feel that relaxation … Now breathe in and fill up your lungs; inhale deeply and hold your breath. Study the tension … Now exhale and let the walls of your chest grow loose as the air is pushed out automatically. Continue relaxing, breathing freely and gently … Feel the relaxation and enjoy it … With the rest of your body as relaxed as possible, fill your lungs again. Breathe in deeply and hold it again … That's fine. Now breathe out and appreciate the relief. Just breathe normally … Continue relaxing your chest and let the relaxation spread … to your back … shoulders … neck … and arms. Just let go … and enjoy the relaxation.

Now pay attention to your abdominal muscles, your stomach area. Tighten your stomach muscles, making your abdomen hard. Notice the tension … and relax. Let your stomach muscles loosen and notice the contrast … Once more, press and tighten your stomach muscles. Hold the tension … study it … and relax. Notice the general well-being that comes with relaxing your stomach …

Now draw your stomach in. Pull your stomach in and feel the tension this way … Relax again. Continue breathing normally and easily and feel the gently massaging action all over your chest and stomach … Now pull your stomach in again and hold the tension … Now push it out and tense like that; hold the tension … Once more pull in and feel the tension … and now relax your stomach completely. Let the tension dissolve as the relaxation grows deeper. Each time you breathe out, notice the rhythmic relaxation both in your lungs and in your stomach. And as you do, notice how your chest and your stomach relax more and more … Try to let go of all muscular tension throughout your entire body …

Now direct your attention to your lower back. Arch your back away from the chair, making your lower back quite hollow; feel the tension along your spine … and settle down comfortably, relaxing your lower back … Arch your back up again and feel the tension as you do so. Try to keep the rest of your body as relaxed as possible. Try to localize the tension in your lower back area … Relax once more, relaxing further and further. Relax your lower back … relax your upper back … spread the relaxation to your stomach … chest … shoulders … arms and face. These parts relaxing further … and further … and further … and ever deeper.

With your legs straight, point your toes downward, away from your face. Study the tension in your legs … and relax. Feel your legs becoming heavier as you allow your legs to relax … more and more. This time, again with your legs straight, bring your toes up toward your face. Bring your toes right up! … Relax again. Keep relaxing for a while … Now let yourself relax further all over. Relax your feet … ankles … calves … and shins … knees … thighs … and buttocks and hips. Feel the heaviness of your lower body as you relax still further …

Now spread the relaxation to your stomach … waist … and lower back. Let go more and more. Feel the relaxation all over. Let it proceed to your upper back … chest … shoulders … and arms … right to the tips of your fingers. Keep relaxing more and more deeply. Make sure that no tension has crept into your throat. Relax your neck … and your jaws … and all the muscles in your face. Keep relaxing your whole body like that for a while … Let yourself relax …

You can become more relaxed than you are now by merely taking in a long, slow, deep breath and slowly exhaling. Take in a long … slow … deep breath … and let it out very … very slowly … Feel how heavy and relaxed you have become. In this state of perfect relaxation, you feel unwilling to move a single muscle in your body. Think about the effort that would be required to raise your right arm. As you think about raising your right arm, see if you can notice any tension that might have crept into your shoulder and your arm … Now you decide not to lift your arm but to continue relaxing. Observe the relief and the disappearance of the tension …

I'm going to say the word "calm" at this time, and each time I say the word "calm," I want you to become even more relaxed … even more relaxed … letting all the muscles of your body go. In a few moments, I'm going to want you to say the word "calm" silently to yourself, without moving your lips. Then, in situations other than this, you can say the word "calm" to yourself and it will assist you in returning to the deep state of relaxation that you feel right now. I'm going to say the word now … and each time I say it, I want you to become more aware of your present state of relaxation … Become even more relaxed … Calm … Calm … You're very relaxed, very comfortable … Calm … Calm [softer] … Calm [softer]. In just a moment, I'll want you to say the word "calm" silently to yourself. And as you say it … be more aware of how relaxed and how comfortable you feel … Now silently say the word very slowly … Say it again … And each time you say it, feel more and more relaxed … Again … You're very comfortable … and very relaxed … very … very relaxed … Now just carry on … relaxing like this. (The last paragraph is reprinted from Knox [1971], with permission of David Knox.)

If you're recording the relaxation instructions, turn off the recorder now so that the next paragraph, directing the client to open her eyes, isn't on the recording, in case she wants to use the recording to help her fall asleep.

Now I'm going to count backwards from four through one, and when I reach one, I want you to open up your eyes … wide awake, refreshed, and very, very calm … Four … Three … Two … One … Open your eyes … wide awake, refreshed, and very, very calm … very, very calm.

Resume the session recording, not the PMR recording.

How do you feel? Almost always, clients report that they feel relaxed. On those very rare occasions that a client reports she isn't more relaxed, it's usually because she wasn't comfortable or didn't think she was safe with her eyes closed. If this happens, tell the client in a matter-of-fact way that the therapy office is a safe place. Also, emphasize the importance of focusing solely on bodily sensations when doing the relaxation and not focusing on distracting thoughts, especially worry-related thoughts suggesting that something bad is going to happen while her eyes are closed.

4.7. Assigning PMR Homework

Give the client a copy of the recorded PMR exercise, whether prerecorded or made during the session, to keep and use to practice PMR. I want you to play the relaxation recording twice a day. Always play it at bedtime. This won't eat into any of your waking time, and it will help you fall asleep more quickly and sleep more deeply. The other time during the day when you play the recording is more at your discretion. One good time is when you wake up in the morning. It will give your day a good start, and there are no negative side effects.

You can also do PMR without the recording; for example, while you're riding the bus. Many people use driving or travel time as "worry time" because they have nothing to do but think. Consider doing some deep breathing or muscle relaxation while driving, instead. Make it your goal to be more relaxed when you get to your destination than when you got into your car or on the bus. Optional humor: One caution, however: Don't close your eyes tightly while driving! (A recording of PMR is available at our website, www.treatingptsd.com. If you wish, you may download it to give to clients or simply ask clients to download the recording themselves.)

4.8. Instruction on How and When to Do a Body Scan

It's also very important that you do a similar exercise, tensing and then relaxing, after experiencing stress. When something stressful happens, such as being caught in traffic, having a disagreement with someone, or being reminded of the trauma, do a body scan to identify where in your body you are experiencing tension.

I'll explain how to do a body scan so you'll know how to do it anytime you experience stress. First, take a deep breath and hold it for five to ten seconds … Now breathe out and relax, and continue to breathe easily and freely. Scan your body and focus on any tension you feel in the major muscle groups in your body … Focus on any tension you may feel in your forehead … Now focus on your eyes … cheeks … mouth … and jaws … look for tension in your neck … shoulders … upper back … and down into your lower back … Look for tension in your chest … stomach … upper arms … lower arms … and right down to the tips of your fingers … Focus on your thighs … calves … and right down to the tips of your toes …

Where in your body did you notice the most tension? … Now over-tense muscles where there's tension and hold them at a peak of tension as long as you can … And now let go of the tension … Repeat this sequence if necessary, with the goal of bringing yourself down to the level where you were before the stressful event occurred.

The reason I start the body scan exercise with holding your breath for five to ten seconds is because when you experience anxiety, your breathing likely becomes disrupted, and you may start to hyperventilate. By holding your breath for a while and then concentrating on breathing slowly and easily, you may be able to restore your normal rate of breathing, and in so doing, you may be able to become more relaxed. And when you're more relaxed, it will be easier for you to identify where in your body you're experiencing tension.

Many people become upset about something and then remain stressed all day. Let's say that something happens that brings you up to a score of 70 on your tension thermometer. You don't have to stay at 70 all day. You can bring yourself down 20 or 30 points in five to ten minutes. One client often tensed and relaxed her stomach muscles during meetings at work if she felt tense. There are plenty of opportunities throughout the day to tense and relax your muscles so that you stay calm and feel better.

If, during any of our sessions, I notice that you're particularly tense or anxious, I'll ask you to do a body scan to identify which muscles are the most tense. Then I'll want you to tense and relax your muscles until you come down 20 or 30 points.

Why would I take five to ten minutes of valuable session time, when we have so very much to cover, to do this? [rhetorical question] I do this with clients to reemphasize how important it is for you to over-tense and relax your muscles whenever you experience stress, particularly during the time in between sessions. Once again, you don't have to stay at 60 or 70 all day. If you're relaxed, not only will you feel better, you'll also think more clearly.

CONCLUDING REMARKS

Most clients are conscientious in practicing the PMR exercises as assigned, and many report improvements in sleep and concentration after completion of this module. In addition, many clients seem less hyper after completing modules 3 and 4, on stress management.

Trauma History Other Than Partner Abuse

Most CTT clients have experienced traumatic events in addition to partner abuse, and it may be important to address these other traumatic experiences for clients to achieve the full benefit of therapy. In this module, therapists query clients about any traumatic events other than partner abuse they may have experienced. The aim of this module is for the client to gain some relief by talking about other traumas in a comfortable, safe, and trusting environment. In addition, most CTT clients find that talking about these experiences in a nonjudgmental atmosphere removes some of the emotional pain associated with these other traumas.

When CTT is conducted in a ninety-minute session format, this module (inquiry about trauma history other than partner abuse) is conducted as part of session 1, after taking the client's partner abuse history. When CTT is conducted in a fifty-minute session format, which is more typical, this inquiry about trauma history other than partner abuse is conducted here, as module 5.

OBJECTIVES

- To identify trauma issues—other than partner abuse—that may need to be addressed

- For the client to experience a lessening of discomfort as a result of disclosing and talking about these other trauma issues

MATERIALS

- Traumatic Life Events Questionnaire (TLEQ), which the client completed prior to starting treatment

HOMEWORK

- Listen to session audio-recordings.

- Continue to monitor and record negative self-talk.

- Practice PMR while listening to the PMR recording, twice a day (ongoing assignment).

- Do a body scan and over-tense and relax muscles when experiencing stress (ongoing assignment).

PROCEDURES CHECKLIST

1. _____ Inquiry into the client's history of traumas other than partner abuse, dealing with one at a time

---

DETAILED PROCEDURES FOR MODULE 5

5.1. Inquiry into the Client's History of Trauma Other Than Partner Abuse

Refer to the client's TLEQ and ask about each traumatic event in turn. **Now I'm going to ask you about other things that have happened to you—things you reported on the Traumatic Life Events Questionnaire, which you completed before our first session.** Be sure to inquire about all events, one by one, that evoked intense fear, helplessness, or horror.

You indicated that you ... Fill in the sentence with the specific TLEQ event; for example, "experienced the sudden and unexpected death of a loved one due to suicide." **What happened?** For each event, ask, **Do you experience any guilt about that event?**

In describing these events, clients may report specific things that are likely sources of their guilt, such as "If I hadn't gone to that party ..." At those times, ask, **Do you experience any guilt about that?** If the client seems confused or uncertain about whether she experiences any guilt, ask her, **Do you think you should have done anything differently?** The purpose of the guilt inquiry is to identify sources of guilt—other than those related to partner abuse—that may be targeted later, during the guilt intervention in module 10. If any other sources of guilt are identified, be sure to document this information in the client's chart, for later retrieval.

If the client endorsed TLEQ item 14 (assessing intimate partner abuse), don't ask about guilt related to partner abuse. That subject will be probed with the structured guilt assessment interview at the beginning of the guilt intervention module (module 10).

CONCLUDING REMARKS

Make note of any other traumas besides partner abuse that the client has experienced, as it will be in the client's best interest to deal with these later in therapy, after partner abuse has been addressed. Because many clients have never talked about some of their traumas to anyone, sharing them for the first time can be both a relief and quite difficult. If a client is upset or tearful after discussing other traumas, take time to assist her in "letting it all out" to gain maximum relief. For the rare client who remains upset and shows no sign of calming down, employ calming or relaxation tools, such as deep breathing or a body scan and PMR, to help her calm down before ending the session.

Education About PTSD

This module has two major goals. The first is for the client to realize and appreciate that PTSD symptoms are normal human reactions to extremely stressful events. This normalizing of problems clients are experiencing serves to reassure them that they aren't "crazy" and often results in a decrease of symptoms. The second major goal is to motivate clients to do the exposure homework, the topic of the next module. The information conveyed here is intended to help the client see exposure assignments as a way of overcoming or getting rid of PTSD and thereby provide her with a compelling reason for doing the difficult work involved in exposure. Avoidance in its many forms (avoidance of thinking and talking about the trauma and avoidance of activities that serve as reminders of the trauma) is a hallmark feature of PTSD. It is essential to counteract or reverse the normal tendency to avoid in order to overcome PTSD.

OBJECTIVES

■ For the client to understand and appreciate that her PTSD symptoms are normal human responses to extreme stress

■ For the client to understand the rationale for the upcoming exposure homework

■ To motivate the client to comply with exposure assignments

MATERIALS

■ Symptoms of Post-traumatic Stress (handout 1.4)

- Causal Model of Factors Thought to Underlie the Development and Persistence of PTSD (handout 6.1)

- Two-Factor Model of Escape and Avoidance Learning (handout 6.2)

- Identifying Harmless Reminders Survey (handout 6.3)

- *Honolulu Star-Bulletin* article: "Abused Women to Share in New Therapy Project" (handout 6.4)

HOMEWORK

- Listen to session audio-recordings.

- Continue to monitor and record negative self-talk.

- Practice PMR while listening to the PMR recording, twice a day.

- Do a body scan and over-tense and relax muscles when experiencing stress.

- Complete the Identifying Harmless Reminders Survey (handout 6.3).

- Read the article "Abused Women to Share in New Therapy Project" (handout 6.4).

- Read and complete chapters 1 and 7 in *Healing the Trauma of Domestic Violence* (optional).

PROCEDURES CHECKLIST

1. _____ Introduction to PTSD

2. _____ PTSD—a normal reaction to extreme stress

3. _____ How PTSD differs from psychosis

4. _____ PTSD—a disorder with a specific cause

5. _____ Discussion of PTSD symptoms (using handout 1.4, from module 1)

6. _____ Situational factors that contribute to the development of PTSD (handout 6.1)

7. _____ Trauma and the tendency to ask "why" questions

8. _____ "Why" questions and guilt

9. _____ "Why" questions and anger

10. _____ The only good answer to the question "Why me?"

11. _____ "Why" questions and emotional numbing

12. _____ How guilt and anger contribute to the persistence of numbing

13. _____ Why PTSD symptoms may not dissipate with time

14. _____ How PTSD is learned

15. _____ Two-factor model of escape and avoidance learning (handout 6.2)

16. _____ Relief—a very powerful reinforcer

17. _____ The problem with behaviors that lead to temporary relief

18. _____ Examples of maladaptive habits that are maintained by relief

19. _____ Why escape and avoidance habits are hard to overcome

20. _____ How emotional reasoning makes it difficult to overcome escape and avoidance habits

21. _____ Accepting that conditioned stimuli aren't dangerous

22. _____ PTSD and loss

23. _____ Overcoming fears of trauma-related events that aren't dangerous

24. _____ Escape and avoidance busting

25. _____ How emotionally charged words interfere with escape and avoidance busting

26. _____ Homework assignments

   ■ Identifying Harmless Reminders Survey (handout 6.3)

   ■ Article: "Abused Women to Share in New Therapy Project" (handout 6.4)

DETAILED PROCEDURES FOR MODULE 6

6.1. Introduction to PTSD

Now I'll teach you about PTSD. In the course of doing so, I'll explain the rationale for the treatment approach I'm using and why it's important to focus on the trauma and to reprocess what happened. I'll help you understand why trauma produces the same kinds of symptoms or reactions in everyone and help you see that your memories of traumatic events are not dangerous.

I'll explain why thinking and talking about what happened are essential to overcoming PTSD. I'm also going to encourage you to voluntarily experience reminders of the trauma, such as watching stories about violence on the evening news.

We can't change what happened, but we may be able to change your interpretation of what happened. Optional example: For example, many people considered Christopher Columbus to be a great guy for five hundred years, but now he's more often considered to be a creep. Can you see that what Columbus did hasn't changed, but people's interpretation of what he did has?

6.2. PTSD—A Normal Reaction to Extreme Stress

PTSD symptoms can be viewed as normal human reactions to extreme or intense stress. The symptoms you're experiencing are because of what happened to you, not because of something about you or your personality. I'll give you a few examples to illustrate. In a study of rape victims who were assessed every two weeks, starting with their initial visit to the emergency room, 94 percent of the women had symptoms of PTSD two weeks after the rape (Rothbaum, Foa, Riggs, Murdock, & Walsh, 1992). Or consider that almost 40 percent of Vietnam veterans who had high exposure to combat still had full symptoms of PTSD fifteen to twenty years after their tours in Vietnam (Kulka et al., 1990).

In a study conducted at the National Center for PTSD from 1993 to 1995, 255 women with histories of physical or sexual abuse were assessed for PTSD with a structured clinical interview (Kubany, Leisen, et al., 2000). It turned out that 80 percent of the women had PTSD. Similarly, in a study of support groups for battered women, 80 percent of the women had scores on a PTSD questionnaire indicating that they could be diagnosed with PTSD (Kubany, Haynes, et al., 2000).

Just imagine, if you were in a support group with ten other battered women and that group was representative, eight of those other women would have PTSD! You are not alone. If someone else had the same trauma history as you have had, they would probably have PTSD, too, and they'd be having similar symptoms or problems to those you're having. Can you see how PTSD is more about what happened to you than about you?

6.3. How PTSD Differs from Psychosis

Traumatic events don't cause a person to "go crazy." Most of the people who wind up in psychiatric wards have psychotic disorders, like schizophrenia and bipolar disorder. Psychosis is different than PTSD. Disorders like schizophrenia and bipolar disorder have a strong genetic basis, which may be triggered by stress. For example, if both parents have schizophrenia, there's a 50 percent chance that their children will have a schizophrenic episode.

In fact, rates of PTSD among the seriously mentally ill are relatively high—40 percent in one study—and it may have been trauma that activated the psychoses. But if you had the genetic tendency to go crazy, you would have gone crazy already, given what you've been through.

6.4. PTSD—A Disorder with a Specific Cause

Exposure to a traumatic event is considered necessary to develop PTSD. Traumatic events are really terrible or life-threatening events—events that cause injury or death, or awful things that happen to loved ones. They are the kinds of events that cause extreme fear or horror, or leave a person completely helpless to stop something bad from happening.

6.5. Discussion of PTSD Symptoms

Show the client handout 1.4, Symptoms of Post-traumatic Stress Disorder. **In the diagnostic manual of the American Psychiatric Association (2000), there are four types of core symptoms of PTSD:** reexperiencing symptoms, avoidance symptoms, numbness symptoms, and hyperarousal symptoms. **Items 1 to 17 on this list of symptoms are divided into those categories.**

Items 1 to 5 are reexperiencing **symptoms. For example, you get upset when you think about what happened, you have physical reactions when you're reminded of what happened, or you have upsetting trauma-related dreams. Give me an example of a reexperiencing symptom you've had in the past month.**

Items 6, 7, and 8 are avoidance **symptoms, and items 6 and 7 are very conscious, deliberate avoidance. Because you don't like thinking about what happened, you may avoid doing things that will remind you of it. What is something you have been avoiding? What do you do to avoid it?**

Item 8 is involuntary avoidance. **Amnesia or a memory block about some important aspect of what happened is an evolutionary coping mechanism. Many survivors of serious childhood physical or sexual abuse have or had amnesia about their childhood trauma, but it enabled them to function. This is a form of what's known as emotion-focused coping.**

Optional example (very relevant if the client is highly dissociative or has memory blocks): Twenty-five years ago in a city in the northeastern United States, all documented incidents of childhood sexual abuse required that the child be examined at the emergency room. Twenty years later, 120 of these women were interviewed for a study but weren't told the true purpose of the study. About 38 percent of these women couldn't recall the incident that brought them to the emergency room (Williams, 1994). The memory block helped them avoid painful memories.

Items 9 to 12 are *numbing* symptoms, which are very similar to symptoms of depression—things like loss of interest in activities that had been enjoyable and feeling detached or cut off from others. In fact, there's a strong correlation between PTSD and depression. This means that if you see someone who has experienced a trauma and appears to be depressed, it is highly likely the person is suffering from PTSD. The good news is that the depression is usually secondary to the PTSD. So if you get rid of the PTSD, the depression usually lifts.

These symptoms may be experienced as a numbness that prevents the person from having positive or joyful feelings or spontaneous laughter, or it may prevent her from being able to cry. This numbness may reflect a protection against experiencing the pain associated with a loss—and an associated inability to accept and grieve that loss. What sorts of numbing symptoms have you experienced?

Items 13 to 17 are *hyperarousal* symptoms—things like trouble sleeping, trouble concentrating, irritability, or being constantly on guard. There is even some evidence that combat veterans with PTSD have higher resting heart rates than veterans without PTSD. Which hyperarousal symptoms have you experienced? How often do you experience them—only rarely, most of the time, or somewhere in between?

Anger is one symptom that many women with PTSD manifest or express differently from men, especially combat veterans, many of whom are very angry and verbally aggressive. Many women with PTSD don't like arguments and raised voices, and avoid conflict at all costs. Women with PTSD avoid anger and conflict for at least two reasons. First, what do arguments and raised voices remind you of? Right. The trauma—getting hurt. Arguments and anger are trauma reminders, and by avoiding conflict, you are exhibiting a symptom of PTSD, item 7 on this list of symptoms: "Efforts to avoid activities, people, or places that remind you of the event."

Here's the second reason women with PTSD usually try to avoid conflict: In the past, when you got fed up and expressed dissatisfaction, what happened? Right. The argument escalated or you got hit. Your anger or expressions of dissatisfaction were followed by or paired with extremely negative consequences, such as getting hit. As a result, impulses to express dissatisfaction become scary, and because these impulses are scary, you may push down impulses to disagree, argue, or express anger.

Now look at items 18, 19, and 20, which deal with trauma-related guilt, trauma-related anger, and grief, sorrow, or feelings of loss. These aren't considered core symptoms of PTSD, but we think it would be in everyone's best interest if they were!

Trauma-related guilt is unpleasant feelings accompanied by beliefs that you should have thought, felt, or acted differently. Trauma-related anger is unpleasant feelings accompanied by beliefs that you think somebody else should have thought, felt, or acted differently. Trauma-related grief, sorrow, or loss may include tangible losses, such as loss of loved ones, loss of property, injuries, or scars, but there are also symbolic losses, such as loss of identity, self-worth, faith in human nature, optimism, or control. Other possibilities are loss of innocence or loss of time—where did the years go? What losses have you experienced as a result of your trauma?

6.6. Situational Factors That Contribute to the Development of PTSD

Give the client handout 6.1, Causal Model of Factors Thought to Underlie the Development and Persistence of PTSD, and as you go through this diagram, point to the parts of the diagram you're talking about. **This diagram shows how PTSD develops and what a person struggling with PTSD is experiencing. Look at the diamond at the top, on the far left. It shows that certain situational or environmental factors make some negative events more stressful than others and make some traumatic events more traumatic than others. Because events that produce intense distress are most likely to cause PTSD, any situational factor that contributes to extreme distress increases the likelihood that a person will develop PTSD. What are some of these factors? [rhetorical question] Well, the amount of damage that is caused. The more damage or harm, the greater the distress.**

A second such factor is proximity, or closeness, to a negative event. There are two kinds of proximity. One is geographical. For example, it would be more distressing if you saw a really bad accident than if you just heard about it. And if you were the victim, you can't get any closer than that. The second kind of proximity is emotional. For example, if something really bad happens to a loved one, the distress is extreme even if you don't directly witness the negative outcome.

A third situational factor involves negative events that occur without warning and don't fit our view of how the world is supposed to work. These are bad things that occur out of the blue that don't make sense—things we don't get a chance to prepare for. An example would be a woman whose "loving" boyfriend hit her out of the blue and broke her jaw.

6.7. Trauma and the Tendency to Ask "Why" Questions

When trauma is occurring, victims are often in shock or disbelief. When you've experienced trauma, you probably couldn't believe what was happening and were terrified or horrified—your heart racing ninety miles per hour, like pressing the gas pedal to the floor while the car is in neutral. But after the trauma is over and you're safe, you're still agitated. It's like taking your foot off the gas pedal, but it doesn't come all the way back up. You're still upset.

When really bad things happen, people try to make sense out of what happened—to understand why it happened. If you know why something happened, maybe you'll be able to predict when it's likely to happen again and maybe even be able to prevent it.

It's human nature, and even animal nature, to search for meaning in negative events. For example, if I put a mouse on the floor, the first thing the mouse will do is explore the room in order to anchor herself in space and make the environment predictable. People and animals don't like uncertainty or ambiguity. It is a universal tendency for animals, including humans, to act in ways that reduce uncertainty and increase predictability.

Well, what kinds of questions do people ask when they try to make sense out of really bad events? Right. They ask why. "Why me?" or "Why would God do this to me?" But as you'll soon learn, when senseless events occur there is only one good answer to the question why.

6.8. "Why" Questions and Guilt

The thinking involved in guilt typically goes something like this: "Why did I do what I did? I shouldn't have done that!" And the thinking involved in anger often goes like this: "Why did he do what he did? He shouldn't have done that!" This helps explain why guilt and anger are extremely common among trauma survivors.

Trauma is a fertile breeding ground for the development of guilt. This is why, in a study of 168 women in support groups for battered women, only 6 of them experienced no guilt related to their victimization. In other words, 162 of 168 did experience guilt related to their victimization by an intimate partner (Kubany et al., 1996).

Trauma survivors will experience guilt whether they deserve to or not, and usually they don't deserve to experience guilt. We'll work on guilt before we work on anger because guilt is thought to contribute directly to shame, low self-esteem, depression, and social isolation. Let's take a look at how this happens. Guilt often leads to shame due to thoughts like "Why did I do what I did? I shouldn't have done that! ... Stupid. There's something wrong with me." And if you experience guilt and shame, how high can your self-esteem be? [rhetorical question] Not very high. You'll also be depressed. And if you're ashamed and depressed, you'll probably want to isolate yourself and be alone.

6.9. "Why" Questions and Anger

Now let's take a look at the thought process involved in trauma-related anger: "How could you? You shouldn't have. How could someone who is supposed to nurture and protect me hurt me? That SOB." If there are multiple victimizations or multiple betrayals, this often leads to a mistrust, negative views about human nature and religion, and a negative, cynical, and hostile worldview. If you can't trust your stepfather, or your boyfriend, or your husband, how can you trust any man? And if you can't trust other people, this also leads to social isolation.

6.10. The Only Good Answer to the Question "Why Me?"

You've probably asked a lot of "why" questions about your trauma: "Why did this happen to me? What did I do to deserve this? Am I jinxed?" There is only one good answer to these sorts of "why" questions. Do you have any idea what that answer might be? Damn bad luck. You were in the wrong place at the wrong time. If you ask one hundred small children to cross a busy freeway, some of them will make it across. Tragically, some of them won't. What happened to you was tragic, and you didn't deserve it. You were just unlucky. Something like winning a lottery— only you didn't walk away with millions of dollars. As one client said, "Yeah, the shit lottery."

I could give you countless examples of damn bad luck. A woman who lived in San Francisco was terribly traumatized by the 1989 earthquake. She then moved to Los Angeles, where she lived through the 1992 riots and was traumatized again. In September 1992, she went to Kauai, one of the Hawaiian Islands, for a vacation—just in time for Hurricane Iniki, which caused a great deal of destruction. This woman was a basket case when they escorted her off the island. Because of her history, she erroneously concluded that what happened had something to do with her, but it didn't. It was just really, really bad luck.

On the other hand, combat veterans who have no guilt related to combat have philosophical beliefs like "War is hell. In war, people die. My buddy died because he was unlucky. It didn't have anything to do with me." This is healthy thinking—the kind of thinking you want to be striving for.

6.11. "Why" Questions and Emotional Numbing

"Why" questions that search for meaning in senseless events—situations where there are no good answers—often lead to emotional numbing. The inability to accept the loss manifests itself as numbing. That is, numbing reflects the inability to grieve and accept some loss, for example, "I can't believe it really happened. I can't understand why."

Emotional numbing may be experienced as an emotional deadness, an inability to experience positive emotions, such as joy, happiness, tenderness, or spontaneous laughter, and sometimes an inability to cry. The numbing is a protective barrier that keeps the person from experiencing the pain of the loss, but this prevents grieving and acceptance of the loss. It's like a painkiller that protects you from feeling the pain of a wound or injury, but in the case of emotional injuries, it's important to feel and process what happened so that you can heal.

6.12. How Guilt and Anger Contribute to the Persistence of Numbing

Guilt and anger contribute to the persistence of emotional numbing. Guilt is so painful that survivors don't like to think about what happened because when they do, they feel guilty. But if you don't think about what happened, how can you reprocess what happened and grieve the loss? Right. You can't.

And anger is the only emotion you can experience that's compatible with numbing. Have you been to a funeral lately? Are people at funerals more likely to scream or more likely to weep and cry? Right. Weeping and sobbing, but not anger, are incompatible with numbing. In fact, there is some scientific evidence that anger may interfere with the grieving process. In a study of prolonged exposure therapy, anger interfered with recovery compared to individuals who exhibited facial expressions of distress and grieving (Foa, Riggs, & Massie, 1995). **People who are angry after a trauma have a harder time overcoming the effects of the trauma because anger interferes with the healthy grieving process.** This concludes the explanation of the causal model. Ask the client, **Does this model or portrait of PTSD fit for you?** Clients usually indicate that the model fits or applies completely and always indicate that it fits at least partially.

6.13. Why PTSD Symptoms May Not Dissipate with Time

You may wonder why you can't get over your trauma, especially things that happened a long time ago. Here's one way to look at it: Have you ever sung karaoke, where the music of songs is played and the lyrics are presented on a monitor so you can sing along, even if you don't know the song? Let's say you go to sing karaoke to distract yourself from your trauma. You turn on the karaoke machine, but it's not playing songs. It's playing your trauma. And the words on the monitor are saying, "I could have prevented this. I never should have gone out with him. I should have left sooner. How foolish. That monster. How could he do that to me? How could anyone who is supposed to love me be so cruel?"

These words are psychological shocks that recharge the images with emotional energy. **This is why memories of the trauma may never lose their ability to make you feel bad—even after many years. Does this model or portrait of PTSD fit for you?** Clients usually indicate that the model fits or applies completely and always indicate that it fits at least partially.

6.14. How PTSD Is Learned

Now I'm going to show you how PTSD is learned and how emotions play a big part in this learning. This model also suggests a way to treat PTSD, because if a person can learn to be afraid of something that isn't dangerous, she can be taught to unlearn her fear. We'll be talking about negative emotions and avoidance, but the model also applies to positive emotions and developing skills.

These principles are applied every day at marine parks. Animal trainers use principles of emotional learning, also known as Pavlovian conditioning and positive reinforcement, to teach dolphins to do tricks, like doing flips and jumping through hoops. When the dolphin does what the trainer wants her to do, the trainer gives the dolphin a fish as a reward. The trainer may also blow a whistle or ring a bell just before giving the dolphin a fish, and after a while the dolphin starts to like the sound of the whistle or bell. At that point, the trainer can use the sound of the whistle or bell itself as a reward, just like Pavlov's conditioning of a dog to salivate at the sound of a tone.

6.15. Two-Factor Model of Escape and Avoidance Learning

Give the client handout 6.2, the Two-Factor Model of Escape and Avoidance Learning. This enclosure, called a shuttle box, has a hurdle in the middle separating the two sides. And here we have a mouse, whom we will call Millie. Millie can shuttle back and forth from one side to the other. When she's first placed in the box, Millie vastly prefers the side with the light because it's air-conditioned and has plenty of food and water, mouse magazines, a light to read by, a cot, and maybe even a mouse companion. Millie doesn't like the other side because it's dark and humid and she's only fed bland food and warm water once a day over there. Unfortunately, the side with the light also has a floor with an electrified shock grid that the mouse trainer in this laboratory can turn on or off.

Let's say the mouse trainer turns the light on and then gives Millie a shock—and then does this again five or ten times. What will Millie start thinking about the light? What will her attitude about the light be? Will she like the light? Right. She won't like the light. She will learn to dislike the light.

This is emotional learning, or Pavlovian conditioning. If you repeatedly pair or associate something neutral with something that has the power to evoke positive or negative feelings without prior experience, after a while the neutral event will also evoke positive or negative feelings. For example, you don't need prior experience with shock to dislike shock, but if you pair the shock with something neutral or even positive, like a light, after a while the light will also evoke negative feelings.

The same kind of conditioning works with people. Say we were to put a picture of an extremely handsome man on the wall. If you get a shock in the seat of your chair every time we illuminate the picture, would you like this guy? Of course not.

And if I told you I wanted you to meet somebody, and then a handsome man comes into the room and you see his resemblance to the man in the picture, would you want to meet this guy? No, you wouldn't.

6.16. Relief—A Very Powerful Reinforcer

After a while, what will Millie learn to do when the light goes on? Right. She'll jump to the other side. And what does Millie get that she likes when she jumps to the other side?

Ask as many Socratic questions as necessary to get the client to figure out the answer. Here are some examples: **What is the big reward that Millie gets for jumping to the other side? What does she get that she likes by jumping to the other side? What is the mental and emotional state that she gets when she jumps to the other side? How will she feel when the light goes on? And how will she feel when she gets to the other side, where there is no light? If I turned on the light in here and it was repeatedly paired with a shock, how would you feel when the light went on? And how would you feel once you got outside?**

Right. She gets relief by going to the other side. And relief is a very powerful reward, or reinforcer. When in pain, people will do almost anything to get relief. Relief is such a powerful reward that at least two antacid commercials have used the word "relief" in the slogan. Do you know what they are? Right. Alka-Seltzer: "Plop, plop, fizz, fizz. Oh, what a relief it is." And Rolaids: "How do you spell relief? R-O-L-A-I-D-S."

A reinforcer is anything that someone likes, wants, and is willing to work for. Deprived of food, a mouse likes, wants, and is willing to work for food. In states of severe pain, people like, want, and are willing to do almost anything to get relief.

6.17. The Problem with Behaviors That Lead to Temporary Relief

One of the problems with relief is that it only feels good for a little while. For example, how many people would say that the best day of their life was the day they got over a bad case of the flu? Sure, it felt great to wake up without a headache and be able to breathe freely for the first time in a month, but what about three days later? Are they still remembering how good it felt when they woke up three days ago? No.

Relief feels good because it is right next to pain and is immediately associated with the termination of pain. Imagine a group of people trying to decide what to do on Saturday night, and one person says, "I know. Let's go to the pharmacy and buy a six-pack of aspirin." Sounds odd, doesn't it? But if you had a severe headache, hardly anything would sound more appealing. Some people will do almost anything to get relief.

A major problem with relief is that behaviors that provide immediate relief usually aren't good for a person. In fact, relief-seeking behavior is the major reason why people come to psychotherapy. They are acting in ways to get immediate gratification or relief, but the long-term consequences of their actions are negative or self-destructive. Let's take a closer look at how this works.

6.18. Examples of Maladaptive Habits Maintained by Relief

For example, consider alcoholism or drug addiction. When experiencing withdrawal symptoms, a drug addict will do almost anything to get relief, even if all the long-term consequences are negative, such as going to jail, becoming more severely addicted, or engaging in behaviors that violate fundamental values, like stealing—including stealing from family—and even prostitution.

Or, to look at it another way, consider obsessive-compulsive disorder, a problem that's well-explained in terms of relief-seeking behavior. You might wonder why a person would keep washing her hands up to a hundred times a day. It's because it feels good when she does it; it gives her relief from the idea that she's dirty or contaminated. Even though it may have felt good a hundred times on any given day, now her hands are red and raw. It isn't in her long-term best interest to engage in the behavior just because it gives her temporary relief, and it doesn't address her underlying and erroneous belief that she's contaminated.

You may be surprised how many rape victims take long or frequent showers because they "feel dirty" and are extremely motivated to get relief. Here's another example: More than a few battered women repeatedly give in to badgering to engage in unwanted sex or unwanted sex acts, such as extremely long sex, anal sex, group sex, or even prostitution, to get relief from the badgering. They give various reasons—"to get it over with … to get some peace … to get through the day … so I can get some sleep"—even though the long-term consequences of giving in are deep resentment, shame, and low self-esteem.

In the most general sense, it is basic human nature to maximize pleasure and minimize pain. Yet some people think that drug addicts and women who stay in abusive relationships are masochistic—that they want to suffer. Nothing could be further from the truth. Such individuals are just the opposite—they're *hedonists*! They're motivated to maximize pleasure and minimize pain—in the short term. Because short-term relief provides pleasure, or immediate gratification, people often opt for relief even when it isn't in their long-term best interest. For example, women who stay with an abusive partner may get relief from all sorts of things—thoughts of poverty, guilt associated with thoughts of leaving, or anticipation of partner retaliation, to name a few.

Look at it this way: Would a three-year-old child rather have a small candy bar today or the offer of a large candy bar tomorrow? Of course. A small candy bar today.

Children have to learn to tolerate delayed gratification, and to save rather than to spend right now. It's not something that comes naturally.

Let's get back to Millie and how this plays out with her. At first, she learns to escape the light. Then, after a while, she also learns to avoid the light. In fact, given a choice, Millie will never go near the compartment with the light again.

6.19. Why Escape and Avoidance Habits Are Hard to Overcome

Escape and avoidance habits are very durable and resistant to efforts to overcome them. Let's say the trainer starts feeling sorry for Millie and throws the shock machine away. Nevertheless, Millie will keep jumping to the other side over and over again, and she may never stop—even though she never gets shocked again. Her escape and avoidance behaviors are maintaining her symptoms and preventing her from overcoming her fear of the light.

Now that the trauma is over and the situation is no longer dangerous, the major problem with this persistent escape and avoidance behavior is that it perpetuates Millie's PTSD. Escape and avoidance are relief-seeking behaviors, but the relief is actually serving to keep Millie afraid. The relief strengthens her symptoms—her fear and her desire to escape and avoid—by giving her a big dose of relief. This positive reinforcement is what makes escape and avoidance habits so much more difficult to break than positive skill habits. For example, how many times do you think a dolphin will jump through a hoop after hearing a bell or whistle, in the absence of being conditioned by receiving a reward of fish? Not many.

Escape and avoidance habits are very durable for at least three reasons: First, each time Millie jumps over the hurdle she gets a big dose of relief, which feels really good, and this makes it more likely she will continue to jump. A second important reason Millie doesn't overcome her fear of the light is that she doesn't stay around long enough to find out that the light isn't dangerous.

6.20. How Emotional Reasoning Makes It Difficult to Overcome Escape and Avoidance Habits

A third important reason why Millie doesn't overcome her fear and still wants to escape and avoid has to do with emotional reasoning. Let's assume Millie has the power of language—that she can talk. When the light goes on, Millie notices her heart beating faster, then she says, "I don't feel safe. I wouldn't be afraid of the light if it wasn't dangerous. My heart wouldn't be racing unless that light was dangerous. I'd better get out of here." So Millie jumps to the other side, and when she notices her heart rate slowing down, she says, "I feel safer now. I feel better, and I feel relieved when I get away from the light. That's additional proof it's safer over here, and that the light on the other side must be dangerous."

When the light went on, even though there was no shock, Millie used her increase in symptoms and her thought that she felt unsafe as evidence that the light was dangerous. When she jumped to the other side, she interpreted her reduction in symptoms and her thought that she felt safer as evidence that the light must be dangerous. Why else would she feel better and safer now?

But is the light dangerous? No. The shock machine is long gone, and logically Millie knows she hasn't been shocked for a long time. She's erroneously using her negative feelings and how they increase and decrease as evidence. But feelings are not evidence. The fact that Millie felt unsafe wasn't evidence that she was, or wasn't, unsafe. The fact that she later felt safer wasn't evidence that she was, or wasn't, safe. Millie might think she couldn't possibly be so scared if she weren't in real danger, but the intensity of her fear of the light simply isn't proof that she is in danger, just as the intensity of fear in a bad dream isn't evidence that someone is in danger.

6.21. Accepting That Conditioned Stimuli Aren't Dangerous

Now, what does this all have to do with PTSD? Images, and memories, and other reminders of traumatic events are just like the light. They're conditioned stimuli, and they aren't dangerous.

Here's an example: A therapist was doing guided imagery with a woman who was afraid of swimming in deep water. The therapist asked her to close her eyes and visualize herself swimming in water that was over her head. When he asked her to open her eyes, she said she hadn't conjured up the requested image. The therapist asked her to try again. After several seconds, the woman exclaimed, "I can't! I can't!" Her therapist then said, "*Imagining* yourself swimming in deep water isn't dangerous."

Any neutral or even positive event that is associated with a traumatic event may become disliked and avoided. For example, many women who were raped in the shower won't take showers. Or if they do, they take really short ones, because while they're taking a shower they feel anxious, and when they get out they get relief reinforcement.

Similarly, many women who were assaulted in their beds won't sleep in that bed anymore, preferring to sleep on a couch or even the floor, and many battered women who were beaten up at the beach won't go to the beach anymore. One woman who was raped in a studio apartment even vowed never to live in a studio apartment again.

6.22. PTSD and Loss

So far, we've been talking about a fear model of PTSD. But, in trauma, there are also losses. For example, a woman who was assaulted in her shower said she used to love taking showers. She said that in the old days, "Nothing was more refreshing than a long, hot shower." Now if she takes a shower, it's a fast one. She feels anxious while taking the shower and gets out quickly so she can get relief. This loss of some-thing she used to enjoy needs to be grieved, or better yet, her willingness to take and enjoy showers needs to be rekindled in some way.

Another example would be women who have been assaulted in their beds. Some of them say that before the assault, nothing was more enjoyable than a good night's sleep in their own bed. Now many of these women prefer to sleep on the couch or even on the floor. A woman may say, "I gotta get over this," and force herself to get into bed. But then she just tosses and turns for half an hour and finally gives up and gets out of bed, thereby getting relief, and goes to sleep on the couch or the floor. This loss of a formerly enjoyable activity needs to be grieved, or, preferably, these women need to learn that the bed isn't dangerous so they can once again enjoy that lost pleasure.

In the same way, many women who were assaulted at the beach by their boy-friend or husband used to love the beach. In fact, that's where they may have met their boyfriend, where they had barbecues and beach parties, and maybe where they first began to dream of an ideal future with their "soul mate," complete with chil-dren, an intact family, and growing old together. These dreams have been shattered or lost and need to be grieved or possibly rekindled in some way, in some future relationship.

6.23. Overcoming Fears of Trauma-Related Events That Aren't Dangerous

The reason this model of escape and avoidance is important is that it has impli-cations for the treatment of PTSD. Millie's fear of the light is irrational. There is no longer anything to be afraid of. The other side of the compartment is air-conditioned and has plenty of food and water, a cot, a companion, and a light to read by. Yet Millie prefers the side that's dark, hot, and humid, where she gets bland food and warm water only once a day. If you put her on the side with the light, she'll jump over to the other side. It's just the way all animals, including humans, are wired.

Unfortunately, many women who have been abused respond just like Millie. They engage in chronic avoidance strategies, and they often become increasingly withdrawn and isolated. They end up in a state of chronic avoidance and relief-seek-ing behaviors, which often don't feel good anymore, in an effort to get rid of every single reminder of the abuse.

6.24. Escape and Avoidance Busting

So what can be done? Let's say you're the new mouse trainer, and you know that Millie is being extremely irrational. Your job is to teach Millie to get over her irra-tional fear of the light. How are you going to teach her that the light isn't dangerous? Remember, the light is just a light. It isn't dangerous or capable of directly causing

pain. But somehow, it has all this power. The correct responses are closing off the side with the light, perhaps by extending up the hurdle or wall separating the two sides, or putting a light on the formerly dark side of the enclosure. If the client doesn't come up with the answer right away, give her some hints, as follows.

Hints: **Imagine that you're an architect or home designer and can rearrange things however you want. How can you rearrange the compartments so that Millie can't get away from the light? And how will Millie act at first when the light goes on? Right. She'll freak out. And how do you think she'll be acting after two or three hours? If nothing else, she'll be exhausted. She'll probably look up at the light and say, "Well, I'll be darned. It isn't dangerous."**

This approach, called escape and avoidance busting, involves exposing trauma survivors to harmless reminders of the trauma until the reminders no longer evoke negative feelings. At first Millie will go "wild," frantically running around if she can't get away from the light. But after a while the light would lose its emotional charge and its ability to elicit negative feelings.

All programs shown to be effective for treating PTSD include escape and avoidance busting as an important component of treatment. All of these programs involve exposing people to reminders of the trauma that are just like the light: scary, but not dangerous.

6.25. How Emotionally Charged Words Interfere with Escape and Avoidance Busting

Escape and avoidance busting is an important part of the cognitive trauma therapy program, too. Escape and avoidance busting is one of the paths to recovery from PTSD. However, there is one circumstance under which Millie could be repeatedly exposed to the light and still not get over her fear of the light. Do you have any idea what that might be?

It's something like this: She's put in the compartment and the light goes on. When it does, she says to herself, "Damn light! I never should have come into this box. I wasted the best years of my life. How stupid! I could have prevented all this. And that mouse trainer. What a monster! He promised he would be good to me. How cruel!"

These negative words are psychological shocks that recharge neutral memories and images of the trauma with negative energy, a process called *higher-order language conditioning.* If you pair neutral things with negatively evaluative words, the neutral things will start to make you feel bad. That's why one of the first things we did in your therapy was help you "clean up your language" by monitoring and breaking habits of negative self-talk. If you stop using negatively evaluative words when you think about the trauma, at first you may still feel anxious or sad, but eventually those feelings will go away.

6.26. Homework Assignments

I'm going to give you a homework assignment to identify reminders of your trauma that evoke anxiety and that you avoid—reminders that aren't dangerous. To help you with this assignment, here's a worksheet on identifying harmless reminders. Give the client handout 6.3, the Identifying Harmless Reminders Survey.

This worksheet lists twenty-two common categories of reminders that battered women often avoid. For each category, you'll indicate the extent to which you avoid that type of reminder. You'll also provide an example of each type of reminder that you escape or avoid. The first category is looking at pictures that remind you of the abuse, such as pictures of your abusive partner. How often do you do that? Clients almost always say seldom or never. Do you think I'm surprised? Not many of my clients like to look at pictures of their ex-partners. In fact, many throw them away. But remember, pictures of your abusive partner are just like the light Millie tried to avoid. They are no more harmful than the light, and it's irrational to be afraid of them.

In another session, I'll negotiate with you to do an exercise in which you voluntarily experience trauma reminders that aren't dangerous. It is important for you to know that I will never ask you to do anything you're unwilling to do. Occasionally, clients say something like "Do I have to?" Do you know what I say in response? I say, "I hope you never have to do anything again as long as you live." I only want you to do things I ask you to do if you voluntarily choose to and think it's a good idea—only if you think it's in your best interest and will promote your long-term happiness.

Give the client handout 6.4, the article "Abused Women to Share in New Therapy Project." I'd also like you to read this article, which relates to the exposure assignment I'll give you a bit later in the course of your therapy. The article, which is about cognitive trauma therapy for battered women, profiles two of the first women who completed the program—a mother and her adult daughter. Their therapist asked these two women to do something they would have never done on their own: to intentionally experience reminders of their trauma. They said, "Why on earth would I want to do that?" But they did, and they both got rid of their PTSD. I want you to read the article and tell me what you think about it next time.

CONCLUDING REMARKS

We have found that after this module is conducted, most clients are willing to do the exposure homework assigned in the next module without putting up any resistance. As a result of the education on PTSD in this module, most clients understand why the exposure assignments are important and see that avoidance only serves to perpetuate or exacerbate PTSD. Once in a great while, however, a client is somewhat reluctant to do the exposure homework. In the next module, we mention some things therapists can say to overcome this reluctance.

Handout 6.1

Causal Model of Factors Thought to Underlie the Development and Persistence of PTSD

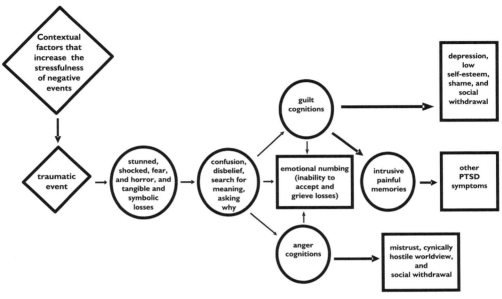

Handout 6.2

Two-Factor Model of Escape and Avoidance Learning

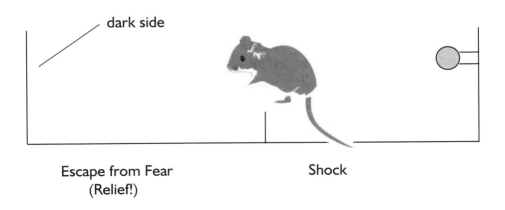

Handout 6.3: Identifying Harmless Reminders Survey

Client Initials: _____   Date: _____

Many formerly battered women continually avoid or try to escape from scary or anxiety-evoking events that are *not* dangerous in order to preserve or obtain a state of relief. Please circle the answers that best reflect how much you avoided the types of events listed below in the past month (the last 30 days). For each type of event that you escape or avoid, please provide an example of what you escape or avoid or the circumstances under which you do so.

1. **Pictures of your abusive partner(s)**

   Don't   Avoid   Avoid   Avoid   Avoid
   avoid   slightly   moderately   considerably   completely

Examples/under what circumstances?

2. **Imagining yourself staring or looking at your abusive partner(s)**

   Don't   Avoid   Avoid   Avoid   Avoid
   avoid   slightly   moderately   considerably   completely

Examples/under what circumstances?

3. **Certain tastes, textures, or odors** (for example, beer, cologne, sweat, or marijuana)

   Don't   Avoid   Avoid   Avoid   Avoid
   avoid   slightly   moderately   considerably   completely

Examples/under what circumstances?

4. **Certain songs or types of music**

   Don't   Avoid   Avoid   Avoid   Avoid
   avoid   slightly   moderately   considerably   completely

Examples/under what circumstances?

5. **Certain kinds of movies or programs on TV**

| Don't avoid | Avoid slightly | Avoid moderately | Avoid considerably | Avoid completely |

Examples/under what circumstances?

6. **Certain kinds of articles in newspapers or magazines**

| Don't avoid | Avoid slightly | Avoid moderately | Avoid considerably | Avoid completely |

Examples/under what circumstances?

7. **Certain kinds of activities** (for example, exercise, going to movies or restaurants, or taking showers)

| Don't avoid | Avoid s lightly | Avoid moderately | Avoid considerably | Avoid completely |

Examples/under what circumstances?

8. **Going to certain places** (for example, shopping malls, certain stores, the beach, or certain parks)

| Don't avoid | Avoid slightly | Avoid moderately | Avoid considerably | Avoid completely |

Examples/under what circumstances?

9. **Wearing certain kinds of clothes or makeup**

| Don't avoid | Avoid s lightly | Avoid moderately | Avoid considerably | Avoid completely |

Examples/under what circumstances?

10. **The telephone** (for example, answering, keeping the phone turned on, or not changing your phone number)

Don't avoid	Avoid slightly	Avoid moderately	Avoid considerably	Avoid completely

Examples/under what circumstances?

11. **Disagreements, arguments, or conflict**

Don't avoid	Avoid slightly	Avoid moderately	Avoid considerably	Avoid completely

Examples/under what circumstances?

12. **Showing emotional upset or raising your voice**

Don't avoid	Avoid slightly	Avoid moderately	Avoid considerably	Avoid completely

Examples/under what circumstances?

13. **Other people's arguments**

Don't avoid	Avoid slightly	Avoid moderately	Avoid considerably	Avoid completely

Examples/under what circumstances?

14. **Someone raising their voice or showing upset or anger toward you**

Don't avoid	Avoid slightly	Avoid moderately	Avoid considerably	Avoid completely

Examples/under what circumstances?

15. **Expressing dissatisfaction or telling other people what you want or what you would like them to do**

Don't avoid	Avoid slightly	Avoid moderately	Avoid considerably	Avoid completely

Examples/under what circumstances?

16. **Hearing someone swearing or using profanity**

Don't avoid	Avoid slightly	Avoid moderately	Avoid considerably	Avoid completely

Examples/under what circumstances?

17. **Certain types of men** (for example, certain body types, certain races, men in uniform, certain kinds of mannerisms, certain kinds of facial features, and so on)

Don't avoid	Avoid slightly	Avoid moderately	Avoid considerably	Avoid completely

Examples/under what circumstances?

18. **Certain family members, certain friends, or certain types of people**

Don't avoid	Avoid slightly	Avoid moderately	Avoid considerably	Avoid completely

Examples/under what circumstances?

19. **Imagining yourself accidentally running into or seeing your abusive partner**

Don't avoid	Avoid slightly	Avoid moderately	Avoid considerably	Avoid completely

Examples/under what circumstances?

20. **Imagining yourself seeing your abusive partner in court**

| Don't avoid | Avoid slightly | Avoid moderately | Avoid considerably | Avoid completely |

Examples/under what circumstances?

21. **Displaying affection** (for example, hugging, kissing, or giving compliments) **or accepting compliments**

| Don't avoid | Avoid slightly | Avoid moderately | Avoid considerably | Avoid completely |

Examples/under what circumstances?

22. **Other nondangerous things that you make efforts to escape or avoid**

| Don't avoid | Avoid slightly | Avoid moderately | Avoid considerably | Avoid completely |

Examples/under what circumstances?

Handout 6.4: Abused Women to Share in New Therapy Project

by Helen Altonn

NO LONGER "A WORTHLESS PERSON": CONFRONTING HER ISSUES LEADS DAUGHTER TO SUCCESS

Christie Corpuz says she was molested as a child and had a succession of abusive relationships starting when she was 12 years old.

"There was no one to say or teach me differently," she said. "Anyone in a different lifestyle, they were not normal to me."

She was involved with four abusive men, she said, noting she met the first one through her church. "The pastor knew and did nothing. That's why I'm not worshipping there anymore."

She didn't try to get away from any of her partners, who eventually left her. "When you try and run, you get it even worse than before if they catch you, and they do catch you."

She became pregnant at 17 and didn't tell her mother. "I didn't think she could handle it. She couldn't protect herself. How could she protect me?"

When her parents divorced, her mother was ordered to go to a counseling program with the children, Corpuz said. "Everything started opening up. I was 19 or 20."

She met Julie Owens, an abuse victim and therapist with the PTSD therapy program, who was working with battered women.

Owens encouraged her to see Dr. Edward S. Kubany in the trauma therapy project.

"She's a fabulous person, smart and articulate. She's a great mother. She has everything going for her, but her life was stalled badly," Owens said.

"I was really scared about addressing any issue," said Corpuz, who began seeing Kubany in March before the project began officially. "I was able to bottle it up. I thought I was all right with it. Dr. Kubany opened my eyes to a lot of stuff I was doing that I didn't know I was doing."

She said she avoided 10 or more things associated with her abusive partners, including four different colognes and the beach. "My first boyfriend had done a lot of violating on the beach because he lived in Waianae."

She has since gone to the beach several times with a companion.

Her worst fears were related to Old Spice men's cologne, she said.

"Dr. Kubany told me to just try to sniff it, to buy a bottle and keep it in my room … My heart started beating fast. I started sweating, just thinking, 'Oh my God, he wants me to buy a bottle.'"

Her mother got a bottle for her, she said. With the top still on, she smelled it and started getting dizzy, she said.

"I just had to keep telling myself it's just cologne; it can't hurt me. It's a nasty smell, but it doesn't affect me like it used to."

Corpuz said she had major guilt feelings because of her abusive partners. "I felt guilty about loving them and staying with them, making excuses for them … I always thought there was something wrong with me because I kept getting involved with these idiots."

She also had a "horrible traumatic experience" when

she was raped by a neighbor, she said.

She said she's not ready for a relationship anytime soon, but she knows the signs now of a potential abuser: "if he doesn't like it when I try to bring out my opinions, or if he doesn't respect my opinions, if he tries to force intimacy too fast, if he doesn't respect my privacy and personal space."

Corpuz said she's happy just to be with her children, 7 and 3 years old, and work toward becoming a high school counselor. "It was so many years all the things were belted into my head— 'I'm worthless; I'm a slut,'" she said. "I have to use the tools (from therapy) the rest of my life. I'm a worthy person. I don't deserve to be hit."

"IT WENT FROM HELL TO HELL TO HELL" FOR MOM

Gloria Riveira said she endured an abusive childhood on the Big Island knowing "once I was 18, I would be out of that house."

One week after high school graduation, she left for Oahu and cut herself off from all of her family except one brother, she said. She has three brothers and two sisters.

"I grew up hating my mom because she was the abuser," Riveira said. "My dad abused the family as a whole and physically abused my mom on a continuous basis. Everybody was abused."

She also was molested by an uncle on Oahu when she was 17, she said.

"I grew up very unloved. I felt so worthless that I don't deserve even to have the breath of life because if my own parents don't love me, who's going to love me?"

After moving to Oahu, she worked at Fort DeRussy, went to an airline school, then got a job as a tour escort and met her ex-husband, a tour driver.

"If I knew the red flags I know now … Within a week he announced to all the tourists on the bus that we will be married."

They were married for 20 years and had three children. "He was very abusive right away," she said. "Within the first week he was calling me all kinds of names. He started hitting me within a month with such rage. He choked me until I'd pass out."

She ran away once and stayed all day at Ala Moana Beach Park. When she returned home, "He said all the things I wanted to hear, that he loved me," she said.

"He told me a number of times, 'If you ever leave me, I'll kill you.'

"He clicked a gun in my face one time and said, 'If I don't have you, no one else will.' He pulled a knife on me in front of my children." Riveira said she thought of killing herself or him. "But what was going to happen to my children?"

She called a shelter once but was frightened when a man answered the phone, she said. "I felt I was in *Catch-22*."

She said her husband "fooled around. He cleaned me out. He pretty much abandoned the family."

Still, her pastor told her that "a bad father is better than no father" and that she should try to "win him back," she said. "So it went from hell to hell to hell."

She said they were evicted twice. "I was trying to support three kids. I worked for the state but it was not enough. He wasn't providing anything. I was still hanging onto the marriage, trying to win him back."

She learned he had a mistress, and still she "didn't want to be the bad guy to file divorce and take the kids away from the father."

Then her son told her: "He's not going to change. You've got to do something."

"I had permission from the kids," she said. "I told him to stay the hell away."

She was divorced seven years ago. The court sent her and the children to counseling because of allegations of abuse. But she continued to have PTSD, she said.

Since joining the trauma therapy program, she said, "Dr. Kubany helped me with a lot of my thinking and avoidance issues."

She had a picture of her ex-husband with two grandchildren and had put a sticker over his face. "He told me to take the sticker off.... This picture no longer can hurt me."

She said she asked her youngest son to invite his father to his high school graduation. "Before therapy I wouldn't have done it.... I had no butterflies whatever. He was no longer a threat to me.

"I have never felt more complete," she said. "I have

God, my health, my children and my life. And I have just finished building my own house with my children."

Riveira said she has asthma, which is aggravated by emotional anxiety, and the therapy "has helped me be more healthy. It has given me a healthier outlook on life.

"It's a piece of gold I'm going to keep in my heart.... I'm no longer a worthless person. I'm a person of value."

The above article appeared in the September 6, 1999, issue of the *Honolulu Star-Bulletin* and is reprinted with the permission of editor Frank Bridgewater.

MODULE 7

Exposure Homework

In this module, clients are asked to systematically experience nondangerous reminders of their abusers and the abuse as a way of significantly reducing, if not eliminating, their negative emotional responses to these reminders. This approach differs from prolonged exposure in that the focus is on decreasing emotional responses to harmless reminders of the trauma rather than to memories of the actual trauma.

OBJECTIVES

- For the client to master a method shown to break avoidance habits

- For the client to learn that she has control over reminders of the trauma and that they need not continue to be scary to her

- For the client to significantly reduce or eliminate negative emotional responses to her trauma reminders

MATERIALS

- Escape and Avoidance Busting Exposure Homework Agreement (handout 7.1)

HOMEWORK

- Listen to session audio-recordings.

- Continue to monitor and record negative self-talk.

■ Practice PMR while listening to the PMR recording, twice a day.

■ Do a body scan and over-tense and relax muscles when experiencing stress.

■ Do the exposure exercises outlined in the homework agreement (handout 7.1).

■ Read and complete chapter 14 in *Healing the Trauma of Domestic Violence* (optional).

PROCEDURES CHECKLIST

1. _____ Introduction and discussion of the Identifying Harmless Reminders Survey (handout 6.3)

2. _____ Exposure to reminders of the abuse and abuser

3. _____ Looking at pictures of an abusive partner or visualizing looking at him (handout 7.1)

4. _____ Enhancing the reality of looking at pictures of an abusive partner and visualizing him

5. _____ Ways to regulate tension levels during exposure exercises

6. _____ Watching movies that portray domestic violence

7. _____ Guidelines for watching *Sleeping with the Enemy* and *Once Were Warriors*

8. _____ Identifying important similarities between the batterers in *Sleeping with the Enemy* and *Once Were Warriors*

9. _____ Engaging in activities and going to places that are reminders of the abuse or the abuser

10. _____ Exposure to other avoided reminders

11. _____ Some exposure success stories

■ A woman who started to enjoy visualizing a former boyfriend

■ A woman whose deceased abusive husband had an identical twin

DETAILED PROCEDURES FOR MODULE 7

7.1. Introduction and Discussion of the Identifying Harmless Reminders Survey

In the previous session, you learned that your efforts to avoid thoughts or memories of your abusive relationship have given you temporary relief, but this has inadvertently contributed to the persistence of your PTSD. You also learned that one of the paths to recovery from PTSD is to deliberately experience reminders of your abusive relationship.

At this point, I'm going to request that you deliberately and voluntarily experience harmless reminders of your abuse and your abuser as a means of helping you get rid of your PTSD. However, I only want you to choose to do what I suggest if you think it's a good idea and will benefit you in the long run.

At the end of our last session, I asked you to complete the Identifying Harmless Reminders Survey, which lists twenty-two types of potentially anxiety-evoking activities that aren't dangerous, but which many battered women avoid in order to preserve or obtain a state of relief. An example would be watching movies or reading articles about domestic violence. After they complete this survey, many of my clients are amazed at how many activities they avoid, how constricted their lives have become, and how much energy it takes to chronically avoid things. I want you to take your life back and realize your full potential. I believe that if you can find the courage to face reminders of pain from the past and do things you didn't think you could do, you'll feel empowered and liberated, with enhanced self-esteem and peace of mind. Did you read the *Honolulu Star-Bulletin* article? What did you learn from reading it?

7.2. Exposure to Reminders of the Abuse and Abuser

In prolonged exposure, the most widely used exposure therapy, people are asked to repeatedly reexperience the trauma in visualizations until memories and images of the trauma no longer evoke anxiety or fear. Unlike what happens in prolonged exposure, I won't ask you to visualize, reexperience, or dwell on specific incidents of abuse. Instead, I'll ask you to engage in four types of indirect exposure exercises, which may or may not trigger memories of abuse.

The first type is to look at pictures or photographs of your abusive ex-partner, if you have any, and imagine yourself looking at him. The second is to experience smells, tastes, and songs that remind you of the abuse or your abuser. The third is to watch movies that portray domestic violence. And the fourth is to engage in other activities or go to places that remind you of the abuse or your abuser.

7.3. Looking at Pictures of an Abusive Partner or Visualizing Him

Do you have any pictures of your ex-partner? If you don't, I'm not surprised. Many clients destroy such pictures or throw them away because they don't want to be reminded of their abuser and what he did to them. If you have pictures or access to pictures of your former abuser, would you be willing to look at them for five minutes a day? If yes: **Great!**

If no: Do you want your ex-partner to be able to continue to get a rise out of you or control how you feel? For example, if he were looking at you, would you want him to see you get upset just talking about him? Of course you wouldn't. If you run into him on the street or at the store, would you rather be calm and relaxed or anxious and panicky? Of course you'd rather be relaxed, because if you're relaxed, you're much less likely to do something rash or impulsive.

Also, remember that nothing about your ex-partner's physical appearance is dangerous. It's just like our mouse Millie and the light. If the trainer showed Millie a picture of your ex-partner every time he shocked her, she wouldn't want to look at him either. However, just as the light itself couldn't inflict pain on Millie, your ex-partner's physical appearance can't inflict pain on you. You may not want to look at pictures of your ex-partner because his face and physical appearance are associated with the mean and hurtful things he did. But our goal here is to neutralize everything about your partner that can't hurt you. Would you reconsider your decision and agree to look at pictures of your ex-partner for five minutes a day? If yes: **That's great!**

If the client's answer is still no: **If you're still unwilling to look at pictures of your ex-partner, I respect your decision. You don't have to do anything you choose not to do. Perhaps you'll reconsider at a later time. Perhaps not. But you are the captain of your own ship, and I respect the direction in which you choose to go. As your advocate, I can only make recommendations regarding what I think is in your long-term best interest, but the final decision is up to you.** If the client persists in saying no to exposure homework, skip the rest of this module and move on to module 8.

Assuming the client has agreed to do exposure therapy, give her handout 7.1, Escape and Avoidance Busting Exposure Homework Agreement. **Please write "I will look at pictures of [abuser's name] for five minutes a day" on line 1 of the homework agreement.** If you have lots of pictures of your ex-partner, I'd like you to select some pictures that remind you of the best times with him and some that remind you of the worst times. Looking at pictures that remind you of the best times is likely to help you feel sad but will help you grieve the loss of the hopes and dreams you once had for the relationship. Looking at pictures that remind you of the worst times is likely to evoke anxiety, which will gradually dissipate.

You're more likely to do an activity that's scheduled than one that isn't, so don't just plan to get around to it; set a specific time. Times that usually work well are in the morning or the evening, rather than in the middle of the day. What time each day would you be willing to look at pictures of your ex-partner? Write the time on the second line on the homework agreement.

I usually recommend that clients perform this exercise in the bathroom, where there is privacy. Unless there's a reason why the bathroom wouldn't be a good place to do this exercise, please look at pictures of your ex-partner for five minutes each day in the bathroom.

Now let's talk about visualizing your abuser. Are you good at visualizing things? For example, if I asked you to imagine yourself in the supermarket, would you be able to make it fairly real—almost as if you were there? The more real you can imagine something happening, the more effective visualization can be as a technique for overcoming your anxiety or fear of anything that isn't actually dangerous.

Would you be willing to visualize looking at your ex-partner for five minutes a day, immediately after looking at pictures of him for five minutes? If the client doesn't have any pictures of her ex-partner, ask her if she'd be willing to visualize him for ten minutes a day. **Please write "I will visualize myself looking at [name] for five [or ten] minutes a day" on the next blank line of the homework agreement, and on the following line, write down when you'll do this.**

7.4. Enhancing the Reality of Looking at Pictures of an Abusive Partner or Visualizing Him

The more sensory dimensions, such as smells, sounds, sight, or touch, that you can create in a simulated experience, the more effective the simulation will be for reducing your level of fear or anxiety when faced with the actual situation. For example, to teach pilots to function at a high level during hazardous flying conditions, trainers utilize a flight simulator, in which pilots practice in a real cockpit, with realistic visual and auditory effects, and with the cockpit shaking like a real airplane would in hazardous flying conditions. But even if the simulated plane "crashes," the pilot will be unharmed because the simulated reality wasn't actually dangerous. The same thing is true when you look at pictures of your ex-partner or visualize him.

If possible, I would like you to add some dimensions of sound and smell to your experience of looking at pictures of your ex-partner and visualizing him. Did he wear any kind of deodorant, cologne, or aftershave lotion that reminds you of him? If yes: Would you be willing to buy a small container of [whatever he wore] and smell it while looking at pictures and visualizing him? If yes: Please write, "I will smell [name of scent] while visualizing and looking at pictures of [his name]" on the next line of the homework agreement.

If your ex-partner drank beer or hard liquor, does that smell remind you of him or the abuse? If yes: Would you be willing to buy a bottle of [whatever he drank], pour it on a towel, and smell it while looking at pictures of your ex-partner and visualizing him? If yes: Please write, "I will smell alcohol while visualizing and looking at pictures of [his name]" on the next line of the homework agreement.

Is there any type of music or are there any particular songs that your ex-partner liked and that remind you of him? If yes: What type of music did he like or what songs did he like? Would you be willing to listen to his favorite type of music or a song or songs that he liked while looking at pictures of him and visualizing him? If yes: Please write, "I will listen to [type of music or songs he liked]" on the next line of the homework agreement.

I congratulate you for having the courage to engage in these exercises. Now let's discuss ways you can control your level of tension and distress while doing these exercises.

7.5. Ways to Regulate Tension Levels During Exposure Exercises

Here are some techniques for regulating your tension level while visualizing your abuser and looking at his photos: First, be super aware of your level of tension, and if you notice increased muscle tension in any part of your body, take a couple of long, slow, deep breaths, tense the affected muscles for five to ten seconds, and then concentrate on letting go of the tension. Second, be very aware of the thoughts going through your mind and make your best effort to avoid any negative self-talk. And third, try to avoid any value judgments, negatively evaluative words, or editorializing about the meaning of your abuser's behavior or intentions. For example, if you interpret his gaze as sinister or evil, characterize him as having a serial killer mentality, refer to him as a pig or a monster, or ask yourself why, you're just going to get yourself worked up into a fit of anger. As I mentioned earlier, emotionally charged words are psychological shocks that can recharge thoughts and memories of abuse and your abuser with negative energy.

If engaging in any of these exposure exercises causes you to recall incidents of abuse you haven't thought about for a long time, don't be alarmed. Having such memories surface will give you the opportunity to take the charge out of them and reduce the negative effects they may have had on you without your awareness. In the unlikely event that you experience intense distress that you can't manage or regulate while engaging in the exposure exercises, you may want to stop doing the exercises for the time being.

How long do I suggest you do this? If you look at pictures and do the visualizations diligently, on a daily basis, for three or four weeks, you'll probably get to the point where it won't bother you much, if at all, to look at pictures of your ex-partner or imagine yourself looking at him. Plus, you'll probably be much less anxious if you actually see or run into him after doing these exercises than you would be now. Would you be willing to do the visualization and looking at pictures exercises for thirty days? If yes: Please write, "I will do the visualization and looking at pictures exercises for thirty days, or until I am not bothered at all doing this exercise" on the next blank line of the homework agreement.

7.6. Watching Movies That Portray Domestic Violence

I always ask clients to watch at least two movies on domestic violence: *Sleeping with the Enemy* and *Once Were Warriors*. Have you seen *Sleeping with the Enemy*? In this movie, Julia Roberts plays a battered woman married to a wealthy man who, beneath a facade of sophistication and charm, is quite cruel and vicious. Are you willing to watch *Sleeping with the Enemy*? If yes: Please write, "I will watch *Sleeping with the Enemy*" on the next blank line of the homework agreement. Then, on the next line, write down when you will watch it.

Once Were Warriors is probably the most graphic movie on domestic violence ever produced. The movie is fictional but very realistic in the way it portrays domestic violence in New Zealand among the native Maoris. Are you also willing to watch *Once Were Warriors*? If yes: Please write, "I will watch *Once Were Warriors*" on the next blank line of the homework agreement. Then, on the next line, write down when you will watch this movie.

I'd like to tell you a little bit more about *Once Were Warriors* before you watch it so you won't be surprised or caught off guard. There's one scene in which the children are terrified and huddled together in their bedroom as they hear their father berate and beat their mother. In a scene toward the end of the movie, the teenage daughter is betrayed and raped by a favorite uncle, a trauma that has far-reaching and tragic consequences. These scenes may be difficult for you to watch, especially if you experienced family violence or sexual abuse while growing up.

7.7. Guidelines for Watching *Sleeping with the Enemy* **and** *Once Were Warriors*

If the client hasn't agreed to watch the movies, skip to section 7.9; or, if she agrees to watch only one of them, modify the following script as needed. **There are several guidelines I would like you to follow in watching *Sleeping with the Enemy* and *Once Were Warriors*.** First, when watching these movies, keep in mind that these are only *movies*, not real life, and no one is getting hurt. The violence is only simulated. For example, in *Sleeping with the Enemy*, Julia Roberts doesn't get real bruises when her husband kicks her in the stomach.

Second, it's important that you watch each movie all the way to the end. If you don't finish the movies, there's a chance you'll be giving yourself relief reinforcement that will actually strengthen rather than weaken your PTSD avoidance symptoms. It's perfectly all right to take breaks from watching the movie as long as you return and eventually watch it all the way through. And when you do get to the end, pat yourself on the back and congratulate yourself for doing something that may have been difficult at first or that you didn't think you could do.

Third, after you have watched each movie, go back and rewatch scenes that were distressing for you and keep watching them until they no longer bother you. And finally, be very aware of how your body is reacting as you watch the movies. If you notice increases in tension, take a couple of long, slow, deep breaths, tense the affected muscles for five to ten seconds, and then concentrate on letting go of the tension.

7.8. Identifying Important Similarities Between the Batterers in *Sleeping with the Enemy* **and** *Once Were Warriors*

In certain respects, the batterers in *Sleeping with the Enemy* and *Once Were Warriors* are very different. The batterer in *Sleeping with the Enemy* is wealthy and sophisticated, and he controls and violates his wife in very manipulative and premeditated ways. By contrast, the batterer in *Once Were Warriors* is uneducated, alcoholic, extremely impulsive, and violent both in and out of the marriage. Now that I've pointed out the differences between these two men, I want you to figure out—after you've watched both movies—how the two men are similar. There are at least two important similarities between these two abusive men that transcend their differences.

The following script is to be used in the client's next session after she has watched both movies. Make a note to come back to this section (7.8) and use the following script once the client has watched the movies: **When you watched *Sleeping with the Enemy* and *Once Were Warriors*, did you come up with any similarities between the two batterers, who seemed so different outwardly?** Allow the client to describe the similarities she noticed, then explain what these similarities indicate: **First, both characters were extremely selfish, egotistical, and self-centered. Second, neither had any empathy, compassion, or even the slightest concern about the suffering he caused the woman he claimed to love. Certainly, both of them had absolutely no guilt. Third, both were deceitfully charming when they wanted to be. Wrapping this all up, both of these guys were full-on sociopaths.**

7.9. Engaging in Activities and Going to Places That Are Reminders of the Abuse

Many formerly battered women avoid a variety of activities and places that remind them of the abuse or their abuser. Examples of activities some of my clients have avoided include exercising, watching sports on TV, reading articles that deal with violence, watching the news or TV programs that depict violence, eating certain kinds of food, and wearing makeup, jewelry, or certain kinds of clothes. Examples of places clients have avoided include certain beaches, parks, restaurants, or shopping centers.

Have you been avoiding any activities or places that would remind you of the abuse or your abuser? If yes: What activities or places have you been avoiding? Are you willing to engage in any of these activities or go to any of these places? If yes: Please write these activities and places on the next blank lines of the homework agreement, and also indicate when you'll engage in these activities or go to these places.

7.10. Exposure to Other Avoided Reminders

Is there anything else you've been avoiding because it's related to your experience of abuse and might make you anxious or uncomfortable? If yes: What have you been avoiding? Are you willing to [do whatever the client has been avoiding]? If yes: Please write down what you agree to do on the homework agreement, along with when you are going to do it.

7.11. Some Exposure Success Stories

In two studies to evaluate the effectiveness of cognitive trauma therapy, 90 percent of the 105 women who completed therapy no longer had PTSD at their post-therapy assessments. The great majority of these women had successfully performed exposure exercises and were no longer avoiding reminders of their abuse or abusers. Let me give you a few examples of exposure success stories.

Janette had been doing an exposure exercise of visualizing her abusive ex-boyfriend for a couple of weeks. At her next session, her therapist asked Janette how this exposure exercise was going, and Janette said, "I'm actually enjoying it." Surprised by Janette's response, her therapist asked for an explanation. Janette replied, "He really was quite good looking, you know." Janette had completely severed the connection between her ex-boyfriend's physical appearance and the abuse he inflicted. She was able to appreciate her ex-boyfriend's good looks without associating them with the type of person he was and what he did to her.

Here's another example: Fran was haunted by memories of her deceased husband, who had abused her for many years. In therapy, it came to light that Fran's husband had an identical twin, Walter, who was always very nice to her but whom she hadn't seen for several years. Fran's therapist suggested she visit Walter, who would definitely remind her of her husband, and Fran agreed. Reporting on what happened, she said, "When Walter opened the door, I started shaking like a leaf. It was as if my husband had risen from the dead." After a pleasant meeting with Walter, she invited him—at her therapist's suggestion—for a barbecue at a beautiful beach where Fran's husband had beaten her badly—a place she had been avoiding. At the following therapy session, Fran said that she and Walter had a wonderful time at the beach and that she was no longer bothered by memories of her deceased husband. Her therapist then said, only half joking, "It would be great if all my clients had an abusive partner who was off the planet and had an identical twin who was a nice guy."

CONCLUDING REMARKS

It ordinarily takes no more than two to five weeks of doing exposure homework on a daily basis to significantly weaken clients' negative emotional associations with reminders of their abuser and the abuse. In some cases, clients actually start enjoying activities they had been avoiding. Once in a great while, a client will report considerable distress that does not decrease after two or, in rare cases, even three weeks of doing the exposure assignments. Under these circumstances, reassure the client that her emotional responses will eventually diminish if she sticks with the exercises. We've had several clients who had strong emotional responses at first but whose emotional responses diminished greatly after no more than four or five weeks of doing the exposure exercises.

Handout 7.1: Escape and Avoidance Busting Exposure Homework Agreement

Client Initials: _____   Date: _____

I agree to engage in the following escape and avoidance exposure exercises to overcome anxieties and fears about abuse- and abuser-related reminders that aren't dangerous.

1. I will _____

    When: _____

2. I will _____

    When: _____

3. I will _____

    When: _____

4. I will _____

    When: _____

5. I will _____

    When: _____

6. I will _____

    When: _____

7. I will _____

    When: _____

8. I will _____

    When: _____

9. I will _____

    When: _____

10. I will _____

    When: _____

Learned Helplessness and How to Overcome It

In this module, clients learn that many battered women who have experienced repeated partner abuse come to believe that they are trapped in the relationship and are helpless or powerless to stop the abuse. This is when they shift their focus from trying to solve their problems to trying to tolerate or make the best of a bad situation (or from problem-solving coping to emotion-focused coping). Even once they're out of an abusive relationship, many women continue to rely on an emotion-focused coping style and allow themselves to be taken advantage of and mistreated by other people. In this module, clients learn about the importance of adopting a solution-oriented or problem-solving coping style as a way of empowering themselves and counteracting a thinking style characterized by learned helplessness or a focus on obstacles.

OBJECTIVES

- For the client to realize that emotion-focused coping makes sense when escape from painful situations is thought to be impossible

- For the client to learn that an obstacle-oriented attitude, such as focusing on reasons problems can't be solved, is unhelpful when solutions may exist

- For the client to adopt a solution-oriented or problem-solving thinking style as a general way of coping with current and future problems

MATERIALS

- Learned Helplessness (handout 8.1)

- A Solution-Oriented Attitude (handout 8.2)

HOMEWORK

- Listen to session audio-recordings.

- Continue to monitor and record negative self-talk.

- Practice PMR while listening to the PMR recording, twice a day.

- Do a body scan and over-tense and relax muscles when experiencing stress.

- Read and complete chapter 8 in *Healing the Trauma of Domestic Violence* (optional).

PROCEDURES CHECKLIST

1. _____ Introduction to learned helplessness

2. _____ Learned helplessness training with Millie (handout 8.1)

3. _____ Millie's thinking shift—coping to survive

4. _____ Women in abusive relationships—coping to survive

5. _____ Trying to make "the best" of a bad situation

6. _____ Results of prolonged powerlessness

7. _____ Examples of coping to survive: deer on frozen lake; lost in the Arctic

8. _____ Emotion-focused coping versus problem-solving coping

9. _____ Aron Ralston's story

10. _____ How learned helplessness overrides reality

11. _____ Learned helplessness training with elephants and with humans

12. _____ How to overcome learned helplessness

13. _____ Learned helplessness and battered women

14. _____ A woman who rolled up into a ball

15. _____ A woman who thought she was overwhelmed

16. _____ Optional examples of learned helplessness: A woman who pretended to be asleep on the beach and a woman who didn't fight back even though she was much bigger and stronger than the rapist

17. _____ Focusing on obstacles and reasons why problems can't be solved

18. _____ Empowerment through solution-oriented thinking

19. _____ Finding a way out (handout 8.2)

DETAILED PROCEDURES FOR MODULE 8

8.1. Introduction to Learned Helplessness

Now I'm going to teach you about a model of learned helplessness, or learned powerlessness, that has been widely used as an explanation for depression or "give-up-itis." You'll also learn why many battered women continue to believe they are powerless even after they're safely out of an abusive relationship.

This model of learned helplessness can also be seen as a model of coping—which seems kind of contradictory, doesn't it? But a little later on, I'll explain why there's no contradiction here. I'll also teach you about the importance of cultivating a solution-oriented or problem-solving thinking style. This will empower you and facilitate your recovery from PTSD.

8.2. Learned Helplessness Training

Give the client handout 8.1, Learned Helplessness. **Assume that Millie has been placed in the same shuttle box she was in before. But now I want you to assume that Millie has never been in the shuttle box before. The difference this time is that the wall is already up, so there are no escape routes to the other side of the enclosure, as shown in diagram 1. In fact, Millie doesn't even know there's another side to the box.**

The trainer turns on the light and then gives Millie a shock. Let's say he does this one hundred times today. And he turns the light on and shocks Millie one hundred times tomorrow and the day after that, too. What will Millie do at first when she's placed in the box and shocked? Right. She'll freak out. She'll run frantically all over, trying to find some way to escape or get away from the shock.

And how will Millie behave after two or three days of getting shocked over and over again? If you were looking at Millie, what would she be doing? Right. She won't be doing anything. She'll appear to have given up, like in diagram 1.

This is exactly what dogs did in the initial research on learned helplessness, which was conducted in the 1950s, before the establishment of current ethical standards for conducting research with animals. After prolonged exposure to inescapable shocks, the dogs would just lie down and moan when the shock was turned on. Similarly, studies have also shown that if you stimulate a leg reflex in a dog and continually shock the dog when it engages in the reflex, the reflex will eventually stop occurring.

8.3. Millie's Thinking Shift—Coping to Survive

Even though Millie stops trying to get away from the shock, has she really given up? Let me ask you this: Would it make sense for Millie to continue to try to get away if escape is impossible? Right. It wouldn't make any sense.

Look at it this way: If you were tied to a chair and someone was beating you with a stick, would it make sense for you to focus on how much it hurts each time you got hit? Or would it make more sense for you to dissociate—to numb out, daydream, or try to distract yourself in some way—to minimize the impact of the beating and the pain? Of course it would make more sense to distract yourself in some way.

In Millie's situation, if she can't escape, would it make sense for her to use up the little precious energy she has left? Of course it wouldn't. It's something like letting a laptop computer go into sleep mode when it's on batteries to make its limited amount of power last longer.

So Millie hasn't really given up, has she? Rather, she has shifted her focus from efforts to escape to efforts to survive. This is coping to survive.

8.4. Women in Abusive Relationships—Coping to Survive

Something very similar happens to many women in abusive relationships. Early on in the relationship, many battered women come to believe they are in the relationship permanently or can't escape or get out of the relationship for a variety of reasons. Maybe because of beliefs that marriage is supposed to be forever or that the children need their father. Maybe because of the abusive partner's threats to harm or kill her if she tries to leave. And many women who grew up with domestic violence may believe that all relationships are likely to be violent, and that if they leave, the next relationship will be just as bad—and maybe even worse.

Did you ever go through a period of time when you thought that you were going to be with your abuser forever—that there was no way that you would be able to get out of the relationship? If yes: What were your reasons for believing that you would not be able to end the relationship or leave your partner?

8.5. Trying to Make "the Best" of a Bad Situation

Back when they believed they were stuck in an abusive relationship, many of my clients were very creative and kept trying to come up with new ways to stop the abuse. Perhaps they felt this was really within their power. After all, in many cases their partners repeatedly blamed them for the abuse and would ask questions like "Why do you keep making me hit you?"

For example, one client said, "I stopped having an opinion. I stopped bringing up things that bothered me or issues that mattered to me because it would only infuriate and enrage him. If I noticed he was in a bad mood, I would avoid him. Another way to avoid it was to participate in his drinking or smoking. So I did things that went against my upbringing. In essence, I lost myself to try to avoid it … But the abuse just got worse and worse." What are some of the ways you came up with to try to get your partner to stop abusing you?

Eventually, most women learn that there's nothing they can do to stop the abuse. More than one client has said, "I could do absolutely nothing, and he would still beat me up." One client was in a relationship with an abusive man who came and went as he pleased. He came home one day after being gone for several days, and she was terrified about what he might do. She said absolutely nothing and went into her bedroom and sat on the bed. He came into the bedroom, watched her for half an hour without saying anything, then beat her up.

Here's an extreme example of a woman who believed she was trapped in an abusive relationship and was completely powerless to prevent even the worst possible outcome. Marie, who lived in Hawaii, was using numbness and dissociation to cope with what she perceived as a completely hopeless situation. One day her boyfriend said, "I'm going to kill you today" as they were driving to the North Shore of Oahu. A short time later, he stopped and went into a convenience store to buy some beer and left Marie in the car with the doors unlocked and the windows down. She made no attempt to get away. She just sat in the car and stared off into space. Fortunately, Marie wasn't killed, or I wouldn't be able to tell you her story. It's an extreme example of how women who believe they're trapped in abusive relationships don't engage in problem-solving coping and instead use emotion-focused coping to minimize the emotional impact of painful situations they perceive to be unsolvable.

8.6. Results of Prolonged Powerlessness

Let's take a moment to summarize: Many battered women think they are powerless to get out of the relationship. Eventually, they also come to believe that they are powerless to stop the abuse. This is when they shift their focus from efforts to escape or stop the abuse to efforts to survive. At this point, many women start numbing out and start focusing on the "bread crumbs" of good things about the relationship to make the best of a bad situation. They may go so far as to say, "He isn't always mean. He really is a nice guy." One client said, "I would inflate every little positive thing about him. Everyone at work thought he was so great. He's very religious, and he's a great cook. And he really does have a good heart. I would puff up all the good things about him in my mind."

What are some of the positive little things that you focused on to make the best out of a bad situation? Many people don't understand why a battered woman would focus on the positive, and they may wonder why she doesn't leave. But if a woman believes she can't get out of an abusive relationship and is powerless to stop the abuse, wouldn't it be pointless to focus on the abuse? Right. It would make more sense to dissociate and focus on something else.

8.7. Examples of Coping to Survive

I'd like to give you an example from the real world. This happened in winter at a frozen-over lake. During the day, the surface thawed a little bit, but then it got really cold and the ice became very slippery. A deer who ventured out to the middle of the lake kept falling down because of the slippery ice. Finally, she stopped trying to get up. Two men approached the deer, and she made no attempt to get away. The men more or less carried the deer off the ice to shore. Interestingly, the deer just stood there staring at the two men, who misinterpreted her behavior as appreciation and establishment of a bond. After about thirty seconds, the deer turned and slowly walked into the forest.

What do you think would have happened if the deer had continued to try to get up before the two men rescued her? She might have used up all of her remaining energy—and died from exhaustion. In a very real sense, the deer was coping to survive when efforts to escape would have been worse than pointless—they might have been fatal.

Here's another example: There have been stories of people who were lost in the Arctic and survived for weeks without food or water. They survived by focusing on preserving precious resources and moving as little as possible. These efforts to cope clearly weren't efforts to escape, but they were efforts to survive.

8.8. Emotion-Focused Coping vs. Problem-Solving Coping

We've been talking about coping—coping with adversity. "Coping" can be defined as "acting to minimize the impact of adverse or painful events." There are two very different ways of minimizing the impact of physically or emotionally painful events. The first is problem-solving coping, which involves placing your focus on overcoming difficulties, eliminating problems, finding solutions, or otherwise removing some irritating or aversive stimulus.

The second way of coping, emotion-focused coping, involves placing your focus on finding ways to get immediate relief from the impact of negative events—without doing anything to remove the painful stimulus or solve the underlying problem. Emotion-focused coping involves finding ways to feel better, or at least less bad, about a physically or emotionally painful situation that may be perceived as unsolvable. Examples of emotion-focused coping include avoiding memories of traumatic events, emotional numbing, dissociation, use of alcohol or drugs, overeating or bingeing and purging, and even self-mutilation.

8.9. Aron Ralston's Story

One of the best examples I can think of to illustrate the distinction between problem-solving coping and emotion-focused coping is the story of Aron Ralston, who in May 2003 was pinned by an eight-hundred-pound boulder that fell on his arm in a remote slot canyon in Utah. After five nights of being trapped, Ralston escaped by cutting off his arm below his elbow with a pocketknife.

Ralston said that he spent the five days considering various plans and evaluating each option. Despite being literally stuck between a rock and a hard place, he simply never gave up and never stopped trying to find a solution. What Ralston did is an ultimate example of problem-solving coping in a situation most people would perceive as hopelessly unsolvable. In his shoes, most of us would probably cope by shutting down, becoming numb, or dissociating and becoming delirious, which almost assuredly would be fatal in a situation such as Ralston's, where rescue was highly unlikely.

8.10. How Learned Helplessness Overrides Reality

Let's say the mouse trainer wants to give Millie a break and takes down the wall so that escape is possible, as shown in diagram 2. Millie sees the other side and says, "Wow, I didn't know there was another side to this box." What will Millie do when the light goes on and then she receives a shock? Will she stay where she is, or will she jump to the other side? And why does she stay or why does she jump?

If the client answers that Millie jumps to the other side, say, **We'd like to think that Millie will jump to the other side, but she doesn't. Why not? Why do you think she doesn't jump?**

Millie doesn't jump because she doesn't think it will do any good. All of her prior efforts to escape were futile, so she's acquired the pervasive belief that she has no power—that she's incapable of stopping bad things from happening through her own efforts. Therefore, it would be pointless to focus on the pain and to try to get away.

8.11. Learned Helplessness Training with Elephants and with Humans

Learned helplessness training is sometimes used to make domesticated elephants more compliant. The trainer chains the elephant's leg to a cage or some other immovable object, and each time the elephant tries to get away the chain hurts the elephant's leg. Eventually, the elephant stops trying to get away because not only is it futile, it also causes pain. At that point, the trainer can chain the elephant to anything, even just a peg in the ground, and it won't try to escape.

Can you see why an elephant tied to a peg in the ground wouldn't try to get away—even though it has the power to easily get away? Perceived reality is more important than actual reality. This is similar to the situation of many battered women, whose efforts to stop the abuse or to escape from the relationship not only don't work, they also result in an escalation of the abuse or other negative consequences.

In laboratory studies, humans have been taught to believe they are helpless, too. For example, human subjects have been taught to endure a mild shock and not try to escape—even though they can potentially escape the shock. In one study (Rosenhan & Seligman, 1989), subjects were asked to put a finger on a table, and when they did, they received a mild electrical shock. When they picked up the finger, which was the reflexive thing to do, they continued to receive the shock. After a while, the experimenter arranged it so that if subjects raised the finger, the shock would stop. However, subjects who had learned that raising their fingers didn't do any good continued to keep the finger on the table and receive the shock—even though they could now escape the shock.

8.12. How to Overcome Learned Helplessness

Because Millie doesn't try to get away from the shock, she doesn't have an opportunity to learn that going to the other side will bring relief. To encourage Millie, let's say we coax her to the other side, where she gets relief from the shock. "Wow, that feels great," she says.

Now we put her back on the side with the light and turn on the light, and the shock. What will Millie do? Many clients say that now Millie will jump to the other side. Unfortunately, though we'd like to think that Millie will now jump, she doesn't. Why do you think Millie won't jump to the other side, even after she's had the experience of obtaining relief when she gets to the other side? If we could interview Millie to find out why she didn't try to get away from the light, she might say something like "What would be the point?" If we pressed the issue and reminded her that she got relief when she was on the other side, she'd probably say something like "Yeah, I noticed. That was great!" If we were to ask her why she thinks the shock stopped, it's likely that she'd say something like "I don't know, but it didn't have anything to do with me. Was that mouse trainer having a good day? Or did he find some other mouse to pick on?"

The point here is that Millie has acquired the pervasive belief that she's powerless—that she can't stop bad things from happening. She sees no connection between her actions and a potential solution to the problem.

After training in learned helplessness, animals are slow to learn that they aren't actually powerless—that they can get away from the shock once it's no longer inescapable. This "unlearning" is slow even if you coax them to the other side of the compartment and they experience the termination of the shock. Left to themselves on the side with the shock, they may remain curled up on the floor and endure the shock repeatedly. Eventually, however, they will figure out that they don't need to endure the shock. That's the good news.

8.13. Learned Helplessness and Battered Women

Now, what does this all have to do with formerly battered women? [rhetorical question] Many battered women are in a similar situation after they are safely out of an abusive relationship. They still don't think they're very powerful, influential, or capable of solving their problems. They may think that if they get involved in a new relationship, they still won't be able to get their needs met and will be taken advantage of—or worse. I'll give you a couple of examples.

8.14. A Woman Who Rolled Up into a Ball

Mary had a very good marriage for about ten years. Then something awful happened to one of her husband's close friends, and this activated memories of a terrible trauma from his own childhood. Overnight, he turned from a nice guy to a "screamer." He would repeatedly scream at Mary, six inches away from her face. Mary believed he was sick and thought it was her duty to see him through his illness. So she would just take it and dissociate or shut down to minimize the impact of the screaming. Mary shut down so much, in fact, that she could only remember about one month of a two-year period of time. If her husband wasn't home by 9 p.m., Mary knew that he was drinking and that she would be in for it when he got home. On these occasions, she'd go into the closet, crawl under a pile of clothes, and roll up into a ball, as if trying to shrink and disappear.

When she started therapy, Mary was divorced, safe, and had a good job. She was under a lot of stress, however, and her PTSD symptoms were acting up. One day Mary misplaced her keys three times and was being highly self-critical, saying things like "What's the matter with me? Why can't I get over this?"—which didn't help the situation. To make matters worse, her coworker, who was generally a very nice guy, started making fun of her, saying things like "How can anyone misplace their keys three times in one day in a small office like this?" Mary didn't think he was being funny, however, and referred to his behavior as "picking on me." She said, "Why do people always pick on me?"

That evening, her coworker drove Mary home after work, as he often did, and went with her into her apartment to have a cup of coffee, also as he often did. When Mary entered her apartment, she walked right through the living room, went into her bedroom, closed the door, and rolled up into a ball! She acted as if she was just as powerless as she truly had been when she was trapped in her marriage. It never even occurred to Mary to say something like "Hey, get off my case," "You could at least help me look for my keys," or "I don't think your teasing is funny, and I would appreciate it if you stopped."

A related story about Mary further illustrates just how powerless or uninfluential she believed herself to be. She described other coworkers in her office as if they were extremely malicious and exploitative, saying things like "They really have it in for me." Mary's therapist started talking to her about the importance of being assertive and standing up for her rights. Her therapist said, "People can't read your mind and won't know what you want or what bothers you if you don't tell them," and encouraged Mary to start advocating for herself. Mary's first reaction to this suggestion was to recoil in fear. She said that if she started being assertive, it not only wouldn't help, it would actually make matters worse. "Then, they will really have it in for me," she said. Can you see just how powerless Mary perceived herself to be?

8.15. A Woman Who Thought She Was Overwhelmed

A second example is Yuki, a formerly battered woman who continued to believe that she wasn't in control of her life even though she had been out of an abusive relationship for three years. She was dreading having to move, and at first her therapist couldn't figure out why. One day Yuki came to therapy reporting great shame for something she had done. A friend who was going to help her move called at the last minute and said she couldn't help because she just got a job. Yuki said that she "felt overwhelmed" when her friend told her she couldn't help, and she ended up taking some illegal drugs to try to deal with her feelings. As a result, she felt like a bad mother to her two young boys. (By the way, from monitoring your own negative self-talk, you might recall that statements like "felt overwhelmed" and "felt like a bad mother" are both inaccurate and unhelpful. We'll take an in-depth look at this in our next session.)

Yuki's therapist asked her to recall the first time she felt overwhelmed. Almost instantly, Yuki said that she first felt that way when she was five years old and living with an abusive stepmother. She said that on one occasion her stepmother was going out and told her "to do this, and this, and this, and this," giving Yuki a series of impossible tasks. Yuki knew she would be beaten when her stepmother returned home no matter how much she did. Was Yuki overwhelmed in that situation? She certainly was. She had absolutely no power and couldn't do anything to prevent the bad things that were going to happen to her. Now Yuki thought she was just as overwhelmed about having to move as she was when given all those impossible tasks by her stepmother. Yuki's therapist asked, "How is having to move as an adult similar to being given an impossible task as a small child?" Yuki answered, "They aren't the same at all. Except that I felt the same way: overwhelmed!"

Yuki was using emotional reasoning to conclude that she was just as powerless as an adult as she was when she was a small child. As her present situation was analyzed, Yuki realized that she wasn't overwhelmed and did in fact have many options. She realized that instead of taking drugs, it would have been in her best interest to relax and then prioritize the tasks involved in moving. By the end of the session, she laughed after concluding that she could make moving even easier by giving half of her things away.

8.16. Optional Examples of Learned Helplessness

Here are a few optional examples that may be used if learned helplessness is a major issue for the client, or if she's having difficulty with the concept. A woman who pretended to be asleep on the beach: Carla had a long history of physical and sexual abuse. She had a phobia about raised voices and was intimidated by other people's anger. For example, Carla would perspire profusely and visibly tremble if someone got even slightly mad at her. On one occasion, Carla was lying in the sun on a secluded beach and had fallen asleep. When she woke up and opened her eyes, there was a man lying right next to her wearing a sweat suit and a hood over his head. What do you think Carla did? She closed her eyes again and "pretended to be asleep." When asked why she didn't say or do anything, Carla said, "I didn't want to be rude."

A woman who didn't fight back even though she was much bigger and stronger than the rapist: Here's yet another example: Celeste befriended a neighbor. One evening he invited her over to watch TV and then made advances and forcibly raped her. Celeste didn't fight back. She told her therapist, "I don't know why I didn't fight back. I was bigger and stronger than he was. I should have fought back. How stupid!"

You can understand why Celeste didn't fight back once you know her history with two abusive boyfriends when she was an adolescent. Both boyfriends were sexually violent and would beat her up if she resisted their forceful sexual advances in any way. When her neighbor assaulted her, Celeste went numb and froze, which had been adaptive in the past, when she was assaulted by her two much bigger and stronger boyfriends.

8.17. Focusing on Obstacles and Reasons Problems Can't Be Solved

An attitude of learned helplessness focuses on obstacles and reasons why problems can't be solved. For example, what are your chances of getting over a high wall if you focus or dwell on how high it is, citing reasons why you can't get over it? Based on past experience, you might say, "I tried getting over that wall. It didn't work then, and it won't work now." But what are your chances of getting over the wall if you think this way? Right. Slim to none—not good at all. With that kind of thinking, you'll only get over this wall if you get lucky, and that wouldn't have anything to do with you or anything you have control over.

When asked about her chances of getting over the wall if she didn't think she could, one client said, "I wouldn't even think about the wall!" This is a classic example of learned helplessness, where the emphasis is on emotion-focused coping. It's adaptive or helpful if you can't escape from a bad situation, but unhelpful if escape routes exist.

8.18. Empowerment Through Solution-Oriented Thinking

Now I want to help you develop a different attitude—an attitude I have that helps me not get depressed because of working with battered women and other trauma survivors. Can you imagine how depressing this kind of work would be if I focused on how painful my clients' problems are? It would be all too easy to think, "Oh my god, you're never going to be able to recover from this. You might as well give up and drop out of therapy right now. You're wasting your time. And I'm wasting my time too! I've got a headache. I need a drink. I need to get out of this line of work."

Wouldn't this be a terrible job if this was my attitude? The reason this kind of work isn't depressing to me is that I'm always focusing on how problems can be solved and how obstacles can be overcome: "How can I get over that wall? How can I get around that wall? How can I get through that wall? How can I get *under* the wall?" If you spend your time thinking about ways obstacles can be overcome and problems can be solved, you may or may not succeed. But what are your chances of success if you focus only on the negative and give up? Right. You'll only be successful if you get very lucky. My attitude is always solution-oriented. I try to focus on changing the present and the future, rather than dwelling on the past and things I can't change.

8.19. Finding a Way Out

Give the client handout 8.2, A Solution-Oriented Attitude. **I'm going to illustrate this problem-solving or solution-oriented attitude with this cartoon of two men shackled to the wall in a dungeon with only a tiny window. It looks like a completely hopeless situation—about as bad as it can get. But notice that one of the prisoners is smiling. What could he possibly be smiling about? Maybe something that reflects a solution-oriented attitude? Let's see. Perhaps he's saying something like "There must be some way to get out of here. I know I can figure it out. At least there are two of us here. Two heads are better than one. Let's brainstorm possible solutions."**

Do you have any ideas about what he could be saying? One of the most creative responses I've heard is "I know where I can get a good attorney!"

Here's what I think he's saying: Write the sentence "Now, here's my plan!" in the bubble over the man's head, then say it out loud and ask the client to read it aloud.

This problem-solving orientation is the same kind of attitude that prisoners of war use to survive imprisonment. They never give up hope, and they never stop trying to come up with ways to escape. Developing a solution-oriented attitude is going to facilitate your recovery from PTSD, and it's necessary for your recovery. Coming up with ideas for possible solutions is incompatible with "give-up-itis" and perceptions of powerlessness.

Does this make sense? Can you relate to this? Can you see how a problem-solving attitude is going to be helpful or useful for you?

CONCLUDING REMARKS

The information provided in this module makes good sense to most, if not all, clients. After being educated about learned helplessness, most clients recognize that they have come to rely on an emotion-focused coping style. They usually acknowledge that a solution-oriented or problem-solving coping style is much more likely to promote their long-term best interest.

Handout 8.1: Learned Helplessness

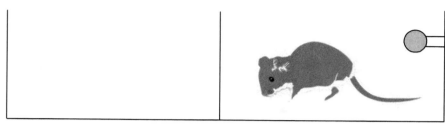

Inaccessible area
(escape **impossible**)   Shock

Diagram 1

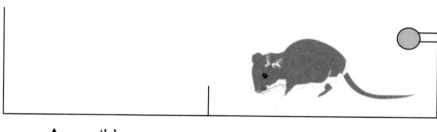

Accessible area
(escape **Possible**)   Shock

Diagram 2

Handout 8.2: A Solution-Oriented Attitude

Education About Negative Self-Talk

The most important reason for having a module on negative-self-talk education is to heighten clients' motivation to break their habits of using negative self-talk and encourage them to conscientiously do the self-monitoring homework. While self-monitoring can be an important and effective tool in breaking any undesirable habit, it will only work if it's used. To the extent that clients appreciate how detrimental negative self-talk is, we believe they will be more conscientious about doing the self-monitoring assignment and will be more successful in breaking negative self-talk habits.

OBJECTIVES

- For the client to acquire a full understanding of how negative self-talk is detrimental to her emotional well-being

- To motivate the client to break negative self-talk habits and do the self-monitoring homework

MATERIALS

- Negative Emotional Experiences (handout 9.1)

HOMEWORK

- Listen to session audio-recordings.

■ Continue to monitor and record negative self-talk.

■ Practice PMR while listening to the PMR recording, twice a day.

■ Do a body scan and over-tense and relax muscles when experiencing stress.

■ Read and complete chapter 5 in *Healing the Trauma of Domestic Violence* (optional).

PROCEDURES CHECKLIST

1. _____ Introduction to negative self-talk

2. _____ The word "should"

3. _____ The phrases "should have" and "could have"

4. _____ "Why" questions

5. _____ Shame-related put-downs of one's entire self, personality, or intelligence

6. _____ Saying "I feel" in statements that aren't about emotions

7. _____ Relatively pure negative emotions (table 1 in handout 9.1)

8. _____ Hybrid emotions (table 2 in handout 9.1)

9. _____ Ideas, opinions, and value judgments (table 3 in handout 9.1)

10. _____ Emotional reasoning (table 4 in handout 9.1)

11. _____ "I feel responsible"

12. _____ "I feel obligated"

13. _____ "I feel overwhelmed"

14. _____ "I don't feel safe"

15. _____ Emotional reasoning and decision making

16. _____ Strong motivation—a prerequisite for breaking bad habits

DETAILED PROCEDURES FOR MODULE 9

9.1. Introduction to Negative Self-Talk

You've been monitoring your negative self-talk for a while, but now I'd like to explain in-depth why this is so important. Let's take a look at the power of negative self-talk. Negative self-talk is like a cancer, and the more you realize how personally harmful it is, the more motivated you'll be to break this habit. And the more motivated you are, the more quickly you'll break this harmful habit. In your self-monitoring, you've been keeping track of four categories of self-talk in speech and thoughts. These four categories encompass almost all the ways you can talk disrespectfully to yourself. Just to recap, category 1 is "should," "should have," "could have," and "why?" Category 2 is put-downs of your entire personality or character. Category 3 involves using "I feel" in statements that aren't about emotions. And category 4 is apologies. Let's take a closer look at all of these, starting with category 1.

9.2. The Word "Should"

Using the word "should" when deciding what to do often leads to decisions that aren't in your best interest. What does it mean to say "I should do something"? Right. It means that you're *obligated* to do something. You're *supposed* to do something. You have to do something. Unfortunately, from the time they are girls, women are taught many "supposed to" beliefs that lead them to believe they are supposed to do all kinds of things that aren't in their best interest and only maintain the existing social order of male dominance and female subordination.

Hence, "shoulds" are "supposed tos," but it may or may not be in your best interest to do what you think you should do. Here's an example: "Should I give him another chance? Should I stay? I guess I should. After all, he apologized, and I'm supposed to be a forgiving person. And marriage is supposed to be forever, after all. I should stand by my man. On the other hand, is it a good idea to forgive him and act like it never happened? I don't know. But, I should. I'm supposed to."

When trying to decide what to do, instead of asking yourself what you should do, instead ask, "What course of action is most likely to be in my long-term best interest? What is most likely to promote my long-term happiness? What good things and bad things are likely to happen if I do this? What good things and bad things are likely to happen if I do something else?" In other words, when you're thinking "I wonder what I should do?" rephrase the question.

Millions of women would have ended an abusive relationship sooner or would have been less likely to go back after leaving had they made their decisions based on an intellectual analysis of the likely consequences of leaving or staying, rather than on the basis of an irrational "should." In summary, the word "should" can be harmful to you, and you do not need to use it to communicate or to make smart decisions. I refer to "should" as "the S word."

9.3. The Phrases "Should Have" and "Could Have"

The self-talk phrases "should have" and "could have" aren't good for you for at least three reasons: they reflect guilt, they make you feel bad, and they often indicate a put-down of your entire self. Let's look at the first issue—guilt.

Statements that include the phrases "should have" or "could have" usually signal the presence of guilt, and guilt, of course, is a source of emotional pain. But it's worse than that, because when you say "I should have" or "I could have," it usually signals guilt that has no rational basis. You're usually making a thinking error that causes you to draw a faulty conclusion about your role in a negative event. When you say or think the phrase "should have" or "could have," it's likely that you're falsely remembering an unforeseeable negative outcome as foreseeable. And if the outcome was foreseeable, it was also preventable, right? If you're remembering the negative outcome as preventable, yet you allowed it to happen, can you see where that goes? Right. Straight to guilt. This tendency to remember unforeseeable outcomes as foreseeable is called hindsight bias. I'll have a lot more to say about hindsight bias when we start working on guilt issues.

A second reason the phrases "should have" and "could have" aren't good for you is that they make you feel bad. Saying "I should have" or "I could have" is self-criticism or self-punishment that makes you feel bad and lowers your self-esteem. What if a friend or relative says, "You could have prevented the abuse," "You shouldn't have gotten together with him," "You should put it behind you and get on with your life," or "You shouldn't feel that way." Would you feel better? Of course not! You wouldn't feel better because it's criticism, and criticism doesn't feel good. These words have the same negative effect when you say them to yourself as when someone else says them to you.

A third reason the phrases "should have" and "could have" aren't good for you is that they are often followed by or lead to the second category of negative self-talk—shame-related put-downs of your entire personality, character, or intelligence; for example, "I shouldn't have done that. I was stupid and I have bad judgment. There's something wrong with me." And put-downs of your entire self can be even more painful than the phrases "should have" and "could have." Again, the bottom line is that it is in your long-term best interest to give yourself the same kind of respect that you would like to get from other people.

9.4. "Why" Questions

Now I'm going to elaborate on reasons that "why" questions aren't good for you. One reason is because these questions often lead to "should have" statements and guilt. For example, when you ask "Why did I do something?" you will often then say or think "I shouldn't have done that." Do you see how "should have" statements often follow from "why" questions?

Similarly, "why" questions can also give rise to anger. When you ask why others did what they did, it can lead to "should have" statements associated with anger, such as "Why did he do that? He shouldn't have done it!" or "Why did the criminal justice system fail me? It's unfair. I shouldn't have been treated unfairly by the system!" When it comes to anger, spending your time on the things you can't change is nothing more than a loss of time you could spend on improving your life. That's one of the reasons I'm going to help you stop asking "why" questions that lead to anger. Asking why does you no good at all. The next time you find yourself asking why, ask yourself a "what" question instead, such as "What am I going to do about it?" If your answer is "nothing," change the subject, because you're wasting your time.

The third set of statements on the self-advocacy strategies handout (handout 1.2) is particularly relevant here. I'll read it to you: "It does not promote my long-term happiness to think or talk about things I cannot change, such as dwelling on the unfairness of the system or past injustices. The time I spend on such things is time I can't spend working on things I can control, change, or do something about. In business, they call this an opportunity cost. Time spent doing things of little value costs us the opportunity of spending that time doing something more worthwhile. In other words, spending time on things I can't change does not belong on my daily to-do list."

Let's see, what are you going to do tomorrow? Go to work. Read. Have some fun. Spend some time with a friend. Cook. And spend fifteen minutes asking why? If something isn't going to improve your life in some way, don't waste your valuable time doing it.

Another problem with "why" questions is that they can keep you stuck in the past. There is no problem solving involved because knowing why can't change what happened. It just keeps you stuck in pain, helpless anger, or helpless rage. You cannot control or undo what happened in the past.

You may think that the answers to "why" questions will make you feel better, but this is seldom true. As a formerly battered woman, you may wonder, "Why was he so brutal and cruel? Why would someone who said he loved me treat me that way? Why did he keep lying to me? Why didn't he realize that he was destroying my love for him?" But knowing the answers to these questions won't change fact that you were betrayed. Knowing why won't undo what happened, and it won't change your abuser into a loving, caring, faithful, and compassionate partner. It's usually a fantasy when a person thinks, "If I just find out why, I'll feel better."

9.5. Shame-Related Put-Downs of Your Self, Personality, or Intelligence

I'll only talk briefly about the second category of negative self-talk—put-downs of your entire self—because it's so obvious that this kind of self-talk does nothing but drag you down and keep you down. Statements such as "I feel stupid and inadequate," "I'm an emotional mess and a wimp," "I feel ashamed," or "There's something wrong with me" are all expressions of shame. Shame can be defined as an unpleasant feeling plus a negative evaluation of your entire self, personality, intelligence, or character. Shame is often expressed as an "I feel" statement, like "I feel inadequate." Shame-related negative self-talk not only makes you feel bad, it also lowers your self-esteem. Why would you want to lower your self-esteem?

You can verbally communicate the experience of shame in a seemingly infinite number of ways; for example, by saying things like "I feel like I'm a nobody" or "I'm damaged goods." Would putting yourself down in these ways make you want to try harder or make you want to get down on all fours and crawl away? It bears repeating: It is in your best interest to start giving yourself the same kind of respect you would like to get—and deserve to get—from other people.

9.6. Saying "I Feel" in Statements That Aren't About Emotions

Give the client handout 9.1, Negative Emotional Experiences. **How you feel is obviously extremely important, and communicating to others how you feel is extremely important too. However, it's also important to only use the phrase "I feel" in regard to relatively pure feelings or emotions. Let's take a closer look.**

9.7. Relatively Pure Emotions

There are only a small number of relatively pure emotions or feelings. These relatively pure emotions are positive or negative feelings that are vague and diffuse. They don't have much content or meaning attached. You can be in a good mood or bad mood regardless of what is going on around you, like waking up in the morning and feeling anxious, sad, in a bad mood, or down even if you have every reason to be in a good mood. You could think of it as just having a bad biorhythm day. Conversely, you can be in a good mood even though you have reasons to be in a bad mood. We've all had days like these.

The primary relatively pure negative emotions are listed here, in table 1. I'd like you to say "I feel" and then finish the statement with a few of the emotions listed here. (Emotions listed are distressed, upset, hurt, sad, frustrated, disappointed, unhappy, anxious, and scared.)

9.8. Hybrid Emotions

All other emotional experiences are combinations of the pure emotions with certain attributions, explanations, or interpretations. Read the title of table 2. ("Hybrid negative emotions, which have a feeling part and a thinking part.") **What pure emotion from table 1 do you have when you experience guilt? Some type of distress, right? Or perhaps upset or unhappiness.**

And what kinds of thoughts run through your mind when you experience guilt? A lot of women say things like "I should have done something differently," "I screwed up," or "It's my fault." All of these boil down to pointing a negative finger at yourself for acting in a way you think you shouldn't have acted.

I could just as easily ask you "What do you think guilty about?" as "What do you feel guilty about?" because guilt has a thinking part as well as a feeling part. It would be most accurate to say, "I *experience* guilt" because this statement acknowledges that guilt is a combination of feelings and thoughts. The same holds true for other hybrid emotions. Anger and shame, for example, also have a thinking part as well as a feeling part.

Some therapists think it's their job to help clients sort out their feelings. But in cognitive trauma therapy, we don't see it this way. In cognitive trauma therapy, the therapist's job is to help clients think more clearly. Our approach also maintains that people can only have one emotional experience at a time, although different emotional experiences can certainly follow one another in rapid succession. For example, consider the following sequence of statements made by a Vietnam veteran: "I never should have fired into that village. I should have known there were women and children there and that the enemy was long gone. I'm a horrible person for firing on that village. That damn lieutenant! He never should have told us to fire at that village." In those five brief sentences, he transitioned from guilt to shame to anger.

That same sequence of emotional experiences is reflected in this statement by a battered woman: "I never should have married him. I should have seen the signs. What an idiot. I was so stupid. But why did he deceive and manipulate me? He never should have done that. Jerk!" However, even though the negative feelings are the same in each case, the emotional experiences are different because the two people are having different thoughts.

9.9. Ideas, Opinions, and Value Judgments

Now look at table 3 and read the title aloud. ("Examples of thoughts or beliefs, which require evidence or proof.") **Now read the words in the first row aloud.** ("Responsible, obligated, overwhelmed, unsafe.") **These words are not emotions. They are ideas, beliefs, opinions, or conclusions that can only be determined to be true or false based on evidence or proof.** We know these ideas are true or not based on factual evidence—not feelings. Let's examine the words in the top row of table 3.

First, consider the word "responsible." Responsible isn't a feeling or an emotion. To say that someone is responsible means that the person caused something to happen. Whether a person is responsible or not can only be determined based on evidence. Do you think a judge wants the jury to tell him how they *feel* about the defendant—to say something like "Your Honor, we just have a gut feeling the defendant is guilty"? I don't think so. The judge wants the jury to weigh the evidence to determine whether the defendant was responsible for committing the crime.

Now consider the word "obligated." An obligation is a debt. If you charge something on your credit card, you are obligated to restore the balance. If you hire someone to clean your apartment, you are obligated to pay them. An obligation means that a person has a moral or legal duty to do something. To determine whether a person is obligated to do something, it's necessary to analyze the facts.

Next, consider the word "overwhelmed." It means that a person is totally overpowered and completely helpless to prevent something bad from happening. Only slaves, prisoners, children, and victims of abuse are overwhelmed. Like a woman trapped in an abusive relationship or a child who is physically abused by a parent. The child has no power to stop the abuse. She is overwhelmed. This isn't an emotion. It is a cold, hard fact.

Finally, consider the word "unsafe." Is your home or apartment safe from intruders? Does it have locks on the doors and windows? Do you have a smoke alarm and a security alarm? Are you living with someone who might be able to protect you? Do you have neighbors you can trust? Do you live in a safe neighborhood, where there is very little crime? Whether your home is relatively safe or unsafe can only be determined based on an analysis of factual evidence. The state of being safe isn't a feeling, is it?

9.10. Emotional Reasoning

Now look at table 4. Read the title and subtitle out loud. ("Examples of 'I feel' statements that aren't about emotions. The feelings that accompany these words are not evidence for the conclusions.") Now read aloud the phrases on the top row of the table. ("I feel responsible. I feel obligated. I feel overwhelmed. I don't feel safe.") Isn't it interesting? All of a sudden, the words in table 4 now sound like emotions, don't they? But they aren't emotions. We've already established this fact.

Just because you said "I feel" with these words doesn't make them emotions, does it? In addition, the feelings that accompany these words aren't evidence for the truth, accuracy, or validity of the conclusions that these statements convey. Using feelings associated with an idea as evidence for the truth of that idea is called emotional reasoning. Now please read the sentence below table 4 out loud. ("These types of phrases are also called emotional reasoning, because the conclusions are based on feelings, which are not evidence for the conclusions.")

Emotional reasoning could also be called lazy thinking, because when you say "I feel" with words that aren't emotions, you typically don't challenge the conclusions. You just accept the conclusions as true without looking for evidence of whether or to what degree the statement is true. This may be particularly common among women as a result of socialization that women receive from an early age. Women are often taught early on that feelings are the realm of females while thinking is the realm of males. It follows then that women also learn to pride themselves on their intuition and making decisions or coming to conclusions based on gut feelings.

Here's an example of lazy thinking where a woman didn't think critically and didn't question or challenge her reasons for believing that she abandoned her children. Her therapist asked her what she did that constituted abandonment of her children. She said that she had been planning to leave her abusive marriage when her eleven-year-old son fell off a horse, broke his back, and needed to be in traction for several months. So she decided to get a job to make it easier for her to support her children and be independent when she was able to leave. Unfortunately, there were no jobs in the small town where they lived, so she temporarily moved to Dallas, where work was available. Unfortunately, due to events that were unforeseeable at the time, she didn't get her kids back for two years. But did she abandon her children? Of course not. She uncritically accepted the conclusion that she abandoned her children simply because she felt that she'd abandoned them. She didn't challenge her conclusion or weigh the evidence to see if her conclusion made sense.

9.11. "I Feel Responsible"

Let's take a closer look at the four statements in the top row, since they're very common among battered women. Dr. Kubany, the person who developed cognitive trauma therapy, first became interested in "I feel" language when he started helping clients with their guilt issues in 1990. At the end of a session, clients would often say something like "I see where you're going with this and intellectually it makes sense, but I still *feel* responsible."

When you say "I feel responsible," you're falsely using your feelings as evidence for the conclusion that you're responsible. "I feel responsible" probably seems more true than "I think I'm responsible" because the word "feel" taps into the very real feeling, probably anxiety or sadness, that you feel immediately after thinking you're responsible. Adding the word "feel" gives the conclusion a false ring of truth and makes the idea expressed *feel* more true. However, responsible is not an emotion, and you won't find it in any textbook on emotion.

Once again, feelings are *not* evidence. For example, if I tell you that I love the law of gravity, does that make the law of gravity more true? Or if I tell you that I have an anxiety attack anytime anyone mentions the law of gravity, does that make the law of gravity false? In the same way, your emotions about something are not evidence on which to base conclusions or decisions.

9.12. "I Feel Obligated"

Consider the statement "I feel obligated." Many battered women say they feel obligated to stay or reconcile with their abusers in spite of repeated abuse. Did you ever feel obligated to your abuser? In what ways did you feel obligated to him? What is the evidence that you were obligated in this way? And what is the evidence that you were *not* obligated? If you were obligated to him, that would imply that he was doing more of the giving, and you were doing more of the taking, making you obligated to pay him back in some way to restore the balance. Is that the way it was? Not likely. It's more like you cleaned someone's house and then felt you had to pay the person for the privilege of cleaning it.

9.13. "I Feel Overwhelmed"

Now consider the phrase "I feel overwhelmed." This kind of statement reflects learned helplessness. As we've discussed, this is the persistent learned belief that you are powerless to prevent bad things from happening and the associated belief that it doesn't make sense to even try to escape from intolerably bad situations, even if you aren't actually helpless or powerless.

The phrase "I feel overwhelmed" is one of many similar statements ingrained in the vocabulary of battered and formerly battered women. Because of their experiences of victimization, they think they have no power or options for solving their problems. Have you ever felt overwhelmed? How often? Under what circumstance?

Here are some other "I feel" statements that reflect perceived powerlessness: "I feel trapped," "I feel cornered," "I feel stuck," "I feel helpless," "I feel out of control," "I feel like I'm suffocating," "I feel like my back's against the wall," and "I feel like I've run out of options." Sound familiar? But what's the evidence that you have no options? Like everyone else, you can't do everything, so it's important to prioritize. You may have a lot to do, but you are not without options.

9.14. "I Don't Feel Safe"

Now consider the statement "I don't feel safe." If you don't feel safe, that doesn't mean you aren't safe. Similarly, if you feel safe, it doesn't mean you actually are safe. One of the things that shelter workers shudder to hear a battered woman say is something like this: "He apologized and agreed to go to anger management. He never agreed to go to anger management before. Maybe I should go back. I think I will. After all, I *feel* safe." In this scenario, is *feeling* safe evidence that a person is safe? No. What if the woman's history offers more evidence? What if her husband has apologized countless times and this isn't her first time at the shelter. Based on the evidence, is she safe?

Here's an example: A woman named Elizabeth went to a support group but didn't go back because she didn't like hearing the other women talk about incidents of abuse. But she did get one thing out of the group—the importance of an emphasis on safety. Unfortunately, she translated this emphasis on safety to mean that anything that made her feel safe was a good idea, and that anything that made her feel unsafe should be a signal to take action. Her abusive ex-boyfriend had broken into her apartment in the middle of the night one time about three years ago. So ever since she went to the support group, she tried to sleep during the day, when she felt safe, and to stay awake at night, when she felt unsafe. Did this make any sense?

Elizabeth also engaged in a ritual common to a surprising number of formerly battered women. When she got home from work, she would immediately look under the bed (and get relief reinforcement when she found no one there), look in the closet (getting a couple more seconds of relief), and then look behind the shower curtain (getting relief once again). But she also did something even more extreme. After she was home for a while, she'd get a gut feeling that her ex-boyfriend was in the bedroom, so she'd go look in the bedroom. A bit later, she might have a feeling that he was in the kitchen, so she'd go look in the kitchen.

Elizabeth had a twelve-year-old daughter, and she was afraid that her ex-boyfriend might try to kidnap her, even though she had no evidence that he might do this. When she dropped her daughter off at school, she would sometimes have a feeling that her abuser was lurking nearby, so she would drive around the block for reassurance that he wasn't there. Sometimes she'd get a feeling that she'd just missed him, so she'd drive around the block again. Her therapist asked her, "Why stop at twice? Why not three or four times? Why not keep circling until your daughter gets out of school?" Elizabeth would also spend about ten minutes driving around the parking lot at Safeway because she had a feeling her ex-boyfriend might be there. Was this a good use of her time?

Here's another example: Two women lived in different rooms in the same boarding house. One didn't feel safe with her door unlocked. The other didn't feel safe with her door locked. Ordinarily, you might think the women would be safer with their doors locked, but neither woman's feelings provided evidence that she was safer with the door locked or unlocked. That can only be evaluated on the basis of objective evidence.

For each woman, her feeling of being safe had more to do with past experiences than with the present facts. What do you think could have happened in the past to the woman who didn't feel safe with the door unlocked? In this case, the woman had been sexually assaulted by a man who walked into her apartment through an unlocked door. And what do you think might have happened in the past to the woman who didn't feel safe with the door locked? This woman was severely beaten in her apartment because the door was locked and she couldn't escape.

Upon hearing this story, one client said, "I do that. I don't lock my car doors. In fact, I don't lock my house doors, either." Further questioning revealed that this woman had been assaulted and nearly killed by her boyfriend in his locked pickup truck. But before discussing it, she didn't have the slightest idea why she wasn't locking her doors, which actually jeopardized her safety, other than her sense of feeling safer with unlocked doors. Reliance on her emotions in coming to conclusions was getting in the way of her ability to think clearly and logically.

9.15. Emotional Reasoning and Decision Making

Research has shown that if we induce negative emotions in people—for example, making them feel anxious or angry—they tend to make self-defeating decisions (Leith & Baumeister, 1996). Bad moods interfere with your ability to think clearly and make decisions that are in your best interest. For example, when people are in a bad mood, they tend to make decisions based on what they think will make them feel better immediately rather than an analysis of what is in their long-term best interest. Such decisions tend to be self-defeating. I'll give you an example to illustrate.

A thirty-year-old woman was taking part in a study to assess participants' prior exposure to traumatic life events. Joan had been terribly abused—both physically and psychologically—by her first husband when she was in her early twenties. Now she was married to someone who wasn't physically abusive but was extremely controlling and even more psychologically abusive than her first husband. She was extremely unhappy and suffered from severe PTSD. As part of the study debriefing, the assessor engaged her in a brief decision-making exercise in which she was asked to identify the likely short-term and long-term positive and negative consequences of two courses of action: staying with her second husband or moving with her two small children to live closer to her family. Anyone who looked at Joan's responses on this exercise would see that her only hope of future happiness would be to leave her husband. But at the end of the exercise, when the psychologist asked Joan what she was going to do, she said, "If I leave him, I'll feel like I'm abandoning him."

Decisions that lead to short-term or immediate relief from negative feelings usually aren't logical. This is an important reason why it's inadvisable to make major decisions when your emotions are running high. If you need proof, consider this all-too-common example of the decision-making process of battered women when considering whether to reconcile with their abuser: "I feel sorry for him. He misses me and he's falling apart at the seams. He says he'll never do it again. I feel sorry for him. Maybe I should go back. You know, I'll probably feel better if I go back. I'm going to give him another chance."

In this scenario, relief is just a short-term payoff. This is not a good way to make a decision. A much better way would be to ask, "What course of action is most likely to be in my best interest?" Be sure to analyze each potential course of action. It might play out like this: "What's likely to happen in the short term if I go back? Well, I'll probably experience less guilt. But what if he hits me again? Then I'd feel guilty because I went back!" Doing something to get rid of guilt in the short term is no guarantee that you'll be free of guilt in the long term. It bears repeating: Decisions that are driven by emotional impulses are virtually never in a person's best interest. If decision making is an important issue for you, toward the end of therapy we'll devote a session to this topic.

9.16. Strong Motivation—A Prerequisite for Breaking Bad Habits

Most clients are engaging in less and less negative self-talk within three or four weeks of starting to monitor their negative self-talk. Once in a while, however, a client will still be engaging in a great deal of negative self-talk after several weeks of self-monitoring. And, as mentioned previously, when negative self-talk stays at a high level, PTSD symptoms almost always also remain at moderate to high levels. Often the problem is that the client isn't sufficiently motivated to break these self-talk habits. It simply doesn't bother her enough when she continues to engage in negative self-talk.

We've found that it sometimes takes a pep talk to sufficiently increase a woman's motivation, commitment, or determination to break negative self-talk habits. In such cases, the therapist might look for opportunities to say things like "Did you hear what you just said? You just did it again. You just said you were stupid and went right on talking." The client may say something like "I know. I've been beating myself up all day." The therapist might then say something like "It will take strong motivation to break these habits. **When you catch yourself in negative self-talk, say something like this to yourself: 'Shoot! I did it again. Darn! How frustrating! I'm going to break these habits if it's the last thing I do. I *know* it's not good for me!'"**

Given everything you've learned about negative self-talk, are you now more motivated to stop using negative self-talk and more determined to break these habits? Was this discussion of self-talk useful?

Let's end this discussion of negative self-talk on a light note. I want to tell you a story about Peggy, who was receiving cognitive trauma therapy. She was telling her therapist about a negative interaction she had with a coworker and said, "It started when she gave me this look with a *smirk* on her face." When her therapist asked, "What do you mean by 'smirk'?" Peggy answered, "Well, I'm tempted to use the F word." When her therapist reassured her that she didn't have to censor her language, Peggy said, "You mean I can say 'I feel'?"

CONCLUDING REMARKS

At the conclusion of this module, almost all clients are more motivated than they have ever been to stop using negative self-talk. Given that so much negative self-talk is related to guilt and shame, this leads naturally into the next module, in which we address guilt and attempt to alleviate it. When clients experience a reduction in guilt, they will be even less likely to engage in negative self-talk.

Handout 9.1: Negative Emotional Experiences

Table 1. Relatively Pure Negative Emotions		
Distressed	Upset	Hurt
Sad	Frustrated	Disappointed
Unhappy	Anxious	Scared

Table 2. Hybrid Negative Emotions, Which Have a Feeling Part and a Thinking Part				
Guilt	Anger	Resentment	Ashamed	Regret

Table 3. Examples of Thoughts or Beliefs, Which Require Evidence or Proof			
Responsible	Obligated	Overwhelmed	Unsafe
Abandoned	Helpless	Dirty	Mistrustful
Wrong	Stuck	Weak	Stupid

Table 4. Examples of "I Feel" Statements That Aren't About Emotions			
(The feelings that accompany these words are *not* evidence for the conclusions.)			
I feel responsible.	I feel obligated.	I feel overwhelmed.	I don't feel safe.
I feel abandoned.	I feel helpless.	I feel dirty.	I don't feel I can trust.
I feel that what I did was wrong.	I feel stuck in a hole.	I feel weak.	I feel stupid.

These types of phrases are also called emotional reasoning, because the conclusions are based on feelings, which are not evidence for the conclusions.

Addressing Trauma-Related Guilt

Battered women and other trauma survivors with PTSD typically experience guilt that defies any rational explanation. In this module, therapists help clients identify several thinking errors that lead to four distorted guilt-related beliefs: beliefs about one's ability to foresee and prevent negative outcomes, beliefs about responsibility for negative outcomes, beliefs about justifications for actions taken, and beliefs about wrongdoing or violation of moral values.

This is the longest module and ordinarily takes four to five sessions. For the client's first guilt issue, about one session each is needed for the foreseeability analysis, justification analysis, and responsibility analysis, with the wrongdoing analysis usually taking much less than one session. Second and subsequent guilt issues proceed very quickly.

OBJECTIVES

- For the client to understand that if a negative outcome was unforeseeable, she didn't have the power to prevent the outcome

- For the client to understand that the most justified course of action in any situation is one for which the person had the best reasons—among the actions actually considered at the time

- For the client to understand that most outcomes have multiple contributing causes

- For the client to understand that wrongdoing only occurs when a person intentionally causes harm that was foreseeable

- For the client to be able to apply the knowledge inherent in the first four objectives to all issues that have been significant sources of guilt for her

- For the client to experience reductions in the magnitude of trauma-related guilt such that guilt is no longer a significant problem

MATERIALS

- Attitudes About Guilt Survey (handout 10.1; several copies)

- Aspects of Guilt (handout 10.2)

- Thinking Errors That Contribute to Guilt (handout 10.3)

- Article: "Thinking Errors, Faulty Conclusions, and Cognitive Therapy for Trauma-Related Guilt" (handout 10.4)

- Contributing Causes and the Domino Effect (handout 10.5)

- Causes Contributing to Staying with an Abusive Partner (optional handout 10.6)

HOMEWORK

- Listen to session audio-recordings.

- Continue to monitor and record negative self-talk.

- Practice PMR while listening to the PMR recording, twice a day.

- Do a body scan and over-tense and relax muscles when experiencing stress.

- Read the article "Thinking Errors, Faulty Conclusions, and Cognitive Therapy for Trauma-Related Guilt" (handout 10.4).

- Read and complete chapter 9 in *Healing the Trauma of Domestic Violence* (after completing section 10.9; optional).

- Read and complete chapter 10 in *Healing the Trauma of Domestic Violence* (after completing section 10.44; optional).

PROCEDURES CHECKLIST

1. _____ Conducting a structured interview to identify guilt issues

2. _____ How many guilt issues to address and in what order

3. _____ Completing the Attitudes About Guilt Survey (AAGS; handout 10.1)

4. _____ Guilt incident debriefing for the first guilt issue

5. _____ The good news and the bad news about guilt

6. _____ Examples of trauma-related guilt with no rational basis

7. _____ Education on aspects of guilt using the guilt diagram (handout 10.2)

8. _____ The four guilt-related beliefs (referring to handout 10.1)

9. _____ Guilt analysis as an exercise in logic

FORESEEABILITY AND PREVENTABILITY ANALYSIS

10. _____ Determining what false beliefs the client holds about foreseeability

11. _____ Education about hindsight bias

12. _____ A study demonstrating that people are prone to hindsight bias

13. _____ Examples of trauma survivors who engaged in hindsight-biased thinking

14. _____ Revisiting the meaning of "should," "should have," and "could have"

15. _____ Minefield and two optional examples

16. _____ Inquiry into whether the client would have acted as she did if she knew with certainty what was going to happen

17. _____ *Wheel of Fortune* example

18. _____ Dislodging persistent hindsight-biased thinking

19. ____ President Truman anecdote

20. ____ Re-answering item 1 on the AAGS

21. ____ Discussion of effects of hindsight bias on other guilt-related beliefs

JUSTIFICATION ANALYSIS

22. ____ The importance of remembering which options were actually considered at the time

23. ____ Thinking errors that contribute to faulty beliefs about justification (handout 10.3)

24. ____ Weighing the merits of actions taken against idealized options that didn't exist

25. ____ Weighing the merits of actions taken against options that only came to mind later

26. ____ Inquiry into the client's reasons for acting as she did, other options considered at the time, and why they were ruled out

27. ____ Re-answering item 2 on the AAGS

RESPONSIBILITY ANALYSIS

28. ____ The distinction between causation and blame

29. ____ Explaining that most events have multiple causes using the domino effect (handout 10.5), and that people tend to focus on immediate causes, illustrated with lightbulb example

30. ____ Generating a list of all possible external factors that contributed to the client acting as she did (using optional handout 10.6, if appropriate)

31. ____ Assigning a percentage to each contributing cause

32. ____ Re-answering item 3 on the AAGS

WRONGDOING ANALYSIS

33. _____ Defining wrongdoing

34. _____ Challenging conclusions of wrongdoing

35. _____ The error of attributing wrongdoing based on a tragic but unforeseeable outcome

36. _____ Story about a child with the viluxin virus

37. _____ Accountability vs. the power to cause or prevent outcomes

38. _____ Explaining that the least bad choice is a moral and justified choice, with examples

    ▪ *Sophie's Choice*

    ▪ *The War Within*

    ▪ Two people who were punished if they resisted (and abused anyway)

    ▪ A woman's custody battle

39. _____ Re-answering item 4 on the AAGS

CONDUCTING GUILT INTERVENTION WITH SECOND AND SUBSEQUENT GUILT ISSUES

40. _____ Completing the AAGS and conducting a guilt incident debriefing

41. _____ Foreseeability and preventability analysis

42. _____ Justification analysis

43. _____ Responsibility analysis

44. _____ Wrongdoing analysis

45. _____ Addressing guilt about having emotional responses perceived to be inappropriate

DETAILED PROCEDURES FOR MODULE 10

10.1. Structured Interview to Identify Guilt Issues

Now we'll start focusing on guilt. I'm going to give you a structured interview to identify guilt issues related to abuse by your ex-partner. To review, guilt is an unpleasant feeling with accompanying beliefs that one should have thought, felt, or acted differently. Based on this definition, a person can experience guilt about five different things.

First, she can feel guilty about something she did that she thinks she shouldn't have done. Second, she can feel guilty about something she *didn't* do that she thinks she should have done. Third, she can feel guilty for having certain feelings that she doesn't think she should have had. Fourth, a person can feel guilty for *not* having certain feelings that she thinks she should have had. And fifth, a person can feel guilty for thinking or believing something that she now believes isn't true.

Record the client's responses to this interview to document guilt issues that may need to be addressed. **Do you feel guilty about anything you did related to the abuse that you think you shouldn't have done?** If yes: **Tell me about that … Do you feel guilty about anything else you did that you think you shouldn't have done?** If yes: **Tell me about that … Do you feel guilty about anything you *didn't do* related to the abuse that you think you should have done?** If yes: **Tell me about that … Do you feel guilty about anything else you didn't do that you think you should have done?** If yes: **Tell me about that … Do you feel guilty about any feelings you had that you don't think you should have had?** If yes: **Tell me about that … Do you feel guilty about any feelings you *didn't* have that you think you should have had?** If yes: **Tell me about that …** If the client has guilt about feelings or lack of feelings, this can be briefly addressed right now, or it can be addressed later (see the last section of this module). The analyses for these sorts of guilt issues are different because the client is merely taught that strong feelings are not a matter of choice or willpower. **Do you feel guilty about any beliefs or thoughts you had that you now consider to be false or untrue?** If yes: **Tell me about that … Do you feel guilty about anything else related to the abuse?** If yes: **Tell me about that …**

10.2. How Many Guilt Issues to Address and in What Order

With most clients, it's necessary to address more than one guilt issue to get to the point where guilt is no longer a significant source of emotional pain. In most cases, two or three guilt issues suffice. Only rarely is it necessary to address more than three, for two reasons: First, the psychoeducation provided during the analysis of the first guilt issue is relevant to all guilt issues. Second, the thinking errors that contribute to cognitive distortions and guilt are similar for every guilt issue. For example, hindsight bias typically contributes to distortions about the foreseeability and preventability of most or all events about which people experience guilt, whereas clear thinking associated with the absence of hindsight bias is typically associated with less guilt.

We have found that front-loading a lot of psychoeducation into addressing the first guilt issue usually increases the client's ability to apply clear thinking to other guilt issues, thus reducing the amount of guilt work that needs to be done overall. Typically, however, clients are unable to generalize all of the knowledge gained from analysis of the first issue to all other guilt issues, and that is why it's usually necessary to address more than one guilt issue.

Ordinarily, the order in which guilt issues are addressed doesn't make much difference. The first issue will always take much longer to analyze than subsequent issues because the bulk of the psychoeducation is provided while addressing the first issue. Much of that information doesn't have to be repeated when addressing subsequent issues.

The most common guilt issue among formerly battered women is guilt about not having left the abusive relationship sooner, or variations on that theme, such as guilt about going out with the abusive partner in the first place, guilt about moving in with him, guilt about marrying him, or guilt about reconciling with him after having left. If guilt about not having left sooner is a concern (and it usually is), we almost always address this issue first. If the woman has children, guilt about this issue is often related to problems the children have developed as a result of being exposed to domestic violence. When we alleviate guilt about not having left sooner, guilt about the children usually ceases to be an issue and thus need not be addressed.

If a guilt issue evokes strong negative emotions or tearful grieving (for example, guilt about having an abortion or guilt about the unexpected death of a loved one), it's usually better to address such issues as the second or third issue than as the first issue, to avoid having to provide the lengthy psychoeducation to a distraught client. When covered as the second or third issue, the analysis will typically proceed quickly. For example, it may take three or four sessions to cover the first issue, but analyses of second and third guilt issues can almost always be completed in a single fifty-minute session.

10.3. Completing the Attitudes About Guilt Survey

Once you've identified the first guilt issue to be addressed, give the client a copy of handout 10.1, the Attitudes About Guilt Survey (AAGS) and help her fill it out. If you're sitting side by side with her, you can both look at her copy of the AAGS. Alternatively, you can each have your own copy. (The script for this module uses the acronym AAGS. If you plan to use the acronym when talking to the client, be sure to introduce it now.)

The guilt issue we are going to work on first is [whatever issue you've chosen]. Most commonly, the first issue is some variation on "I should have left my abusive partner sooner." Write this issue on the AAGS, or you can have the client do it.

What negative outcomes could have been prevented? The client may say things like the abuse continuing or problems the children developed as a result of exposure to family violence. Write her response on the AAGS or have her write it in. For each of the questions on the AAGS, you may wish to read aloud the options from which the client can choose.

Look at item 1. To what extent do you think you should have known better and could have prevented or avoided the outcome? Circle the answer that best reflects what you believe.

Now look at item 2. How justified was what you did? That is, how good were your reasons for what you did? Again, circle the best answer—the one that best reflects what you believe today about how good your reasons were for acting as you did.

Look at item 3. How personally responsible were you for causing what happened? If the client's guilt issue is that she should have left her abusive partner sooner, ask her to answer item 3 twice, in two ways: I want you to answer this twice. First, indicate how responsible you were for staying in the relationship by drawing a circle around the best answer. Now, indicate how responsible you were for the abuse and other bad things that happened as a result of having stayed by drawing a triangle around the best answer. And what was your percentage of responsibility—from 0 percent to 100 percent? Fill in your answer just above item 4.

Now look at item 4. Did you do something wrong? That is, did you violate your personal standards of right and wrong by what you did? Circle what you believe. Now let's look at item 5. How distressed do you feel when you think about what happened? Which answer best reflects what you believe?

For item 6, circle the answer that indicates how often you experience guilt related to what happened. And finally, answer question 7. Circle the answer that indicates the intensity or severity of guilt that you typically experience about what happened.

10.4. Guilt Incident Debriefing for the First Guilt Issue

Now give me a slow-motion, detailed description of exactly what happened, starting with the background events that led up to the incident about which you feel guilty. Just tell me the facts, what's on the "front page" not the "editorial page." Try to avoid making value judgments. I only want you to tell me the facts of what happened. What did you see, hear, feel, and smell? Who did what, who said what, and what thoughts went through your mind leading up to that specific point in time— that day, that hour—when you think you should have done something different. The therapist may need to give the client gentle reminders on this last point as she tells the story.

After hearing this descriptive account, ask three additional questions: What was the worst part of the story you just told me? What were your feelings during the worst part? What were your thoughts during the worst part?

10.5. The Good News and the Bad News About Guilt

There's some good news and some bad news about guilt. The bad news is that guilt is an extremely common source of pain and torment among trauma survivors. The good news is that trauma survivors tend to exaggerate or distort the importance of their role in the trauma. They often experience guilt that has no rational or logical basis and are beating themselves up for nothing. So when you change your thinking, you'll get some relief from your trauma-related guilt. For the next several sessions, I'm going to help you learn how to change the thinking that contributes to your guilt.

10.6. Examples of Trauma-Related Guilt with No Rational Basis

I'll give you some examples of trauma survivors who experienced guilt that had no rational basis. Give two or three examples:

Women sexually abused as children (Jehu, 1989): In a study of fifty women in a residential treatment program for women who had been sexually abused as children, forty-three of the women—almost 90 percent—strongly agreed with the following statement: "I was responsible for the abuse because it went on for so long." This is in spite of the fact that almost all of them were first abused before age ten, and almost half before the age of six.

Bank hostage: A woman who was assistant manager of a bank was in charge when a man held up the bank and held her hostage. He had a bomb and threatened to kill everyone. She sobbed as she told her therapist, "The reason I feel so bad is that someone died." Who do you think died? It was the robber. This woman said she felt she was 90 percent responsible for the robber's death because she tiptoed toward the door with him as he held a gun to her side. She was trying to get him away from the cashiers and customers so they would be safer. He was killed by the police as he cracked open the door.

Elephant who trampled its trainer: A woman who went to the circus witnessed a raging elephant trample its trainer and turn toward the crowd before bounding out of the auditorium. She experienced enormous guilt for not going down and giving mouth-to-mouth resuscitation to the trainer. She said she should have because she was trained in CPR and was also involved in health promotion work. Her guilt is particularly irrational when you consider that she was at the circus with her elderly aunt and her four-year-old son, and she was four months pregnant.

Combat medic who waved for assistance: A man who worked as an army medic in Vietnam was assigned to a remote jungle unit of twenty-five men whose mission was to set ambushes. They went out to set ambushes five men at a time, and on one occasion they walked into an underground enemy base camp and were ambushed. They called the rest of the men in, and they were ambushed too. In the melee that ensued, the medic was attending to three men at one time. He waved for a buddy to come help, but on his way, his buddy walked into the line of fire and was killed.

When he filled out this same questionnaire during therapy, how do you think he answered the questions? His answers to every question indicated a maximum level of guilt. On item 1, he answered, "I absolutely should have known better." On item 2, he answered, "What I did was not justified in any way." On item 3, he answered, "I was completely responsible for causing what happened," not even acknowledging the contribution of the enemy! On item 4, he indicated that waving for assistance was "extremely wrong," and his remaining responses indicated that he always experienced extreme distress and guilt about what happened.

Now is the guilt in any of these examples rational? Of course not. Let's say I was conducting a big group therapy session with all of the people from those examples. If we were going around and having everyone tell their story, you would probably be one of the first ones to tell them, "Lighten up. You're being too hard on yourself." But when we get around to you, you'd probably say something like "Well, my story is different because I deserve to feel guilty." I know that right now you probably don't agree that your guilt is irrational, but I'll help you realize that it's just as irrational as the people's guilt in the examples I gave you.

10.7. Education on Aspects of Guilt

Let's take a minute to review what you've already learned about guilt. Guilt can be defined as an unpleasant feeling with accompanying beliefs that you should have thought, felt, or acted differently. So guilt is two things: It involves bad or unpleasant feelings, and it also involves a set of beliefs, thoughts, interpretations, or negative value judgments about yourself. Because guilt has both a thinking part and a feeling part, we could just as appropriately say "I *think* guilty" as "I *feel* guilty." However, it would probably be most technically correct to say "I *experience* guilt," since this takes into account that guilt has both a feeling part and a thinking part.

Give the client handout 10.2, Aspects of Guilt, and point to the diagram at the top. What do you think this is? It's a representation of guilt. It shows that guilt is made up of four interrelated beliefs—negative beliefs about the self—that are fused together by the glue of distress. Very confusing, isn't it? Do you know what a Rubik's Cube is? Guilt is like a Rubik's Cube; it's very hard to figure out. In the next few sessions, we're going to take guilt apart and look at each aspect or component separately. We'll analyze your guilt issues by dealing with one issue at a time and analyzing each part of guilt, one part at a time.

This big gray area surrounding guilt, and shown separately below it, is the distress or emotional pain associated with guilt. We'll put that off to the side. It's not that distress is unimportant—it's extremely important. But strong feelings interfere with your ability to think clearly, and it's very important that you think clearly, especially in regard to guilt.

Down below are the four guilt-related beliefs that combine to create the overall experience of guilt: beliefs about foreseeability and preventability, beliefs about lack of justification, beliefs about responsibility, and beliefs about violation of values or wrongdoing. It may still be difficult to understand guilt when we look at its parts separately, but it's easier to understand than when all of the parts are fused together. For example, look at the part associated with foreseeability and preventability. It still isn't easy to figure out. But look up here. Point to the diagram at the top. Is there any chance of figuring out this aspect of guilt, or even seeing it clearly, when it's mixed together with all of the other parts?

10.8. The Four Guilt-Related Beliefs

Let's look at the four guilt-related beliefs, one at a time. First, consider beliefs about foreseeability and preventability. If a negative outcome was foreseeable, and therefore preventable, yet you allowed it to happen, can you see where that goes? Right. Straight to guilt.

By the way, each of these four guilt-related beliefs is assessed by an item on the Attitudes About Guilt Survey. Bring out the AAGS that the client completed, and refer to her answers in the following passage: Item 1 assesses beliefs about foreseeability and preventability: "To what extent do you think you should have known better and could have prevented or avoided the outcome?" You indicated that you ... Read the client's answer to item 1. The second item assesses beliefs about justification—how good your reasons were for what you did. You indicated that what you did was ... Read the client's answer to item 2. The third guilt-related belief is assessed by item 3: "How personally responsible were you for causing what happened?" To the extent that you think you caused a negative outcome, you will experience guilt.

Looking at responsibility, you can see that it's not just the presence or absence of these beliefs that determines how much guilt you will experience; it's the magnitude of your beliefs. For example, if you think you were only slightly responsible for causing a negative outcome, you would likely experience less guilt than if you thought you were completely responsible. The same principle also applies to the magnitude of distress, which is yet another component of guilt. If distress is profound, as it often is after terrible and tragic events, a person may experience very severe guilt even if she believes she bears only minor responsibility for the negative outcome.

Item 4 assesses wrongdoing. "Did you do something wrong? Did you violate personal standards of right and wrong by what you did?" This is what people usually mean when they talk about guilt: sin or violation of moral values.

Optional: You may tell the client that published research (Kubany, Abueg, et al., 1995) has shown that knowing how a person answers items 1 to 5 on the AAGS can be used to accurately predict how much guilt the person experiences (assessed by items 6 and 7).

10.9. Guilt Analysis as an Exercise in Logic

We are going to engage in an exercise in logic to help you think more clearly about your role in the trauma. We'll examine one guilt issue at a time, and one component at a time. Our goal will be for you to reach an accurate, objective, and realistic appraisal of your role in the trauma—an appraisal that a panel of scientists or experts would agree with. Rest assured, I am not going to try to fool you into believing something that isn't true. If the client is reading and completing chapters in *Healing the Trauma of Domestic Violence* as homework, assign her chapter 9 in the workbook at the end of the current session.

FORESEEABILITY AND PREVENTABILITY ANALYSIS

10.10. Determining the Client's False Beliefs About Foreseeability

The following sequence of questions usually reveals what the client falsely believes she knew prior to a negative outcome that would have enabled her to prevent the outcome: **On item 1 of the AAGS, you indicated** … Read the client's answer to item 1. **What is it that you should have known better? What negative outcomes could have been prevented?** The client may say something like she could have avoided continued abuse if she had left sooner, or that her children wouldn't have developed certain problems if they hadn't been exposed to ongoing domestic violence.

Write down the client's answers to the questions in the following paragraph in order to accurately refer to these answers while proceeding with the analysis. **What is it that you should have done differently? When did it first occur to you to do this? When did you first realize or learn that this would have been a better course of action?** Proceed to the next section if the client responds that it first occurred to her that she should have acted differently *after* she acted as she did.

Occasionally, a client will say she knew she should have acted differently before the outcome was known. An example would be "I knew I shouldn't get involved with him when I first met him." If this happens, ask the client if the negative outcome that she believes was preventable was actually foreseeable. Using the example above, you might say, "Were the years of abuse foreseeable the moment you met him?" The answer is almost always no. *I'm going to help you realize that if a negative event isn't foreseeable, it isn't preventable.*

10.11. Education About Hindsight Bias

Do you see what's happening here? You're remembering yourself knowing something you didn't learn until later. You can't use knowledge acquired *after* making a decision to guide you in making that decision. In other words, something you learn

after making a decision wasn't available to help you make that decision, because you didn't have that information when you made that decision. You can't use knowledge you acquire on Wednesday to help you make a decision on the previous Monday. Finding out that the stock market went up on Wednesday can't be used to help you make an investment decision two days earlier, on Monday.

Did you ever see the TV program *Early Edition?* The star of the program would get tomorrow's newspaper today and spends all day working to prevent some bad thing that's going to happen tomorrow. He can do this because he actually knows what's going to happen tomorrow. Because tomorrow is foreseeable in this show, it's preventable. But in the real world, people can't use knowledge acquired after the fact to help them with decisions they had to make earlier.

This has to do with an extremely important concept called hindsight bias. This is a term you will want to remember. Read the paragraph at the bottom of handout 10.2 out loud. ("Hindsight bias occurs when knowledge of an event's outcome, such as who won a game, distorts or biases a person's memory of what he or she knew before the outcome was known. This type of thinking is evident in statements such as 'I should have known better,' 'I should have done something different,' 'I saw it coming,' 'I knew what was going to happen" (before outcomes were known), and 'I could have prevented it.' As applied to trauma, many survivors falsely believe that the events were foreseeable—and therefore preventable.)

Hindsight-biased thinking is also signaled by phrases such as "There were warning signs," "There were red flags," "There were clues," "At one level, I knew what was going to happen," or "I was in denial." Hindsight-biased thinking is similar to Monday-morning quarterbacking. Do you know what that is? Many women don't. It's more of a guy thing. Literally speaking, it happens on Monday morning, when guys are talking about Sunday's big game and one of them says, "I knew they shouldn't have made that play. In fact, I knew on Friday who was going to win yesterday. I could have told you who was going to win before the game was ever played." It's like having a crystal ball. If I were there, I might go up to that guy and ask him, "If you knew who was going to win yesterday, why didn't you bet ten thousand dollars on the game?"

Here's another way of looking at it: Have you ever been to a fun house and looked into one of those wavy mirrors that distorts the way you look? Hindsight bias is like that. It distorts your recollection of what you knew before the outcome occurred. It's remembering yourself as being smarter than you were capable of being at the time, as if you knew something that you didn't know and didn't find out about until later. It's like remembering yourself having a crystal ball that you didn't have.

Hindsight-biased thinking is extremely common among trauma survivors. But it isn't something that just trauma survivors do. Everyone tends to do it, and this has been demonstrated repeatedly in studies with college students and other populations (Fischhoff, 1975; Hawkins & Hastie, 1990).

10.12. A Study Demonstrating That People Are Prone to Hindsight Bias

I'm going to illustrate the concept of hindsight bias by telling you about one type of experiment that has been used to prove the occurrence of hindsight-biased thinking (e.g., Fischhoff, 1975). In this study, a psychology professor enlists his students to participate in the study. He says, "I'm going to divide you into three groups, and I want you to predict who's going to win the big game tomorrow. I'm going to give you lots of information and statistics to help you predict who will win: win-loss records, the players' heights and weights, their levels of motivation, and more. But I'm not going to let you watch the game. Instead, I'm going to put you up in a hotel to study the information about the teams, then I'll come to the hotel the day after the game and ask you who won."

The day after the game, the professor goes into the room with the first group and says, "Boy, I didn't think the Red team was that good. I didn't think they were going to win. Oops! I shouldn't have told you that. Please disregard what I just said. Just tell me who you think won based on the information I gave you before the game." Then he goes into the room with the second group and says, "I'm really surprised that the Blue team won. Oops! I wasn't supposed to tell you that. Disregard what I just said. Just tell me who you think won based on the information I gave you before the game." Then he goes into the room with the third group and simply asks, "Who do you think won yesterday?" He doesn't give the third group any information about the outcome.

What do you think each of the groups will predict? In coming up with your answer, assume that the teams were very evenly matched based on the statistics given to the students. Here are the actual results: The group that was told the Red team won will say the Red team won. The group that was told the Blue team won will say the Blue team won. And the group that was given no outcome information is likely to say there was a tie score, or half will pick Red and half will pick Blue. Clients almost always answer this correctly, but if they don't, just tell them the outcome. That probably isn't too surprising. But here's what is surprising: When subjects are debriefed and told that knowing the outcome biased their memory of what they knew before the outcome was known, they usually aren't aware of it and may even deny it. They might say, "No. What you told me didn't influence my prediction. That's what I would have said anyway." They are unaware that knowledge of the outcome biased their recollection of what they thought they knew before the outcome was known.

When good things happen, a person can say "I knew that was going to happen" and take some credit. But when bad things happen, it's a recipe for trouble. People start saying, "Oh my god! I could have prevented or avoided it. I could have done something. The signals were so clear."

10.13. Examples of Trauma Survivors Who Engaged in Hindsight-Biased Thinking

Here are a few examples of hindsight-biased thinking exhibited by trauma survivors. The first deals with a thirty-eight-year-old woman who was sexually abused at age twelve by her cousin's husband. She insisted that somehow she must have provoked the abuse. When asked if she had any nieces who were about twelve or thirteen, she said yes. Then her therapist asked, "If you molested one of your nieces, do you think she would be in any way responsible for preventing it?" In a flash of realization, the woman said, "You know what I've been doing? I've been putting my thirty-eight-year-old mind in my twelve-year-old head." She was remembering herself as knowing what she knows now—not what she knew as a naive twelve-year-old girl.

Or consider the woman I told you about who saw an elephant trample its trainer at the circus. She actually said, "I went to the circus during the last performance, when the trainer and the elephant were bound to be tired because that's what was easiest to fit into my schedule. Just irresponsible, I guess." As if there were any way she possibly could have known that the elephant was going to trample the trainer before she went to the circus!

Here's another example: One therapist saw four women in a five-month period, all of them with the same guilt issue, and all exhibiting the same kind of hindsight-biased thinking. As children, all of them had been sexually abused by someone who wasn't scaring them. The women were seven, five, four, and three years old at the time, and their molesters were two father figures, an older cousin, and a neighbor boy. They all claimed that they should have known better than to permit the molestation. One of them said, "I should have known that a daughter isn't supposed to have sex with her father. Yuck!" When asked what they should have done differently, each woman said, "I should have told him, 'No, you can't do that.'" But when asked when she first thought she should have said no, each woman realized that it wasn't until much later that it first occurred to her that she wasn't supposed to permit the sex. For example, it didn't occur to one woman that she could have and should have said no to her father until four years later, in sex education class.

10.14. Revisiting the Meaning of "Should," "Should Have," and "Could Have"

Now let's look at the meaning of the words "should" and "could." To say you should do something means that you have an obligation to do something. That's the definition of "should." However, it's only accurate to say you *should* do something if you're capable of doing it. It wouldn't make sense to say that you should jump up and touch the ceiling if your legs are broken, or to say that you should go to the store and buy some bread if you don't have any money. You can't say that you should read a road sign telling you where to go if the sign is in a foreign language. "Should," which is the past tense of "shall," implies power and capability.

"Should" is related to the word "could." To say that you should have done something implies that you could have done something, that you had the capability to do it. "Could" is the past tense of "can." To say that you can do something means you're capable of doing it. So saying that you could have prevented something means you were able to foresee what was going to happen and had the ability to prevent it. But you can only prevent something if you knew it was going to happen. You're only capable of preventing something if that something is foreseeable. I'll give you an example or two to illustrate.

10.15. Minefield and Two Optional Examples

Let's say there's a minefield right next to us, and I tell you I'm going to shoot you if you don't walk through it. If there are flags designating where the mines are and you walk into a mine and it explodes, could you accurately say, "I should have known better. I could have prevented the explosion"? Of course you could. But let's say there are no flags and you don't know where the mines are. If you start tiptoeing across the minefield very carefully and there's a big explosion, would it be accurate to say, "I should have known better and could have avoided the explosion"? Of course not.

Meningitis example: It's also something like this: Assume there are bacteria in this room that cause spinal meningitis, but you can't see them and don't even know they're there. Do you have the power to avoid getting sick? Of course not. You will only avoid getting sick if you get lucky.

Mugger example: Here's another example: Imagine yourself walking on a sidewalk next to a building. You take a left turn at the corner, where, unbeknownst to you, a mugger is lurking. He pulls a gun on you, grabs your purse, and flees. Were you capable of preventing this outcome if you had no idea the mugger was lurking there? Not unless you were just lucky.

10.16. Inquiry into Whether the Client Would Have Acted as She Did If She Knew What Was Going to Happen

In regard to this guilt issue, if you knew with certainty what was going to happen when you did what you did, would you have done what you did? It's a good idea to personalize the preceding question. For example, "If you knew with certainty that you would end up enduring years of abuse, would you have gotten involved with your partner in the first place?" The answer is almost always no. **That's proof you didn't know what was going to happen. I believe there's no possible way that you knew what was going to happen, otherwise you wouldn't have done what you did.**

10.17. *Wheel of Fortune* Example

I'll give you a final example, from the game show *Wheel of Fortune*. At the end of the program, the winner is going for the grand prize of twenty-five thousand dollars. He has to figure out a short word—only six letters. He gets to pick two con-sonants and a vowel. Demonstrate to the client on paper, as shown below:

— — — — — —

For the consonants, he chooses **h** and **s.** Add the letters as shown:

__ h __ __ s __

He's uncertain about the vowel and is torn between choosing **o** and **e.** Finally he settles on the letter **o.** Sadly, it doesn't come up. He gets ten seconds to figure out the word, but he's at a loss and can't solve it before the buzzer sounds. When the answer is revealed, the vowels come up first. Add the letters as shown:

__ h e e s e

Pause and allow the client to come up with "cheese," then fill in the letter c. (Clients almost always say "cheese." If the client doesn't say "cheese," you say it.)

Can you guess what the man said? He said, "I should have said 'e.'" The host, Pat Sajak, then said something very perceptive. He said, "You can't live on 'should haves.'" If the man had known with certainty that the letter e would allow him to get the word, would he have selected o? Of course not. That's proof that he didn't know with certainty that the letter e would help him figure out the word. He might have had a hunch that the letter e would help him get the word, but people don't usually act on long-shot hunches.

Let's get back into this man's state of mind prior to the outcome and assume his mind is functioning like a computer. Let's say he thinks it's 75 percent certain that o will help him get the word and 25 percent certain that e will help him get the word. Would he say e if he thinks o is much more likely to help him figure out the word? Of course not.

10.18. Dislodging Persistent Hindsight-Biased Thinking

It can be difficult to dislodge hindsight-biased thinking if a client insists that she knew what was going to happen, especially if she actually contemplated options that might have prevented a negative outcome. Thinking errors commonly involved here are failure to realize that acting on speculative hunches rarely pays off and failure to see that occurrence of a low probability event is not evidence that one should have counted on this outcome before it occurred. Under such circumstances, probe for further details about exactly what happened and determine when the client first knew *with certainty* what was going to happen. Help the client see her thinking errors using one or two of the following examples. Preface the examples with a statement such as "Looking at some more examples may help. Sometimes it's easier to be objective about other people's experience than your own."

A woman who said she knew her husband was going to die: Here's a story about a woman from American Samoa whose husband was convicted of drug trafficking and sentenced to twelve years in prison in California. She moved to California and visited her husband in prison every weekend for almost twelve years. Two months prior to his scheduled release, her husband was transferred to a prison in Texas. She had airline reservations to go to Texas, but her husband wasn't feeling well and said he wouldn't be good company. He persuaded her to visit her family in Samoa for Easter instead.

While she was in Samoa, her husband died from complications following surgery for a stomach problem. This woman insisted she knew her husband was going to die. When her therapist asked her how she knew, she said she knew after talking to her husband on the phone a week before his death. She said that when she hung up the phone, she told her friend, "He's going to die." Her therapist then asked, "And that's the last time you talked to him?" She started sobbing uncontrollably, repeating "I knew. I knew!"

Her therapist said, "You know what I'd say? I think you were really worried. You knew he was really sick, and you were afraid that it could be fatal—that it might be. You were really, really worried. But that's different from knowing. If you knew, with 100 percent certainty, that he was going to die, wouldn't you have gone to Texas to be by his side?" She nodded, and her therapist said, "That's proof you didn't know. If you knew, you wouldn't have stayed in Samoa."

A woman who said she knew she should have left her abusive husband sooner: A therapist was addressing a client's guilt issue about not leaving her abusive husband sooner. The woman said, "I knew I should have left him six months before I finally left!" When her therapist asked how she knew that, she said she could remember the exact day when she should have left. It was the day she started counseling, and her social worker told her that if she didn't leave, her husband was going to kill her. She said, "I should have listened to my social worker and left him then."

This woman had waited until her thirties to marry, and marriage was extremely important to her. During their courtship and engagement, her fiancé was absolutely wonderful, but he changed dramatically once they were married. She found this difficult to fathom and thought his abuse was related to his drinking. She believed that if he would just stop drinking, the abuse would stop. She held strongly to the view that marriage is supposed to be forever.

In addition, her father had a chronic illness, and her mother had stood by him all these years, so she believed it was her responsibility to stand by her man too. After all, her husband needed her, and the thought of him being alone made her feel sorry for him. And she did love him and believe that things would eventually get better.

After all, she was a very smart and creative woman, so eventually she would "get it right" and he'd stop abusing her. She thought that if she left, she'd be a quitter and her son would suffer because of being separated from his father.

So as it turns out, at the time she thought she knew she should have left, she actually believed it was likely that things would get better, and that she had more to lose by leaving than by staying. In reality, she didn't believe that her husband would try to kill her, despite what her social worker said.

Over the next three months, her husband continued to abuse her and she was running out of ways to get him to stop. About two months before she finally left, her doubts about whether the marriage would improve started to increase, but she still believed she had more to lose by leaving than by staying. Then, shortly before she left, her husband did indeed almost kill her. Finally, she realized that he wasn't going to change, that she was incapable of getting him to change, and that he was capable of killing her. And as much as her son needed his father, he needed a living mother even more.

That's the point at which she lost all hope and decided to leave him. On the day she started counseling with a social worker, she didn't know what she learned over the next six months.

10.19. President Truman Anecdote

I'll conclude this discussion of hindsight bias with an anecdote about President Truman to illustrate the kind of clear thinking you want to be striving for on all of your guilt issues. It's said that in the late 1940s, President Truman was asked whether he had made the right decision in ordering nuclear bombs to be dropped on two Japanese cities in 1945. If President Truman were a "should've, could've" kind of guy, do you think he might have had guilt and PTSD because of what he did? For example, just imagine how he felt when he saw photos of the victims. But Truman seemed to be doing fine, and the reason was reflected in the way he answered the question. He said something like "Knowing then, in 1945, what I know now, maybe I would have and maybe I wouldn't have made the same decision to drop the bomb. However, knowing today only what I knew in 1945, when I made the decision, I would do exactly the same thing."

President Truman was able to distinguish what he knew when he made his decision from things he learned afterward. He was able to retain a healthy and realistic perspective about what happened, and when he knew what, that served to inoculate him from developing guilt. By the way, President Truman was known as a very decisive person. He might agonize over a decision, but once he decided, he never second-guessed himself. This is the kind of clear thinking you want to strive for on all of your guilt issues.

10.20. Re-answering Item 1 on the AAGS

Bring out the AAGS. Now I'd like you to answer item 1 again: To what extent do you think you should have known better? What's the correct answer? What is the answer that the facts would dictate, the answer that a panel of scientists would conclude is correct? Put a square around the answer you now believe is best. Most of the time, clients select a. If the client doesn't select a, the following script requires modification. **Exactly. There is no possible way you could have foreseen with certainty the negative outcomes that were going to occur. Otherwise, you wouldn't have done what you did.**

10.21. The Effects of Hindsight Bias on Other Guilt-Related Beliefs

One last thing about hindsight bias: Not only does it go straight to guilt, it also contributes to other guilt-related beliefs. For example, hindsight bias contributes to faulty beliefs about responsibility. If a person thinks a negative outcome was foreseeable and thus preventable, yet she allowed it to happen, then to some extent she may conclude that she caused it. This reveals another thinking error. Believing that you could have prevented a negative outcome is not the same thing as causing a negative outcome. One battered woman offered a great insight about this when she said, "You're right. I didn't pull his fist into my face."

JUSTIFICATION ANALYSIS

10.22. The Importance of Remembering the Options Actually Considered

Now we'll analyze justification. The most justified course of action in any situation is the best choice among those you actually considered at the time. You can't berate yourself for failing to choose an option that wasn't even on the table or that didn't occur to you. For example, let's say I'm helping you decide whether to move to Chicago or New York. You make your decision, but you come back to me three months later and tell me I gave you bad advice. "How's that?" I ask. You say, "I should have moved to Los Angeles." Los Angeles? Who said anything about Los Angeles? The most justified course of action has to be moving to either Chicago or New York because these were the only options considered. If you had better reasons for moving to Chicago when you made the decision, Chicago would have been the best choice. If you had better reasons for moving to New York back then, that would have been the best choice. Ultimately, moving to either Chicago or New York might both not turn out well, but at the time, you had to choose among the options under consideration, and on the basis of the information available.

It's something like answering a multiple choice test. The instructions say to select the best answer. You must choose among the options provided, weighing the evidence to decide which is the best answer. What happens if you write in a completely different answer? Do you think you'll get credit? Right. You won't get credit.

10.23. Thinking Errors That Contribute to Faulty Beliefs About Justification

Give the client handout 10.3, Thinking Errors That Contribute to Guilt. **A number of thinking errors can lead to faulty conclusions that contribute to guilt. This list organizes those thinking errors into the four categories of guilt-related beliefs, which relate to foreseeability, justification, responsibility, and wrongdoing. Hindsight bias is the thinking error that contributes to faulty beliefs about the foreseeability and preventability of negative outcomes. As discussed, hindsight bias reflects erroneous beliefs about what knowledge you possessed before a negative outcome was known.**

There are at least eight thinking errors that contribute to faulty conclusions about justifications for actions taken. We'll focus our discussion on two of them. Both involve inserting options that didn't exist when decisions were made.

10.24. Weighing the Merits of Actions Taken Against Idealized Options That Didn't Exist

Read thinking error J1 out loud. ("Weighing the merits of actions taken against idealized options that didn't exist.") **Idealized but impossible options—options that weren't available at the time—cannot be used to evaluate how justifiable your past actions were. I'll give you some examples of trauma survivors who compared what they did against ideal solutions that never existed.**

Consider a Vietnam veteran who experiences guilt about killing several enemy soldiers, even though his only choices were to kill or be killed. Looking back on it, his internal dialogue might sound something like this: "I never should have enlisted. I never should have gone to Vietnam. Then I wouldn't have been there in the first place." That option may have existed previously, but did it exist when he was in Vietnam facing the enemy?

Or consider a woman who was sexually assaulted and didn't fight back. "I survived," she said. "I wasn't injured. I should have fought back." But did the option of fighting back at no risk of getting hurt even exist? The fact that she wasn't hurt doesn't mean that serious injury wasn't a risk at the time.

The tendency to insert ideal solutions as options after the fact may be partly due to our exposure to movies, TV programs, and books where heroes and heroines accomplish the impossible. Consider the exploits of Spider-Man or Xena the warrior princess. Even when faced with seemingly impossible predicaments and excruciating either-or decisions, such characters often find a way to overcome all the obstacles and save the day—usually without significant injury to themselves, and often without seriously harming their archenemies.

10.25. Weighing the Merits of Actions Taken Against Options That Came to Mind Only Later

Read thinking error J2 out loud. ("Weighing the merits of actions taken against options that only came to mind later.") **If you criticize yourself for not following a course of action that only occurred to you later, you aren't being fair to yourself. There's no way you could have chosen to do something you didn't think of at the time.**

I'll give you an example that's based on a true story (Pitman et al., 1991). A Vietnam veteran who was undergoing prolonged exposure therapy was asked to visualize a traumatic event from Vietnam. In the event he chose, his unit was being overrun by the enemy and he saw one of his friends being shot and killed. He wasn't able to intervene and try to save his friend because he was out of ammunition. As he reexperienced the event, it occurred to him that he thinks he could have picked up a rifle belonging to one of the dead. Afterward, thinking he could have saved his friend's life, he spiraled into a suicidal depression. However, did the option of picking up the rifle exist for him twenty years ago? Of course not. In the confusion and intensity of the situation, it never occurred to him, and in fact, it hadn't occurred to him for decades, even though he'd rehashed what happened repeatedly.

If that veteran were here today, I'd ask him, "If you had known that you could have saved your friend's life by picking up a rifle, wouldn't you have done that?" He might say something like "Of course I would have," to which I'd reply, "Well, then, that's proof that it never occurred to you to pick up the rifle." It was a theoretical option that did not exist at the time because it didn't occur to him. For example, if you didn't know there was a door in this room, could you get out? You couldn't. You need to know a door exists before you can open it.

Give the client handout 10.4, the article "Thinking Errors, Faulty Conclusions, and Cognitive Therapy for Trauma-Related Guilt." I want you to read this article. At our next session, I'll ask you to tell me about at least one thinking error you've engaged in that we haven't discussed. Make a note to ask the client about this at the next session.

10.26. Inquiry into the Client's Reasons for Acting as She Did

What were your reasons for doing what you did? Again, try to personalize by referring to the guilt issue being discussed, for example, staying in the relationship or having an abortion. Write down these reasons, as well as the alternative courses the client details after the next question, so you can refer to them later.

What other courses of action did you consider at the time? For each alternative, ask the client the following question: **Knowing only what you knew then, before the outcome was known, what did you think would happen if you acted on that alternative? In other words, why did you rule out that choice or course of action?**

After the client has described the thoughts that caused her to rule out each course of action, ask the following question: **What was the best choice among the options you actually considered at the time?** At this point, clients are often able to recognize that what they chose to do made sense at the time. If you wish to emphasize this point, or if a client is having difficulty with this, read aloud her reasons for acting as she did and for ruling out alternate courses of action. This will usually make it obvious that what she chose to do was the most justified course of action at the time. **What you chose to do made sense at the time.**

10.27. Re-answering Item 2 on the AAGS

Now I'd like you to answer item 2 on the AAGS again. Given everything we've discussed, draw a square around what you now believe to be the correct answer. Clients almost always select "What I did was completely justified." If a client answers with a (or even b), proceed to the responsibility analysis. If not, probe for thinking errors and consider reviewing hindsight bias and the importance of assessing justification on beliefs held and knowledge possessed at the time of the action in question. If you still encounter client resistance, proceed with the responsibility analysis anyway.

Sometimes, what a client did was the *only* course of action considered, so it wasn't really a best-decision kind of situation. For example, it may not have occurred to her to leave when she says she should have left. In this case, the justification analysis is really a one-choice multiple-choice test. In such cases, the therapist can say something like this: "Because you didn't consider doing anything but what you did, what you did was, by definition, the most justified choice. But you have to draw a square around it to get credit."

In such cases, it will also be important to conduct an additional justification analysis comparing what the client did with any alternative courses of action that occurred to her later before asking her to re-answer item 2 on the AAGS: "Even though the alternative action you thought of later wasn't perceived as an option at the time, and therefore wasn't available, let's put it in anyway. At that time, what might you have thought would happen if you had actually done that?"

RESPONSIBILITY ANALYSIS

10.28. The Distinction Between Causation and Blame

In analyzing responsibility, we'll talk about responsibility as *causation*. For example, what causes this pencil to fall to the floor? Drop a pencil on the floor. **We're**

not evaluating whether it's a good idea to drop a pencil. We're simply talking about scientific principles of cause and effect. What causes what? For example, consider gravity. Gravity is a force that can cause things to happen. As to whether it's good or bad, that has more to do with the outcome. When it keeps us from floating off the earth, that's a good thing, but if it results in an airplane crash, that's a bad thing.

10.29. Explaining That Most Events Have Multiple Causes

The following discussion helps clients see that events have multiple causes, some of them far away in time or distance, and some more immediate. **Very few outcomes have a single cause. Most events have multiple causes, which can vary a great deal in how close or far they are from the final outcome along two dimensions—time and distance. Some causes may be quite far away in time and distance, whereas others may be immediate.**

For example, if I have a long row of dominoes on the desk and push the last one with the second-to-last one, it seems like the second-to-last domino is completely responsible for making the last domino fall. And if I push the first domino, it might seem like the first domino, or maybe my finger, is completely responsible for making the last domino fall. However, if we take out one of the middle dominoes and then push the first domino, the last domino won't fall down will it? You may demonstrate by asking the client to examine handout 10.5, Contributing Causes and the Domino Effect. Use the diagram to show how the various factors all contribute to the outcome, and that if you remove one of the factors (or dominoes), the final result does not occur.

Turn a light off, then turn it back on again. **What caused the light to go on? Right. My all-powerful finger. People have a tendency to focus on or overemphasize contributing causes that are right next to the final outcome. But are there other causes? Who else? What else?**

There are almost countless valid answers: the switch, the wiring, electricity, the lightbulb, the electrician who installed the switch, the person who paid the electricity bill, the utility poles, the power plant, the fuel used by the power plant, Benjamin Franklin, Thomas Edison, and so on. If the client struggles to come up with answers, offer some hints: **If the circuit breaker was turned off, would the light go on? If this room were on a small deserted island, would the light go on? If the power plant had to shut down, would the light go on? If some clever person hadn't figured out how to route electricity through wires, would the light go on?** And so on.

10.30. Generating a List of All Possible External Factors That Contributed to the Client's Actions

What external factors—people, history, learning, or other forces outside yourself—contributed to the outcome you feel guilty about? Write down each external factor identified. Alternatively, if the issue is "should have left sooner," you can use optional handout 10.6, which provides examples of common contributing causes for this issue. **What else? Who else?** Generate a list of ten to fifteen contributing factors.

10.31. Assigning a Percentage to Each Contributing Cause

Now let's assign a percentage of responsibility to each outside factor that contributed to the outcome. From 0 to 100 percent, how much was each outside factor responsible for causing or contributing to what happened? Don't worry about making the percentages add up to 100 percent. Just fill in the number that seems right to you for each. Once the client has done this, add up all of the percentages.

10.32. Re-answering Item 3 on the AAGS

Draw a pie chart with a slice showing the percentage of causation the client initially assigned to herself on the AAGS (below item 3); for example, 100 percent. (When the guilt issue is related to "should have left sooner," clients most often initially indicate that they were completely responsible for staying—100 percent.) Then, write down a number outside the pie chart showing the total percentage of all the outside contributing causes added together. **Your answers indicate that all of the external contributing causes add up to ...** (for example, 550 percent). **Combined with the amount you attributed to yourself, ...** (for example, 100 percent), **all of the contributing causes add up to ...** (for example, 650 percent). **But the true total can't add up to more than 100 percent because an event can't be more than 100 percent caused something has to change. Given all of these contributing factors, you need to either reduce your share of responsibility for causing what happened or discredit the contribution of the external factors. With that in mind, go ahead and re-answer item 3 on the AAGS, drawing a square around your new answer, and fill in a new percentage for your share of the responsibility.**

WRONGDOING ANALYSIS

10.33. Defining Wrongdoing

By the time we get to the wrongdoing analysis, most clients' sense of wrongdoing is lessened to a considerable degree because of what they've learned about their guilt thus far: that the negative outcomes were unforeseeable, and hence unpreventable; that knowing only what they knew at the time, what they did was completely justified compared to other options considered at the time; and that they were only minimally or not at all responsible for causing what happened.

When you answered item 4 on the AAGS the first time, what values did you think you had violated? A label or value judgment of "wrongdoing" is usually only applicable when someone intentionally or knowingly causes *foreseeable* harm. In other words, the person deliberately violates personal or societal values, causing harm or damage. For example, let's say that I need a new computer but I don't want to pay for it. I decide to steal one even though I know the people at the computer store will be very upset. Does that qualify as a wrongful act? Of course it does.

10.34. Challenging Conclusions of Wrongdoing

Use the guilt issue that you've been working on in the following example. For example, you might say, "Did you intend to cause the ongoing abuse, and did you foresee that things would get worse, not better, when you decided to stay?" **Did you intend to cause the negative outcome?** The answer is always no. **Did you know what was going to happen when you did what you did?** Again, the answer is almost always no. **Given the definition of wrongdoing, since you didn't intentionally cause the negative outcome and you didn't foresee it, can you see that wrongdoing doesn't apply to you? So we can put that concern to rest. Not guilty. Case dismissed.**

10.35. The Error of Attributing Wrongdoing Based on a Tragic but Unforeseeable Outcome

A common thinking error that contributes to faulty conclusions about wrongdoing is the tendency to conclude wrongdoing on the basis of a tragic negative outcome, rather than on the basis of your intentions before the outcome was known. Hindsight bias is usually implicated in this thinking error.

Here's an example: On a young woman's sixteenth birthday, her parents gave her a party. Because it was early when the party ended, afterward the daughter went out for a couple of hours with so-called friends, who got her thoroughly intoxicated. When she got home, her father saw how drunk she was. But instead of scolding his daughter and ruining her special day, the father just helped his daughter to bed. When he went into her room to check on her the next morning, he discovered she was dead. She had died from alcohol poisoning. He said, "I am going to have to live with myself for the rest of my life knowing that I *murdered* my daughter." But did he murder his daughter? Of course not. When do you think it first occurred to him that it wasn't a good idea to put his daughter to bed when she got home? When do you think it first occurred to him to walk her around until she sobered up? Certainly not until he discovered she was dead, at the earliest. It might not have occurred to him until the police arrived, and possibly not until after the autopsy. As tragic as the outcome was, the father can't be accused of wrongdoing.

10.36. Story About a Child with the Viluxin Virus

I want to tell you a story. A woman's eight-year-old daughter came down with the viluxin virus, so she took her to the doctor and got medication. Her daughter was recovering nicely, but one morning her daughter had an increased temperature and had taken a slight turn for the worse. The mother called the doctor's office but was unable to speak to him because he was with a patient. While awaiting his call back, the mother remembered that she had some Children's Tylenol, is used to reduce a fever. She gave her daughter the minimum dose, then stayed with her, caressing her until the girl drifted off into a peaceful sleep.

What do you think of that story? A responsible, nurturing parent, right? When two nurses were asked what they thought, they both said, "Good call!" But that wasn't the end of the story.

This anecdote was one of six trauma scenarios in a study conducted at the University of Hawaii to test several aspects of a theory about guilt (Kubany & Watson, 2003). In each of the six scenarios, subjects were asked to imagine themselves involved in a tragic event. In the Tylenol scenario, subjects were asked to imagine that they were the mother, who returned to her daughter's room in about fifteen minutes to discover the girl had taken a terrible turn for the worse and was having convulsions. She rushed her daughter to the emergency room, but they didn't make it. Her daughter died on the way there.

In part two of the scenario, the subjects read sometime later that it had just been discovered that Tylenol is not to be given to children who have the viluxin virus, as it has strong side effects that can be fatal in that situation. (This whole scenario is fictitious, by the way. There is no such thing as the viluxin virus.)

What's interesting is that this scenario was rated as evoking more guilt than any of the other five scenarios, in spite of the fact that before the outcome was known, the mother's actions were evaluated as loving and responsible. This is a classic example of the thinking error we were just talking about: the tendency to conclude wrongdoing on the basis of a tragic outcome, rather than on the basis of one's intentions before the outcome was known.

There are a couple of other reasons why this scenario evoked the most guilt. First, the relationship between the subject and the victim was closer than in any of the other scenarios. The death of a child is one of the most distressing and painful events possible, and distress is a component of guilt. A second reason why this scenario evoked the most guilt is that the mother's actions played a role in the causal chain of factors contributing to her daughter's death—even though she was unaware of it. She gave the Tylenol to her daughter.

10.37. Accountability vs. the Power to Cause or Prevent Outcomes

A third reason why this scenario evoked so much guilt has to do with yet another thinking error: the tendency to confuse two different types of responsibility. Responsibility as accountability is very different from responsibility as the power to cause or control outcomes. Accountability often comes with a job or a position of power. But just because you're accountable doesn't mean you can cause or prevent outcomes. Although part of the job of parenting is to try to prevent the child from being harmed, this isn't always within a parent's power. If for any reason something bad happens to a child, most parents think they didn't do their job and that they somehow did something wrong. Similarly, many people falsely believe that when they are given a job or put in charge, they have complete *causal* responsibility for negative outcomes associated with that role.

Here's another example: A platoon was sent on a routine reconnaissance mission a few days before Christmas. The area was thought to be safe, but the unit was ambushed and half of the men were killed. The platoon leader spent Christmas Eve writing letters to the families of the men who died. He was tormented by guilt and shame for not preventing the deaths of the men he was responsible for—so much so that he never told his family what happened and eventually developed a severe drug addiction. Every year, a few days before Christmas he would go up into the hills and wouldn't come back down until after Christmas. Before his therapist helped him analyze his responsibility, he thought he was 100 percent responsible for the deaths of the men in his unit. It had never even occurred to him that the enemy was primarily responsible for the deaths of the men in his unit.

Here's another example. Say you hear that there's a great job available at Veterans Affairs. It pays $150,000 a year, and all you have to do is make certain that everyone comes on time and nobody leaves early. I could give you that job. And I could hold you accountable and fire you if anyone arrives late or leaves early. But would you actually have the power to make certain that nobody gets to work late or leaves early?

10.38. Explaining That the Least Bad Choice Is a Moral and Justified Choice

When relevant, help the client realize that the "least bad choice" is a moral and justified choice if all the available courses of action have negative consequences, such as in catch-22 situations. There's one final common thinking error that contributes to beliefs about wrongdoing that I'd like to discuss. It's the failure to realize that when all the available courses of action have negative consequences, the least bad choice is actually a highly moral choice.

A classic illustration of this type of situation was depicted in the movie *Sophie's Choice* when the lead character, played by Meryl Streep, was faced with choosing which one of her children would live and which would die. A German officer said she could choose to keep one of her children, but that if she didn't choose, both of her children would be sentenced to death. Did this woman have the power to keep both of her children alive? No. Her guilt arose from comparing what she chose to do with the impossible option of keeping both of her children alive.

Let's take a look at a real-life example: The powerful video *The War Within*, produced at the National Center for PTSD residential program in Palo Alto, features the dilemma of a Vietnam veteran, a medic who suffered from severe guilt for ending the life of a buddy in Vietnam. His unit was surrounded by the enemy, who didn't know where they were. His buddy had a severe stomach wound that was being made worse by exposure to the air, and he was starting to scream. They were in a marsh, so the medic filled the wound with mud, injected two syringes of morphine into his buddy, and allowed him to sink below the surface of the water. If he hadn't done this, his unit surely would have been discovered by the enemy, and it's likely that the entire unit would have been killed. So even though the medic took a single life, it was in the interest of the greater good: preserving a number of lives.

Here's another example: A woman who was molested for years by her father experienced guilt about not fighting back or struggling when her father molested her. When asked to describe what happened from the time the abuse first occurred, she recalled that she did fight back in the beginning. But when she did, he beat her and then proceeded to molest her. She learned that she was going to be molested whether she resisted or not, but when she resisted, she'd be beaten and bruised, as well. So she chose the least bad choice: getting molested without being beaten and bruised.

A similar situation was described by a man who was raped by his heinously cruel father for years. He said he felt guilty about cooperating when his father approached him for sex. Upon further questioning, he recalled that when he resisted he was punished in addition to being raped, by being locked in a closet overnight. So he opted for the least bad choice and didn't resist. Although he'd be raped either way, at least he was able to avoid the punishment.

Here's a final example, about a woman who experienced guilt about not disclosing that she was molested by an adult neighbor when she was a girl. During a wrongdoing analysis, her therapist pointed out that disclosing the molestation was fraught with a variety of perceived negative consequences, including family disruption, getting blamed for the molestation, and public humiliation.

When her therapist used *Sophie's Choice* to illustrate the difficult situation she had faced as a child, the woman said, "That's what happened to me!" She said that when she got divorced, she was forced to make a choice between having custody of one of her two children or risking the loss of both children. She and her ex-husband fought over custody of the children for several years, until finally she got custody of their daughter, and her husband got custody of their son. Her son sobbed at the thought of being separated from her and begged her to let him stay with her. The only way this would be possible would be if she went back to court, but if she did so, she'd run a very real risk of losing custody of her daughter, too.

She believed the risk was too great and told her son that he had to go live with his father. She was guilt ridden as her son tearfully boarded the plane to go live with his father. During a subsequent visit by her son, she learned that he was malnourished and had been physically abused by his father. This exacerbated her guilt about not fighting for custody of both children. As she explained all of this during therapy, she finally realized that the option of seeking custody of both children had been burdened by too much risk, and that knowing only what she knew back then, she had made the least bad choice, which was completely justified and highly moral given the circumstances at the time. For the first time, she saw that clearly positive choices were never available to her. As an aside, she did finally obtain custody of her son.

10.39. Re-answering Item 4 on the AAGS

Keeping in mind everything we've discussed about wrongdoing, I'd like you to reappraise your degree of wrongdoing by re-answering item 4 on the AAGS place a square around the best answer. Depending upon the client's response, either probe for uncorrected thinking errors or proceed to the next guilt issue.

Did you intend to cause the negative outcome? Did you know that was going to happen when you did what you did? Because you didn't know the outcome in advance, it's clear that wrongdoing doesn't apply to you. If the client is reading and completing chapters in *Healing the Trauma of Domestic Violence* as homework, assign her chapter 10 in the workbook at the end of this session.

ANALYZING SECOND AND SUBSEQUENT GUILT ISSUES

10.40. Completing the AAGS and Conducting a Guilt Incident Debriefing

Choose a second guilt issue to work on and have the client fill out a new copy of the AAGS. Then conduct a guilt debriefing for the new issue: **Give me a slow-motion, detailed description of exactly what happened, starting with the events that led up to the situation. Give me a little background, then tell me exactly what happened. Remember to focus on the facts, not value judgments. What did you see, hear, feel, and smell? Who did what, who said what, and what thoughts went through your mind leading up to that point in time when you think you should have acted differently?**

After hearing this descriptive account, ask three additional questions: **What was the worst part of the story you just told me? What were your feelings during the worst part? What were your thoughts during the worst part?**

10.41. Foreseeability and Preventability Analysis

As mentioned, analyzing the second guilt issue usually goes much more quickly than the first. And as before, it is important for the therapist to personalize all inquiries and statements to reflect the client's specific guilt issue. **On item 1 of the AAGS, you indicated …** Read the client's answer to item 1. **What is it that you should have known better? What do you think you should have done differently? When did it first occur to you that you could do this?**

Do you see what's happening here? Once again, you're remembering yourself knowing something you didn't learn until later. Remember, you can't use knowledge acquired after **making a decision to guide your decisions about making that decision. You can't use knowledge you acquire on Wednesday to help you make a decision the previous Monday. Like we talked about before, finding out that the stock market went up on Wednesday can't be used to help you make an investment decision two days earlier, on Monday.**

If you knew with certainty what was going to happen when you did what you did, would you have done what you did? Again, that's proof that you didn't know what was going to happen. I believe you couldn't possibly have known what was going to happen. Otherwise, you wouldn't have done what you did.

Bring out the AAGS for the second guilt issue. **Now I'd like you to re-answer item 1. What's the correct answer—the answer supported by the facts?** Again, most of the time, clients select a. If the client doesn't select a, the following script needs to be modified to match the answer selected. **Exactly. There is no possible way you could have foreseen the negative outcome. If you could have, you wouldn't have done what you did.**

10.42. Justification Analysis

Okay, let's move on to justification. What were your reasons for doing what you did? Write down these reasons, as well as the alternative courses of action the client details after the next question, so you can refer to them later. **What other courses of action did you consider at the time?** For each alternative, ask the client the following question: **Knowing only what you knew then, before the outcome was known, what did you think would happen if you acted on that alternative? In other words, why did you rule out that choice or course of action?**

After the client has described her reasons for ruling out each course of action, ask the following question: **What was the best choice among the options you actually considered at the time? Right. What you chose to do made good sense at the time. You had better reasons for choosing that option than you did for doing anything else.** Read the client's reasons for acting as she did and her reasons for ruling out alternative courses of action. Ask the client to choose what she now believes to be the correct answer to item 2 on the AAGS. Depending on her answer, probe for uncorrected thinking errors or proceed to the responsibility analysis.

10.43. Responsibility Analysis

Now let's move on to responsibility. What external factors—people, history, learning, or other forces outside yourself—contributed to the outcome you feel guilty about? Write down each external factor identified.

Now assign a percentage of responsibility to each outside factor that contributed to the outcome. From 0 to 100 percent, how much was each outside factor responsible for causing what happened? Again, don't worry about making the percentages add up to 100 percent. Just fill in the number that seems right to you for each. Once the client has done this, add up the percentages. Then add in the percentage of responsibility the client initially assigned to herself in item 3 of the AAGS. Remind the client that in the real world, the percentages of all contributing causes can't add up to more than 100 percent, then ask her to reappraise her degree of responsibility by answering item 3 on the AAGS once again and filling in a new percentage for her contribution to causing the outcome.

10.44. Wrongdoing Analysis

Once the analysis of the second guilt issue is complete, ask the client if she has any other major unresolved guilt issues related to her trauma. If she does, continue analyzing these issues. While analysis of a third guilt issue is sometimes required, by completion of the second or third issue, most clients are clear on the concepts and their guilt is significantly relieved, and they know how to apply the guilt analyses to other guilt issue.

10.45. Addressing Guilt About Having Emotional Responses Perceived to Be Inappropriate

When clients experience guilt about certain feelings they had, it can usually be alleviated by getting them to realize that strong feelings aren't a matter of choice or willpower. The two most common guilt issues of this nature apply to abused women and combat veterans, respectively. A woman may experience guilt about enjoying or having positive physical responses while being sexually abused in childhood by a person who wasn't scaring her, and a combat veteran may experience guilt about having been afraid during combat.

In the first case, therapists might ask a female client something like "If you could have not responded positively to the sexual abuse, wouldn't you have done that?" When the client answers yes, the therapist may say something like "That's proof you couldn't have, because if you could have not had a positive sexual response, you wouldn't have had a positive sexual response."

Similarly, a combat veteran with guilt about having been afraid might be asked, "If you could have not been afraid during combat, wouldn't you have been unafraid?" When the veteran answers that of course he would have liked to have been unafraid, he might be told something like "That's proof that you had no control over your feelings, because if you could have been unafraid, you would have been unafraid."

CONCLUDING REMARKS

Keep in mind that the goal of the guilt intervention is not to completely eliminate guilt—although this is often the result. The goal is to achieve a reduction in guilt and guilt-related beliefs so that guilt is no longer a significant source of emotional pain. Because guilt can have significant impacts on self-esteem, an additional benefit is enhanced self-esteem.

Handout 10.1: Attitudes About Guilt Survey (AAGS)

Client Initials: _____   Date: _____

Individuals who have experienced traumatic events often experience guilt related to these events. They may feel guilty about something they did (or did not do), about beliefs or thoughts they had (that they now believe to be untrue), or about having had certain feelings (or lack of feelings). The purpose of this questionnaire is to evaluate how you feel about one (and only one) guilt issue.

Please take a moment to think about your experience. Briefly describe what happened and what you feel guilty about:

_____

_____

Briefly describe the negative outcomes that could have been prevented:

_____

_____

I should have or shouldn't have (*circle one and finish the sentence*): _____

_____

In answering each of the following questions, please circle one letter that best reflects or summarizes your view of what happened.

1. **To what extent do you think you should have known better and could have prevented or avoided the outcome?**

    a.   There is no possible way that I could have known better.

    b.   I believe slightly that I should have known better.

    c.   I believe moderately that I should have known better.

    d.   For the most part I believe that I should have known better.

    e.   I absolutely should have known better.

2. **How justified was what you did? (How good were your reasons for what you did?)**

    a.   What I did was completely justified (excellent reasons).

    b.   What I did was mostly justified.

    c.   What I did was moderately justified.

    d.   What I did was slightly justified.

    e.   What I did was not justified in any way (very poor reasons).

3. **How personally responsible were you for causing what happened?**

    a.   I was in no way responsible for causing what happened.

    b.   I was slightly responsible for causing what happened.

    c.   I was moderately responsible for causing what happened.

    d.   I was largely responsible for causing what happened.

    e.   I was completely responsible for causing what happened.

    My percentage of responsibility: _____ %

4. **Did you do something wrong? (Did you violate personal standards of right and wrong by what you did?)**

    a.   What I did was not wrong in any way.

    b.   What I did was slightly wrong.

    c.   What I did was moderately wrong.

    d.   What I did was very wrong.

    e.   What I did was extremely wrong.

5. **How distressed do you feel when you think about what happened?**

    a.   I feel no distress when I think about what happened.

    b.   I feel slightly distressed when I think about what happened.

    c.   I feel moderately distressed when I think about what happened.

    d.   I feel very distressed when I think about what happened.

    e.   I feel extremely distressed when I think about what happened.

6. **Circle the answer that indicates how often you experience guilt that relates to what happened.**

    Never   Seldom   Occasionally   Often   Always   Whenever I
    think about it

7. **Circle the answer that indicates the intensity or severity of guilt you typically experience about what happened.**

    None   Slight   Moderate   Considerable   Extreme

Handout 10.2: Aspects of Guilt

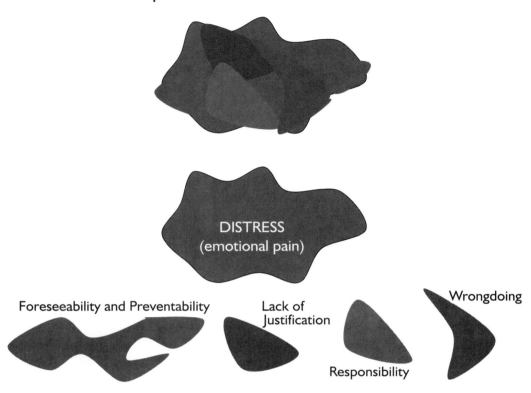

Hindsight bias occurs when knowledge of an event's outcome, such as who won a game, distorts or biases a person's memory of what he or she knew before the outcome was known. This type of thinking is evident in statements such as "I should have known better," "I should have done something different," "I saw it coming," "I knew what was going to happen" (before outcomes were known), and "I could have prevented it." Many trauma survivors falsely believe that the events were foreseeable—and therefore preventable.

This handout is in the public domain. Readers may copy, redistribute, or use as they see fit. This handout is available in color at our website www.treatingptsd.com

Handout 10.3: Thinking Errors That Contribute to Guilt

Thinking error that contributes to faulty conclusions about knowledge possessed before outcomes were known (distorted beliefs about *foreseeability* and *preventability*)

HB: Hindsight-biased thinking

Thinking errors that contribute to faulty conclusions about *justification*, or the validity of reasons for acting as one did

J1: Weighing the merits of actions taken against idealized options that didn't exist

J2: Weighing the merits of actions taken against options that only came to mind later

J3: Focusing only on positive things that might have happened had an alternative action been taken

J4: Tending to overlook benefits associated with actions taken

J5: Failing to compare available options in terms of their perceived probability of success before outcomes were known

J6: Failing to realize that acting on speculative hunches rarely pays off and that occurrence of a low-probability event is not evidence that one should have counted on this outcome before it occurred

J7: Failing to recognize that different decision-making "rules" apply when time is precious than in situations which allow extended contemplation of options

J8: Failing to recognize that in heightened states of negative arousal one's ability to think clearly and make logical decisions is impaired

---

Thinking errors that contribute to faulty conclusions about degree of *responsibility* for causing negative outcomes

R1: Hindsight-biased thinking

R2: Being oblivious to the totality of forces that cause traumatic events

R3: Equating a belief that one could have done something to prevent the traumatic event with a belief that one caused the event

R4: Confusing responsibility as accountability (for example, "my job") with responsibility as having the power to cause or control outcomes

R5: Existential beliefs about accountability and the need to accept the consequences of one's actions—beliefs that fail to take into account the causal power of situational forces

---

Thinking errors that contribute to faulty conclusions about *wrongdoing* or violation of values

W1: Tending to conclude wrongdoing on the basis of outcome rather than on the basis of one's intentions before the outcome was known

W2: Failing to realize that strong emotional reactions are not under voluntary control (not a matter of choice or willpower)

W3: Tending to inflate the seriousness of a minor moral violation when the minor violation leads unforeseeably to a traumatic outcome

W4: Failing to recognize that when all available choices or courses of action have negative outcomes, the least bad choice is a highly moral choice

---

Thinking error that contributes to all of the faulty conclusions

ALL1: Believing that an emotional reaction to an idea provides evidence for the idea's validity

---

Handout 10.4: Thinking Errors, Faulty Conclusions, and Cognitive Therapy for Trauma-Related Guilt

by Edward S. Kubany, Ph.D., ABPP

There is growing recognition that trauma survivors' explanations of their involvement in trauma may contribute to posttrauma symptomatology and interfere with the process of recovery (1,2,3). These explanations often revolve around cognitive aspects of guilt, which is conceptualized as an unpleasant feeling accompanied by a set of interrelated beliefs about one's role in a negative event (2,4,5). My colleagues and I have identified four cognitive dimensions or components of guilt, which include (a) perceived responsibility for causing a negative outcome, (b) perceived lack of justification for actions taken, (c) perceived violation of values, and (d) a belief that one knew what was going to happen *before* the outcome was observed.

Several investigators have noted that trauma survivors tend to distort or exaggerate the importance of their roles in trauma (2,3,6), and trauma survivors repeatedly draw four kinds of faulty conclusions—each of which involves distortion of a cognitive component of guilt (2). First, many trauma survivors exaggerate the degree to which they were responsible for *causing* trauma-related outcomes. Second, many survivors think that their actions were less justified than would be indicated by objective analyses of the facts. Third, many survivors conclude that they are guilty of wrongdoing even though their intentions were consistent with their values. Fourth, trauma survivors often conclude that they "knew" what was going to happen before it was possible to "know."

THINKING ERRORS THAT LEAD TO FAULTY CONCLUSIONS ABOUT ONE'S ROLE IN TRAUMA

We have identified fifteen thinking errors that can lead trauma survivors to draw faulty conclusions about how justified, responsible, and guilty of wrongdoing they were when the trauma occurred. Helping clients correct these thinking errors is a major focus of our structured cognitive therapy approach for treating trauma-related guilt (2,7). The fifteen thinking areas are discussed in considerable detail elsewhere (2) and will be described briefly in this article. Four of the thinking errors may contribute to faulty conclusions about causal responsibility; seven of them may contribute to faulty conclusions about justifiability for actions taken; three of them may contribute to faulty conclusions about wrong-doing; and one of the thinking errors may contribute to all of the faulty conclusions.

Faulty Conclusions About Degree of Responsibility

1. Faulty beliefs about pre-outcome knowledge caused by hindsight bias. Hindsight bias (which is akin to Monday-morning quarterbacking) occurs when knowledge about event outcomes biases or distorts beliefs about knowledge possessed before outcomes were known (2,8,9). Common among trauma survivors, hindsight-biased thinking leads many trauma survivors to believe falsely that they knew what was going to happen before it was possible to know or that they dismissed or overlooked clues or signs that "signaled" what was going to occur. Because they believe they "should have" acted on this "knowledge" to prevent some tragedy, many trauma survivors then conclude that to some extent they *caused* the tragedy. An incest survivor who believed she was partly responsible for causing her own abuse expressed insight about this thinking error when she said, "I was putting my thirty-eight-year-old mind in my twelve-year-old head." She had been remembering herself as being smarter, at age twelve, than she was capable of being.

2. Obliviousness to totality of forces that cause traumatic events. Trauma survivors often seem to be oblivious to the fact that traumatic events often have multiple sources of causation and make no effort to assess the relative contributions of causal factors outside of themselves. For example, one Vietnam veteran who considered himself to be 98% responsible for the death of a buddy from sniper fire had completely ignored causal contributions of the enemy, other soldiers in his unit, the chain of command, the buddy himself, and politicians in the U.S. who were responsible for his being in Vietnam.

3. Equating a belief that one could have done something to prevent the traumatic event with a belief that one caused the event. Many trauma survivors mistakenly equate beliefs that they "could have prevented" a traumatic event with beliefs that they *caused* the event. Even if such individuals "could have" prevented the traumatic outcomes, it does not mean that they actually caused them. This explanation made sense to a formerly battered woman who said, "That's for sure! I didn't pull his fist into my face."

4. Confusion between responsibility as accountability (e.g., one's "job") and responsibility as power to cause or control outcomes. Many trauma survivors think they caused negative outcomes because they equate some job or role assignment with an ability to determine outcomes. For example, one former platoon leader told me he was responsible for the deaths of men in his unit because "I didn't do my job. I was *supposed* to keep my men alive." He confused his social role or position (he was "in charge") with what he was actually capable of accomplishing or causing. This thinking error may be particularly prevalent among parents who have lost children to homicide, suicide, accidents, or serious illness (10).

Faulty Conclusions About *Justification* for Actions Taken

5. Failure to recognize that different decision-making "rules" apply when time is precious than in situations that allow extended contemplation of options. During many traumatic events, brainstorming or extended evaluation of alternatives is not an available luxury, and decisions are often based on an almost automatic summarization and prioritization of options. In fact, failure to act quickly during a crisis can be very risky. For example, a person trapped in a burning building faces increasing risk for every second it takes to decide how to escape. What may seem to have been an "obviously better decision" after years of rehashing may not have been obvious at all during the stressful, precious moments available for deciding what to do during the trauma.

6. Weighing the merits of actions taken against options that only came to mind later. Sometimes, after much rehashing, survivors think of something that might have prevented a tragic outcome, *had it occurred to them during or prior to the trauma.* Pitman and his colleagues (11) described the case of a veteran who realized during therapy that he might have saved the life of a buddy during a Vietnam battle if he had only had the presence of mind to pick up a rifle belonging to one of the enemy dead. (His own weapon was out of ammunition.) However, because he did not think of this option at the time, it *did not exist* and was not available when the battle occurred. It was irrational for the veteran to weigh the merits of his actions against an "option" that first occurred to him twenty years after the battle. Hindsight bias is the mechanism that underlies this important thinking error, which sometimes results in severe self-flagellation (11).

7. Weighing the merits of actions taken against ideal or fantasy options that did not exist. Sometimes, trauma survivors evaluate or judge the goodness of their reasons for acting as they did "against idealized or fantasy choices that would have avoided the rape, prevented the beating, stopped the incest, or kept everyone safe and alive" (2). For example, many soldiers in battle find themselves in situations where their only choices are to "kill or be killed." No matter what they choose to do, someone is going to die. Nevertheless, some veterans weigh the merits of what they did against Superman-like actions that would have produced no violence or death. They may give explanations such as "I should have thought of something. I don't know what I could have done, but I should have thought of something."

8. Focusing only on "good" things that might have happened had an alternative action been taken. Sometimes, trauma survivors glamorize an alternative course of action they contemplated but did not take when the trauma occurred, and they downplay or ignore likely negative consequences of the alternative course. For example, some adult incest survivors who think they were unjustified for not disclosing the abuse as a child dwell on the fact that the abuse *might have* stopped had they complained. At the same time, they may "forget" or disregard what they *believed* would have happened had they reported the abuse (e.g., that they would be blamed, hurt, or punished; that they would disrupt the family; that they would "betray" the offending family member).

9. Tendency to overlook "benefits" associated with actions taken. Sometimes, trauma survivors maintain important values by their actions during trauma and fail to realize that, had they acted otherwise, these values would have been invalidated or violated to some degree. For example, some battered women who refuse to press charges against their partners confirm or validate values (held at the time) that they should "turn the other cheek" and could "change" their partner if they would just try harder.

10. Failure to compare available options in terms of their perceived probabilities of success before outcomes were known. Sometimes, unselected courses of action that seemed to be poor choices when the trauma occurred are "recalled" as less likely to produce negative outcomes than actions taken. Instead of judging their reasons for acting as they did based on the quality or soundness of their decision making (before outcomes were known), some survivors judge their actions solely on the basis of the *outcome*. It is important for clients to know that even good decisions can (and occasionally will) turn out badly (because of laws of probability).

11. Failure to realize that acting on speculative hunches rarely pays off and occurrence of a low-probability event is not evidence that one should have "bet" on this outcome before it occurred. Trauma survivors occasionally say, in retrospect, that they should have acted on "hunches," "intuition," "premonitions," or "gut feelings"—which, if acted upon, might have prevented or avoided a tragic outcome. However, people do not ordinarily act on speculative hunches because they are typically "long-shot" predictions, which experience has shown tend not to be borne out. Furthermore, occurrence of a low-probability outcome that was predicted by a hunch (e.g., "If I trade places with him, maybe something bad will happen") is not evidence that one should have acted on the hunch.

Faulty Conclusions About Perceived *Wrongdoing*

12. Tendency to conclude wrongdoing on the basis of the outcome rather than on the basis of one's *intentions* (before the outcome was known). Sometimes, trauma survivors conclude that they were guilty of wrongdoing, not because they behaved in ways inconsistent with their values, but because of an unfortunate (and unforeseeable) outcome. One client of mine was self-condemning and ashamed for asking a friend (when he was a child) to leave the beach and return with a fishing pole. (The boys had spotted a large school of fish.) On his way to get the pole, the friend fell off a rock jetty and drowned.

13. Failure to realize that strong emotional reactions are not under voluntary control (i.e., not a matter of choice or willpower). Many combat veterans experience guilt about being afraid in battle (12), and many incest survivors experience guilt because they became physically aroused during the sexual abuse. However, strong emotional reactions are not intellectual decisions or moral choices. None of the veterans *chose* to be afraid, and had they been able to make an "intellectual decision" not to be afraid, they wouldn't have been afraid. Similarly, children who are touched in certain ways by adults do not have conscious control over their autonomic nervous system.

14. Failure to recognize that when all available options have negative outcomes, the least bad choice is a highly moral choice. During traumatic events, individuals often confront situations in which *all* available courses of action have unfavorable consequences. Something bad is likely to happen whether a sexual assault victim fights back or does not resist, whether an incested child discloses the abuse or suffers in silence, or whether a soldier in battle shoots to kill or fires over the heads of the enemy. In all of these lose-lose or "catch-22" situations, no unambiguously good choices are available, and the "least bad" choice reflects sound moral judgment by validating an individual's most important values. For example, by shooting "to kill," the soldier may validate his values about the importance of his life and his buddies' lives, and his beliefs about himself as a "patriotic and loyal" citizen.

A Thinking Error That Contributes to All of the Faulty Conclusions

15. Belief that an emotional reaction to an idea provides evidence for the idea's validity. When an idea is associated with affect, the affect appears to give the idea a ring of "truth" or "untruth." For example, a survivor might say, "Intellectually, I agree with you; but I still *feel* responsible" or "Deep down in my heart, I still *feel* that what I did was wrong." The client might be told that "I *feel* responsible is not an emotion. What do you *think* you were responsible for causing?" A battered woman was tempted to reconcile with a boyfriend (who had almost killed her on several occasions) because she "*felt* sorry" for him. The woman was reminded that "how you *feel* when you think about staying away or reconciling *is not evidence* that it is in your best interests to stay away or go back."

COGNITIVE THERAPY FOR TRAUMA-RELATED GUILT (CT-TRG)

The goal of cognitive therapy for trauma-related guilt (CT-TRG) is to help clients achieve an objective and undistorted appraisal of their role in trauma. CT-TRG has three phases: (a) assessment, (b) debriefing or imaginal exposure exercises, and (c) formal CT-TRG, which involves separate procedures for correcting thinking errors that lead to faulty conclusions associated with guilt (2). The thinking errors identified above are addressed in the context of four separate, semistructured procedures for teaching clients to distinguish what they knew "then" from what they know "now," and for reappraising perceptions of justification, responsibility, and wrongdoing (in light of beliefs held and knowledge possessed when the trauma occurred). Space limitations here preclude an elaboration of the phases and procedures of CT-TRG, which are described in detail elsewhere (2,7,13). Clinicians interested in implementing CT-TRG are encouraged to examine these other sources.

REFERENCES

1. Frazier, P. A., & Schauben, L. (1994). Causal attributions and recovery from rape and other stressful life events. *Journal of Social and Clinical Psychology, 13,* 1-14.

2. Kubany, E. S., & Manke, F. P. (1995). Cognitive therapy for trauma-related guilt: Conceptual bases and treatment outlines. *Cognitive and Behavioral Practice, 2,* 23-61.

3. Resick, P. A. (1993). *Cognitive processing for rape victims.* Newbury Park: Sage.

4. Kubany, E. S., Abueg, F. R., Brennan, J. M., Owens, J. A., Kaplan, A., & Watson, S. (1995). Initial examination of a multidimensional model of trauma-related guilt: Applications to combat veterans and battered women. *Journal of Psychopathology and Behavioral Assessment, 17,* 353-376.

5. Kubany, E. S., Haynes, S. N., Abueg, F. R., Manke, F. P., Brennan, J. M., & Stahura, C. (1996). Development and validation of the Trauma-Related Guilt Inventory (TRGI). *Psychological Assessment, 8,* 428-444.

6. Miller, D., & Porter, C. (1983). Self-blame in victims of violence. *Journal of Social Issues, 39,* 139-152.

7. Kubany, E. S. (1997). Application of cognitive therapy for trauma-related guilt (CT-TRG) with a Vietnam veteran troubled by multiple sources of guilt. *Cognitive and Behavioral Practice, 3,* 213-244.

8. Kubany, E. S. (1994). A cognitive model of guilt typology in combat-related PTSD. *Journal of Traumatic Stress, 7,* 3-19.

9. Hawkins, S. A., & Hastie, R. (1990). Hindsight: Biased judgments of past events after outcomes are known. *Psychological Bulletin, 107,* 311-327.

10. Rando, T. A. (Ed.). (1986). *Parental loss of a child.* Champaign, IL: Research Press.

11. Pitman, R. K., Altman, B., Greenwald, E., Longpre, R. E., Macklin, M. L., Poiré, R. E., & Steketee, G. S. (1991). Psychiatric complications during flooding therapy for posttraumatic stress disorder. *Journal of Clinical Psychiatry, 52,* 17-20.

12. Kubany, E. S., Abueg, F. R., Kilauano, W., Manke, F. P., & Kaplan, A. (1997). Development and validation of the Sources of Trauma-Related Guilt Survey— War-Zone Version. *Journal of Traumatic Stress, 10,* 235-258.

13. Kubany, E. S. (1996). *Cognitive therapy for trauma-related guilt.* Audiotape distributed by the National Center for PTSD, Palo Alto, CA.

Published in *National Center for Post-Traumatic Stress Disorder Clinical Quarterly* (1997, 8, 6-8). Reprinted in *Trauma Response* (1998, 4, 20-21). This article is in the public domain.

Handout 10.5: Contributing Causes and the Domino Effect

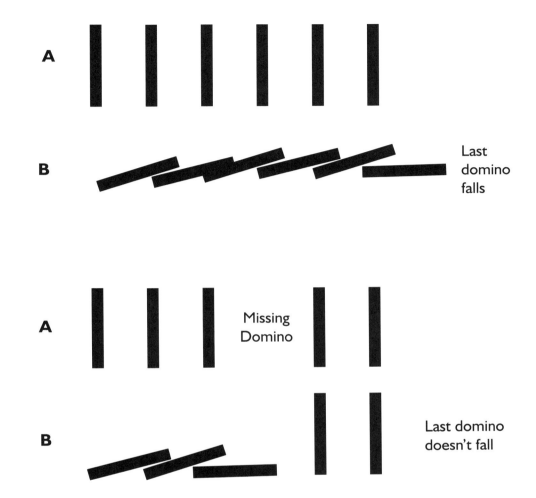

Handout 10.6: Causes Contributing to Staying with an Abusive Partner

Client Initials: _____   Date: _____

Below is a list of factors that battered women have identified as contributing to their decision to stay with an abusive partner. Place a check mark next to each factor that contributed to your staying with an abusive partner. For all checked items, indicate the percentage of contribution of that item. At the end of the list there are several blank lines where you can add additional factors that contributed to your decision to stay.

√   %

____ ____ My history of good times with my partner

____ ____ Socialization or learning history that taught me to believe that marriage is forever

____ ____ A minister or other religious authority who encouraged me to stay

____ ____ The fact that my mother was abused by my father and didn't leave him

____ ____ Socialization history that taught me "if you make your bed, you have to lie in it"

____ ____ My partner saying that I promised I'd never leave him

____ ____ Friends and relatives who encouraged me to stay

____ ____ Socialization history that taught me to believe that children need their father

____ ____ Socialization history that taught me to be prone to guilt, allowing others to influence me with guilt trips

____ ____ Socialization history that taught me to believe that if my relationship doesn't work, I failed

____ ____ Socialization history that taught me to believe that if someone apologizes to me, I am obligated to accept the apology and go back to the way things were

____ ____ Abuse by my partner that resulted in my self-esteem going down so much I didn't think I deserved better

____ ____ My partner telling me I'd never find another man who would accept me for who I am

____ ____ My partner's guilt trips that the children need him

___ ___ My partner's guilt trips that he would fall apart or commit suicide if I left him

___ ___ Social isolation

___ ___ Lack of financial resources

___ ___ Developing PTSD as a result of my partner's abuse

___ ___ PTSD, which impaired my ability to concentrate and make rational decisions

___ ___ My partner's threats that he would physically harm me and/or the children if I left

___ ___ Naivete or lack of knowledge about domestic violence; not even realizing I was a battered woman

___ ___ Socialization history that taught me to believe that all relationships are like mine

___ ___ Socialization history that taught me to believe that if I left the relationship, the next one wouldn't be any better—and might be worse

___ ___ Lack of knowledge about domestic violence resources, such as support groups or shelters

___ ___ Socialization history that taught me to believe that the violence was my fault

___ ___ Low self-esteem due to my trauma history

___ ___ Socialization history that taught me to be so ashamed about the violence that I couldn't tell anyone

___ ___ Continued physical and emotional abuse that caused me to believe it would be impossible to get out of the relationship

___ ___ My partner's threats that he would sue for custody of the children

___ ___ My partner's threats that he would harm my parents or other family members if I left him

___ ___ Socialization history that taught me to believe that my partner would eventually change and stop abusing me

___ ___ Memories of how charming and wonderful my partner was at the beginning of our relationship

___ ___ Drugs or alcohol clouding my judgment and ability to make logical decisions

___ ___ My partner's pressure on me to use drugs or alcohol

___ ___ My partner's repeated apologies and assurances that he would change

___ ___ My child or children, who "needed" me to stay so they could be with their father

___ ___ Dissociation or emotion-focused coping that prevented me from even thinking about how to get out of the relationship

___ ___ Socialization history that taught me to believe that I had to keep my promises

___ ___ Romance novels and movies depicting heroines changing despicable men

___ ___ The social stigma of being divorced and a single parent

___ ___ _____

___ ___ _____

___ ___ _____

___ ___ _____

_____ Grand Total Percent

Challenging Guiding Fictions and "Supposed to" Beliefs

Battered women commonly hold unhelpful beliefs related to relationships, marriage, and women's roles in a variety of contexts. Often these beliefs were taught to them at an early age and have never been critically examined for their accuracy or helpfulness in terms of the client's long-term best interest. In this module, some of the most commonly held and harmful beliefs, or guiding fictions, are brought to the client's attention and the client is led through an examination and refutation of each belief. Although CTT is geared toward women who are no longer in abusive relationships and this will probably be the case for most clients, the discussion of why women stay in abusive relationships is still relevant. It will help clients understand why they stayed in the relationship as long as they did and will also help diminish any lingering guilt related to this issue.

OBJECTIVES

■ For the client to learn that she, like many women, has been socialized to believe she is "supposed to" do all sorts of things for which there is no supporting evidence and that these guiding fictions can influence her to stay in or return to an abusive relationship

■ For the client to challenge and reject several common guiding fictions that keep her subordinate in relationships with men

■ For the client to be willing and able to challenge other people's opinions about what women are supposed to do

MATERIALS

■ Challenging Guiding Fictions That Lead Many Women to Stay in or Return to an Abusive Relationship (handout 11.1; one or two copies)

HOMEWORK

■ Listen to session audio-recordings.

■ Continue to monitor and record negative self-talk.

■ Practice PMR while listening to the PMR recording, twice a day.

■ Do a body scan and over-tense and relax muscles when experiencing stress.

■ Read and complete chapter 11 in *Healing the Trauma of Domestic Violence* (optional).

PROCEDURES CHECKLIST

1. _____ Introduction to the concept of guiding fictions (handout 11.1)

2. _____ Explaining the exercise for challenging guiding fictions

3. _____ Challenging guiding fiction 1: You made your bed and now you have to lie in it

4. _____ Challenging guiding fiction 2: You should be resigned to live out your sentence

5. _____ Challenging guiding fiction 3: Marriage is supposed to be forever

6. _____ Challenging guiding fiction 4: Because you feel sorry for your partner, you should stay in the relationship or go back to him

7. _____ Challenging guiding fiction 5: Because your partner apologized, you should accept his apology and go back to the way things were

8. _____ Challenging guiding fiction 6: If you just try hard enough or get it right, he'll change and you'll be happy

9. _____ Challenging guiding fiction 7: It's your responsibility to make the relationship work

10. _____ Challenging guiding fiction 8: Because the children need their father, you should keep the family together

11. _____ Lessons learned from the guiding fictions exercise

DETAILED PROCEDURES FOR MODULE 11

11.1. Introduction to the Concept of Guiding Fictions

Give the client handout 11.1, Challenging Guiding Fictions That Lead Many Women to Stay in or Return to an Abusive Relationship. If the therapist won't be sitting side by side with the client while doing the following exercise, two copies will be required. **Read the title aloud**. ("Challenging Guiding Fictions That Lead Many Women to Stay in or Return to an Abusive Relationship.") **What do you think the term "guiding fictions" means? In our culture (and many others), the process of female socialization involves teaching girls many beliefs that serve as guidelines or values for determining how they are supposed to think and behave, including in relationships.**

These sorts of "supposed to" beliefs are moral codes in certain respects, not unlike the Ten Commandments or rules of etiquette. In general, their validity, accuracy, or truth is never questioned or challenged; they are simply assumed to be true. For example, many girls are taught that they are always supposed to be polite, nice, and forgiving, which also means they aren't supposed to act in ways perceived to be rude or selfish. Unfortunately, this generally teaches girls not to place their needs ahead of or even equal to anyone else's—that other people's needs are more important.

"Supposed to" beliefs often become inflexible expectations that women have for themselves. They try to live in accordance with these values in order to confirm their self-concept or identity as a woman. When they act in ways that are consistent with these values, they reconfirm who they are. When they act or contemplate acting in ways that are inconsistent with "supposed to" beliefs, they often experience guilt or believe they've lost part of their identity. For example, if a woman has a strong belief that she should always be nice, when she acts in ways she perceives to be rude or unladylike, she will experience guilt and invalidate part of her concept of the kind of woman she aspires to be.

Many of the "supposed to" beliefs that are taught to girls, and which they carry into adulthood, are guiding fictions in the sense that they lead women to believe they are supposed to or obligated to act in ways that are contrary to their best interest. In particular, girls are taught many guiding fictions that influence them to serve men and that keep them subordinate in relationships with men.

In most cultures, men have historically been viewed as being more important than women, who have been viewed as being somehow inferior to men. For example, until recently men were usually considered the head of the household. Even now, some women still accept this particular fiction as true. And to the extent that they act in ways that are consistent with this fiction, they may tolerate mistreatment from their male partners.

There are at least eight major guiding fictions that contribute to many battered women staying with or returning to an abusive partner. Let's do an exercise that will help you examine and challenge these fictions.

11.2. Explaining the Exercise for Challenging Guiding Fictions

Point to handout 11.1. **This handout presents the eight major guiding fictions, each followed by a challenge to the accuracy or truth of the statement. Each guiding fiction is noted with the abbreviation GF, and each challenge with the abbreviation C. We'll go through them one by one. For each, you'll read the guiding fiction aloud, then I'll read the challenge. Then we'll reverse it: I'll read the guiding fiction and you'll read the challenge. Finally, for each one I'll ask you whether you've ever believed that guiding fiction to be true, what you believe about it now, and which of the two statements makes more sense to you—the guiding fiction or the challenge. Depending on your answer, I may elaborate on reasons why that guiding fiction doesn't make sense.** The following scripts assume that the client may have difficulty letting go of each guiding fiction. If the client indicates she agrees with the challenge, the therapist may skip some or all of the script elaborating on that point.

11.3. Challenging Guiding Fiction 1

Read the first guiding fiction out loud. ("You made your bed and now you *have to* lie in it.") After the client reads it, read the first challenge out loud: **"Just exactly what does this mean? You mean if I decide to do something, I can't change my mind?"** Now you read the first guiding fiction and have the client read the challenge.

Have you ever believed this guiding fiction? What do you currently believe about this guiding fiction, and what do you think about the challenge? Which of these two statements makes more sense? If these two statements were two sides of a debate, which side would win the debate?

Did you make your bed today? If you did, does that mean you have to lie in it? When you think about it, it sounds silly, doesn't it? It's just a meaningless cliché, with no evidence whatsoever that it's true. And for many clichés that propose some kind of truism, there's another cliché that proposes the opposite. "Absence makes the heart grow fonder," right? But, what about "Out of sight, out of mind"?

Many women believe that if they say they're going to do something, they have to do it, and if they promise to do something, they have to keep their promise. As one of our clients said, "After all, a promise is a promise!" But ultimately, that's just like saying, "You made your bed and now you have to lie in it." Sure, a promise is a promise, but what the heck does this mean? I've seen clients who stayed in abusive relationships because their partners held them to the promise that they would stay in the relationship forever.

It's important for you to know that you always have the right to change your mind. This is true for everyone. Changing your mind is a right that can't be taken from you. It is yours for your entire life no matter what anyone says. When you make a promise or commit to any course of action, that promise or commitment is based on what you know when you make that promise or commitment. But you may subsequently learn things that indicate it no longer makes sense to keep that promise. When this happens, it's prudent to change your mind and commit to some other course of action that does make sense. I'll describe a couple of scenarios to illustrate this point.

Let's say that NASA plans to send a manned spacecraft to a remote planet. Of course, the trajectory the spacecraft takes is crucial to the success of the mission. So, the decision makers struggle about what to do but finally make a unanimous commitment on the trajectory to use. On a piece of paper, draw a circle depicting a planet, and then a line ending at the circle. **But what if the spacecraft starts going off course? Should they remain committed to the original trajectory? I don't think so. It would make much more sense to make a course correction.**

Here's another example: Let's say you've always believed that you're supposed to spend some time out in the sun to ensure you have plenty of vitamin D. However, what if you read about a large-scale, long-term study that discovered too much sun can cause cancer? Would you continue to believe you were supposed to spend a lot of time sunbathing, or would you change your mind and "break off your relationship" with sunbathing?

Similarly, when you promised you would never leave your partner, did you know how he was going to change and how he would mistreat you? Would you have made that commitment if you knew he was going to become psychologically or physically abusive? Your partner is no longer the nice and charming guy he appeared to be when you said you would never leave. Based on new information, you might want to change your mind about any promise or commitment—and it's your right to do so.

11.4. Challenging Guiding Fiction 2

Now please **read the second guiding fiction out loud.** ("You *should* be resigned to live out your sentence.") After the client reads it, read the second challenge out loud: **"You mean I don't deserve to be happy? How silly is that?"** Now you read the second guiding fiction and have the client read the challenge.

Have you ever believed this guiding fiction? What do you currently believe about this "supposed to" statement, and what do you think about the challenge? Which of these two statements makes more sense? Has anyone ever said something like this to you? Although it isn't as common as "You made your bed and now you have to lie in it," it means essentially the same thing.

Here's a story about a woman who said she was resigned to live out her sentence: Paulette was the eldest of five daughters of a conservative Baptist minister. Paulette said that about a week after she got married, she knew that it had been a mistake. But divorce was unthinkable for her because she believed it would enrage her father, and that her father would never forgive her. Paulette said that she was resigned to live out her sentence. But when one of her younger sisters got a divorce and the world didn't come to an end for her, Paulette realized her mistake in believing that she was obligated to stay and suffer in a bad marriage. Soon afterward, she started divorce proceedings.

11.5. Challenging Guiding Fiction 3

Although this guiding fiction is about marriage, I'm sure you can see how it could apply to any committed relationship. Please read the third guiding fiction aloud. ("Marriage is *supposed to* be forever.") After the client reads it, read the third challenge out loud: **"Even though my husband broke his part of the marital contract over and over again?"** Now you read the third guiding fiction and have the client read the challenge.

Have you ever believed this guiding fiction? What do you currently believe about this "supposed to" statement, and what do you think about the challenge? Which of these two statements makes more sense?

One of the things many women fail to realize is that marital vows and other relationship commitments are for *two* people, not just one. In committed relationships, both parties have obligations and responsibilities. If either person doesn't abide by the contract, it may be considered null or void.

For example, let's say you hire someone to remodel your home and agree to pay the person one thousand dollars each month to complete the work. You keep your end of the deal and pay the person each month for six months, but he never even starts doing the work. Are you going to continue to pay him? Of course not. The other person didn't honor his part of the deal.

Consider some typical marriage vows: The minister or preacher asks a woman to say her vows, and she says, "I promise to love, honor, and cherish … through sickness and in health, for better and worse, till death do us part." Then the minister asks the man to say his vows, and he says, "I promise to do anything I damn well please. I promise to lie to you, swear at you, beat you up, cheat on you, and do anything I damn well please, till death do us part." Was that the kind of deal you made with your partner? I don't think so. In certain respects, you would have grounds for having your marriage annulled, to the extent that your partner didn't fulfill his marital obligations or responsibilities.

The important point here is that a person is only committed to fulfilling her part of any contractual agreement to the extent that the other party fulfills his or her part of the agreement. Why would a woman remain loyal and committed to someone who has shown no commitment to the relationship, has repeatedly been disloyal, and has treated her far worse than even a stranger would?

11.6. Challenging Guiding Fiction 4

Now read the fourth guiding fiction out loud. ("You feel sorry for him, don't you? Therefore, you *should* stay in the relationship or go back to your partner.") After the client reads it, read the fourth challenge out loud: **"Even though staying or going back isn't in my best interest? Even though it won't make me happy in the long run**?" Now you read the fourth guiding fiction and have the client read the challenge.

Have you ever believed this guiding fiction? What do you currently believe about this guiding fiction, and what do you think about the challenge? Which of these two statements makes more sense?

Strategy 23 from the self-advocacy strategies questionnaire [handout 1.2] is very relevant here. I'll read it to you: "When a woman says 'I feel sorry for him,' she is making the other person's problem *her* problem. If I 'feel sorry' for my abuser, I may believe that I'm supposed to do something about it—something he would like me to do, such as go back to him or stay in the relationship. This is faulty thinking! If I do something he wants because I 'feel sorry' for him, I may be putting his wants above my own (and my children's) long-term best interest. It is important to act in my best interest whether or not I 'feel sorry' for him."

Always remember that you are not responsible for solving the problems that your partner caused and for which he is ultimately accountable. Otherwise, he will never learn and will continue to mistreat other women the way he mistreated you. Your greatest obligation is to yourself.

11.7. Challenging Guiding Fiction 5

Now please read the fifth guiding fiction out loud. ("He apologized. Therefore, you *should* accept his apology and go back to the way things were.") After the client reads it, read the fifth challenge out loud: **"You mean I can't accept someone's apology and still choose to have nothing to do with him if it's not in my best interest to do so?"** Now you read the fifth guiding fiction and have the client read the challenge.

Have you ever believed this guiding fiction? What do you currently believe about this guiding fiction, and what do you think about the challenge? Which of these two statements makes more sense?

Beliefs about apologies have kept many battered women stuck in bad relationships. It's related to a very big "supposed to": turn the other cheek. Millions of women have stayed in or returned to an abusive relationship because they thought they were obligated to accept the apologies of an abusive partner and act as if the mistreatment never happened—even though the apologies almost always prove to be nothing more than hollow words and empty promises. An apology implies an attempt to make amends for some wrongdoing, as well as an accompanying commitment to refrain from committing the same wrongdoing again. But most batterers apologize repeatedly and yet still continue to engage in the same wrongful acts over and over and over again.

It is relevant here to paraphrase strategy 13 from the self-advocacy strategies questionnaire, which addresses apologies: Just because someone apologizes to you for some wrongdoing does not mean you are now obligated to do what that person wants or go back to the way things were, whether or not you forgive the person.

To forgive means "to pardon or release from punishment." To forgive someone does not imply being obligated in any way to go back to the way things were. The phrases "forgive and forget" and "turn the other cheek" simply do not apply to women who have been battered by an intimate partner.

A governor can pardon a convicted criminal and release him from prison because he's no longer considered a danger to society and it costs so much to keep him in prison. Does this mean the criminal didn't commit the crime? Does it mean the governor is going to invite him over for dinner? Of course not. Likewise, you can accept your abuser's apology and still choose to have nothing to do with him.

II.8. Challenging Guiding Fiction 6

Read the sixth guiding fiction aloud. ("If you just try hard enough or get it right, he'll change and you'll be happy. If the relationship doesn't work, *you* failed.") After the client reads it, read the sixth challenge out loud: **"No woman will ever be able to 'get it right' with a man who is incapable of having a healthy intimate relationship with anyone."** Now you read the sixth guiding fiction and have the client read the challenge.

Have you ever believed this guiding fiction? What do you now believe about this guiding fiction, and what do you think about the challenge? Which of these two statements makes more sense?

The belief that divorce represents a personal failure has led countless women to stay with or reconcile with an abusive partner. One client said, "I already had two failed marriages. I didn't want to fail at this one too." However, many batterers don't even have a good relationship with animals, let alone women. In fact, it's been estimated that at least 50 percent of batterers mistreat or threaten to mistreat family pets (Ascione, 2000).

In a later session, we'll take a look at how you can identify potential abusers. At that time, I'll ask you whether your partner engaged in various types of antisocial behavior. At the end of that exercise, I'll ask whether you think you could maintain a successful long-term relationship with any man if you did the kinds of things your partner has done. If you're like almost every woman who's completed this exercise, you'll answer with a resounding "No way!" In a very real sense, your relationship with your abusive partner may have been doomed from the start, even though you couldn't see it then.

11.9. Challenging Guiding Fiction 7

Now please read the seventh guiding fiction aloud. ("It's your *responsibility* to make the relationship work.") After the client reads it, read the seventh challenge out loud: **"If two people are in a rowboat and each one has an oar, they both have to row to make the boat move forward. If only one person rows, the boat will go around in circles and won't get anywhere."** Now you read the seventh guiding fiction and have the client read the challenge.

Have you ever believed this guiding fiction? What do you currently believe about this guiding fiction, and what do you think about the challenge? Which of these two statements makes more sense? If these two statements were two sides of a debate, which side would win the debate?

Upon hearing this set of statements, one woman said, "I would just row harder," to which her therapist responded, "Then I guess you would go around in circles faster." For another woman, it reminded her of something that happened when she was still with her partner. She said, "We never went anywhere, but one time he invited me to go on a picnic. What a surprise! We went to a state park, and he kept jumping out from behind trees and scaring me. Some fun! Then we went canoeing on the lake. After ten minutes, I realized we weren't getting anywhere. I was in the front of the boat, so I looked around. He had a big grin on his face and was paddling backward!" Upon hearing this story, another client said, "That's what happened to me on my honeymoon. We went to British Columbia, and we were paddling upriver, against the current. We weren't getting anywhere, so I looked around. My husband was sitting on the floor of the canoe and had his feet up on the seat."

A woman who was considering going back to an extremely cruel partner continued to insist that it was her **responsibility to make the relationship work.** She said, "The way I see it, fixing a marriage is just like fixing a flat tire. If you have the repair manual, you should be able to fix it." Her therapist asked her to close her eyes and to imagine the following scenario. I'd like you to close your eyes and to imagine the scenario too.

Imagine that the biggest problem in your relationship is that you have a car with a flat tire. You and your partner argue about this all the time. If you could just get the tire changed, your relationship would be fine. But you don't know anything about changing tires, and for some reason your partner refuses to do it. One day you see an ad for a new book on changing tires for women who don't know how to change tires. You decide to order the book, and a few days later it arrives. As you start reading it, you're elated to realize, "This is going to be a cinch! Anyone could change a tire with this manual." You eagerly go out, take the tire iron out of the trunk, and start loosening the lugs. All of a sudden, your head feels like a tuning fork. Your partner has come up behind you and smacked the back of your head. Now he has his hands on your face and is trying to scratch your eyes out. Now he's tearing pages out of the book and is trying to gouge the tire with the tire iron.

What are the chances that you could fix the tire, even now that you have the repair manual? No way, of course not! The message in this story is that it takes two people working really hard to make a relationship work, but it only takes one person to destroy a relationship. Similarly, it only takes one person to derail a meeting and keep it from being productive. Have you ever been to a meeting when the disruptiveness of one person prevented everyone else from getting anything accomplished?

11.10. Challenging Guiding Fiction 8

This guiding fiction is geared toward women who have children or who are planning to have children. If you know this isn't the case for a particular client, skip this section. You might, however, explain why you've done so, since it appears on the handout. Assuming this guiding fiction applies to the client, proceed as before: **Please read the eighth guiding fiction aloud.** ("The children need their father. Therefore, you *should* keep the family together.") After the client reads it, read the eighth challenge out loud: **"Do they need a biological father who mistreats me and them? Wouldn't it be better to live in a single-parent home with a mother who's loving and consistent than to live in a two-parent home with a father who's abusive?"** Now you read the eighth guiding fiction and have the client read the challenge.

Have you ever believed this guiding fiction? What do you currently believe about this guiding fiction, and what do you think about the challenge? Which of these two statements makes more sense?

This particular "supposed to" belief is not only embraced by many battered women, it's also imposed on them by society. For example, consider the following interaction between an unenlightened therapist and her client as they address this topic. The therapist tells the woman, "Your kids need their dad. They need a male role model. You should go back to him." The client answers, "Everybody says that. Even my kids' teachers!" The therapist replies, "It's true. They need their father even though he's a terrible role model, and even though the kids are exposed to all kinds of terrible things."

Sometimes this guiding fiction appears in a slightly different form, along the lines of "You're obligated to keep the family together." When considering what's best for your children, keep in mind that the ideal situation is a two-parent home where *both* adults model healthy ways of resolving conflict. However, even a stable single-parent home is far better than a two-parent home burdened by domestic violence and dysfunctional relationships. Both of these guiding fictions send the same message: that the children need their biological father and an intact family, but this is as fictional as it gets if their dad is abusive! Children do not need their biological father in the home just because he has some of the same genes they have. What they need is a loving parental figure who nurtures them and who models a healthy relationship for them to copy or imitate.

These guiding fictions don't take into consideration the harm caused by exposing children to an abusive relationship, a violent father figure, or a mother who tolerates the abuse by staying in the relationship. What are the female children learning? Would you want your daughter to learn that if she ever gets abused by an intimate partner, she's supposed to stay in the relationship, like you did? And what are the male children learning? Would you want your son to learn that it's okay to abuse his girlfriend or wife when he gets older? And what does ongoing domestic violence teach children about how to handle interpersonal problems and resolve conflict in a mutually respectful way? Unfortunately, little or nothing.

II.II. Lessons Learned from the Guiding Fictions Exercise

Now read through the handout and place a check mark next to each of the guiding fictions that you've believed. Even if you no longer believe it to be true, go ahead and check it off. How many of them have you believed? Can you see how these beliefs have influenced many battered women to remain in an abusive relationship?

Clients learn some valuable lessons from completing this exercise: First, it often helps them understand why they stayed with an abusive partner as long as they did. Second, learning to see through these guiding fictions has given many women increased peace of mind that they made the right decision by leaving. And finally, this exercise gives many women the strength to resist efforts by others, including authority figures, to impose "should" or "supposed to" beliefs upon them. This ties in with the next topic we'll be addressing: assertiveness. What you've learned about these guiding fictions and the challenges to each will help you look for evidence about whether it's in your best interest to do what someone else says you should do, are supposed to do, or have to do.

When battered women first contemplate leaving an abusive partner, they experience guilt or anticipate experiencing it because leaving contradicts certain beliefs instilled in them at an early age by female socialization. This, along with the accompanying negative emotions, leads many women to stay in the relationship so they can avoid the guilt. Even when a woman finally makes the decision to leave, she often does so with guilt related to not being the type of person she thinks she's supposed to be.

Has this exercise in challenging "supposed to" beliefs increased your understanding of why you stayed in the relationship as long as you did? Has it reinforced your conviction that you made the right decision by leaving your partner? Has it increased your resolve to resist doing something just because someone else says you should—and to look for evidence to determine what's in your best interest?

CONCLUDING REMARKS

To the extent that battered women believe and act in accordance with the guiding fictions presented here, which may represent central aspects of their identity or self-concept, they may be motivated to stay in an abusive relationship. To the extent that formerly battered women continue to hold these beliefs after leaving an abusive relationship, they are likely to experience guilt. As a client learns to reject or discredit these beliefs, her guilt is expected to diminish or dissolve, reinforcing the work done in module 10.

Handout 11.1: Challenging Guiding Fictions That Lead Many Women to Stay in or Return to an Abusive Relationship

GF = guiding fiction; C = challenge

GF 1:   You made your bed and now you *have to* lie in it.

C: Just exactly what does this mean? You mean if I decide to do something, I can't change my mind?

GF 2:   You *should* be resigned to live out your sentence.

C: You mean I don't deserve to be happy? How silly is that?

GF 3:   Marriage is *supposed to* be forever.

C: Even though my husband broke his part of the marital contract over and over again?

GF 4:   You feel sorry for him, don't you? Therefore, you *should* stay in the relationship or go back to your partner.

C: Even though staying or going back isn't in my best interest? Even though it won't make me happy in the long run?

GF 5:   He apologized. Therefore, you *should* accept his apology and go back to the way things were.

C: You mean I can't accept someone's apology and still choose to have nothing to do with him if it's not in my best interest to do so?

GF 6:   If you just try hard enough or get it right, he'll change and you'll be happy. If the relationship doesn't work, *you* failed.

C: No woman will ever be able to "get it right" with a man who is incapable of having a healthy intimate relationship with anyone.

GF 7:   It's your *responsibility* to make the relationship work.

C: If two people are in a rowboat and each one has an oar, they both have to row to make the boat move forward. If only one person rows, the boat will go around in circles and won't get anywhere.

The last guiding fiction and challenge is for women with children or who are planning to have children.

GF 8:   The children need their father. Therefore, you *should* keep the family together.

C: Do they need a biological father who mistreats me and them? Wouldn't it be better to live in a single-parent home with a mother who's loving and consistent than to live in a two-parent home with a father who's abusive?

Assertiveness Training

Lack of assertiveness may be a factor that contributes to some women becoming involved in an abusive relationship, as unassertive women may be more likely to be taken advantage of or mistreated. Lack of assertiveness may also play a role in negative self-talk and stress; for example, unassertive women are more likely than assertive women to interpret socially stressful situations as threatening or intimidating. Finally, lack of assertiveness may play a role in guilt (that is, people may experience guilt because they think they should have stood up for themselves). The primary goal of module 12 is for clients to become more influential when faced with interpersonal conflict, particularly with people who are being verbally aggressive. A related goal is to increase clients' self-confidence or self-efficacy in managing conflictual interactions and help them not be intimidated when others are verbally aggressive.

OBJECTIVES

- For the client to be able to tell when someone is being verbally aggressive or disrespectful

- For the client to be able to respond to verbally aggressive comments in ways that are assertive and not focus or dwell on the content of aggressive or disrespectful messages

- For the client to understand the importance of being able to refuse requests or say no without giving reasons why

- For the client to understand the importance of communicating wants and needs directly

■ For the client to understand the concept of assertive escalation and the types of situations that warrant assertive escalation

MATERIALS

■ Assertive Behavior, Aggressive Behavior, and How to Take the High Road (handout 12.1)

HOMEWORK

■ Listen to session audio-recordings.

■ Continue to monitor and record negative self-talk.

■ Practice PMR while listening to the PMR recording, twice a day.

■ Do a body scan and over-tense and relax muscles when experiencing stress.

■ Read and complete chapter 12 in *Healing the Trauma of Domestic Violence* (optional).

PROCEDURES CHECKLIST

1. _____ Introduction to assertiveness

2. _____ The communication high road and two low roads

3. _____ Defining assertiveness and aggressiveness

4. _____ The distinction between assertiveness and selfishness

5. _____ The importance of knowing when someone is being aggressive or disrespectful

6. _____ "I" statements

7. _____ Challenging traditional views of assertiveness

8. _____ Expressing anger

9. _____ Studies evaluating the impact of "I" statements versus accusations in expressions of anger and distress

10. _____ A broad view of verbal aggression

11. _____ Aggressive "I" statements

12. _____ Aggressed-upon statements

13. _____ Masked aggression

14. _____ Scorn or character assassination

15. _____ How to respond to verbal aggression

16. _____ How to respond to aggressive questions

17. _____ How to respond to aggressive or disrespectful comments by family members or others who mean well

18. _____ The importance of not tolerating disrespect

19. _____ Practicing assertive ways of responding to verbal aggression

20. _____ The effectiveness of responding to the *style* of verbal aggression, not the content

21. _____ The importance of avoiding verbal aggression

22. _____ Assertive communication basics

23. _____ Refusing requests or saying no

24. _____ Turning down a request for a date

25. _____ Turning down requests from family and friends

26. _____ Turning down requests that you buy something

27. _____ Refusing to talk about something

28. _____ Saying no after you said yes

29. _____ Communicating feelings

30. _____ Making requests and communicating wishes

31. _____ Assertive escalation

32. _____ Assertive escalation in the workplace

33. _____ Assertive escalation in intimate relationships

34. _____ Summary of the keys to assertive communication

35. _____ Additional important benefits of becoming assertive

---

DETAILED PROCEDURES FOR MODULE 12

12.1. Introduction to Assertiveness

Assertiveness is all about empowerment. It's about having influence in social interactions, not tolerating disrespect, and getting your wants satisfied. As we work on assertiveness skills, you'll learn how to identify subtle forms of verbal aggression or disrespect, how to assertively respond to verbal aggression, how to effectively communicate your wants, and how to refuse requests for your valuable time. I'll also teach you about a technique called assertive escalation, which you can use when others aren't responsive to lower-level assertive requests.

12.2. The Communication High Road and Two Low Roads

Give the client handout 12.1, Assertive Behavior, Aggressive Behavior, and How to Take the High Road. **Please read the title of this handout out loud.** ("Assertive Behavior, Aggressive Behavior, and How to Take the High Road.") **What do you think is meant by the "high road" of communication? Right. The assertive road. The honorable road. The superhighway of effective or influential communication. There are two communication low roads we see when people are in conflict; for example, in couples counseling that isn't working. What are the two communication low roads? Right. One of the "low roads" is verbal aggression: screaming, yelling, accusing, being sarcastic, or saying mean things.**

The second low road may be very familiar to you. It also serves to maintain conflict. What is this second low road of communication? Any guesses? It's conflict avoidance: responding to conflict with passivity, opting for "peace" at all costs, sweeping things under the carpet. When confronted by a potentially conflictual situation, you might take the second low road by saying things like "It's not worth the hassle," "Whatever," or "Have it your way."

Have you ever taken this communication low road? In our experience, all clients have. Describe how you've engaged in conflict avoidance ... Now tell me how well

you think this strategy has worked for you … It's almost universally true that relationships go south when one or both parties in the relationship are unwilling or unable to directly communicate about problems in the relationship. And couples counseling never works if either partner is unwilling to talk honestly about problems in the relationship.

12.3. Defining Assertiveness and Aggressiveness

Read the first sentence after the title. ("Assertive behavior is expressing feelings, wants, or opinions in ways that respect the rights and opinions of others.") **This is a definition of assertiveness. The key word here is "respect"—and not just expressing feelings and wants in ways that are respectful. Assertiveness also involves respecting the opinions of others. Everyone has a right to their opinion.**

Aggressiveness is the flip side of assertiveness. Verbal aggression can be defined as expressing feelings, wants, or opinions in ways that violate or disrespect the rights or opinions of others. The key word here is "disrespect": putting someone down, attributing negative qualities or negative intentions to a person, telling others how they should think, act, or feel. Aggressiveness can also involve demanding that others do things you have no right to demand they do. It involves attempting to impose your will, wants, or opinions on others with no regard for their feelings, wants, or opinions.

Certainly, everyone knows that physical violence is aggressive, as is profanity and obviously degrading verbal expressions, such as "slut," "whore," or "bitch." However, verbal aggression also occurs in many subtle forms in all relationships where people are in conflict, not just violent situations. For example, almost all "you" statements with negative content are aggressive, not assertive.

12.4. The Distinction Between Assertiveness and Selfishness

A common myth, perhaps even a guiding fiction, is that assertiveness in women is rude, mean, bitchy, aggressive, unfeminine, unladylike, or selfish. If you hold this belief, it's important to let it go. Assertiveness is none of these things. Assertiveness doesn't violate the rights of other people. Assertiveness is self-advocacy. Assertive people place a strong emphasis on getting their own needs met as a high priority.

12.5. The Importance of Knowing When Someone Is Being Aggressive or Disrespectful

Verbal aggression violates international standards regarding human rights. These standards stipulate that all people deserve to be treated with respect. If someone speaks to you using aggressive or disrespectful language, it reflects badly on that person and says nothing about you. That person is violating your rights by speaking to you in a disrespectful way. This isn't fair; you deserve to be treated with respect.

It's essential that you recognize when someone is talking to you in a disrespectful way. Therefore, one of our goals as we work on assertiveness is for you to learn about some of the subtle ways that verbal aggression is expressed. If you're able to identify when someone is talking to you in an aggressive or disrespectful way, you'll be less likely to absorb the hurtful message and experience emotional pain. The hurtful message will be more likely to bounce off of you if you realize that you don't deserve to be talked to this way. Furthermore, conflict is rarely resolved when people resort to aggressive styles of communication.

A bit later on, I'll also teach you effective ways of dealing with disrespectful words that come out of other people's mouths. Then, once you've identified that a person has spoken to you in an aggressive or disrespectful way, you can respond in a way that neutralizes the disrespect and doesn't make you feel bad.

12.6. "I" Statements

If there's one thing that has come to characterize assertive communication, it's an emphasis on communicating with "I" statements. Put another way, let's say a friend of yours would like to increase her assertiveness because she wants to work out problems with her boyfriend. She asks you, "What do I say to him? How do I bring up the problem?" What would you tell her?

She might try something like "I'm feeling frustrated that we seldom do things that I want to do. I would really like it if we could do something I want to do this weekend." "I" statements are seen as being much more effective than aggressive communication using "you" statements. In your friend's case, the "you" messages might sound like this: "You're frustrating me. You won't do anything I want you to do. Why don't you care about my needs?"

Authorities on assertiveness have generally assumed that all "I" statements are assertive and that they're likely to have a positive impact on the interaction. However, I'm going to challenge both of these assumptions. "I" messages that convey hostility and disrespect should be considered aggressive, not assertive. And as you'll see, "I" messages that convey disrespect influence people negatively.

12.7. Challenging Traditional Views of Assertiveness

Many books on assertiveness recommend certain ways of communicating that are actually quite hostile and likely to evoke anger and antagonism rather than empathy and cooperation. For example, they often encourage people to express anger as long as the anger is expressed with an "I" statement. They've assumed that expressing anger with "I" statements will have the same positive impacts as "I" statements communicating other negative emotions, such as frustration or hurt feelings.

However, research on anger suggests that expressions of anger may evoke hostility and antagonism no matter how the anger is expressed (e.g., Berkowitz, 1984). In other words, even anger expressed as an "I" statement may trigger a hostile response.

12.8. Expressing Anger

Let's take a closer look at anger. What exactly is it? Anger is a negative emotional state that implies hostility, antagonism, or blame. And how is anger different from distress, such as hurt feelings, anxiety, or disappointment? By contrast, distress is a state of suffering, sorrow, or unhappiness, with an implication of needing assistance.

What do angry people do? Right. They fight. They argue. They raise their voices and say mean and hurtful things. They also ruminate about how to hurt someone or see them suffer. This alone is sufficient evidence that expressions of anger are aggressive—not assertive—no matter how the anger is expressed.

12.9. Studies Evaluating the Impact of "I" Statements vs. Accusations in Expressions of Anger and Distress

Edward Kubany, Ph.D., and his colleagues conducted four studies to assess the social impact of using "I" statements versus accusations for communicating both anger and distress (e.g., Kubany, Richard, & Bauer, 1992). In each study, subjects were to imagine they were having a disagreement with their partner. Then they were asked how they would react to several statements spoken by their partner. Each statement was presented on a separate page of a booklet.

First, subjects were asked to rate how sympathetic and how angry they would feel after their partner made the statement. Then they were asked to rate how likely they would be to respond in a conciliatory way, such as by speaking calmly or suggesting a solution, and how likely they would be to respond in an antagonistic way, by raising their voice or saying something hostile, for example. Subjects rated their reactions to sixteen different statements of negative feelings. Half the statements were expressed with "I" statements, and the other half were expressed with accusatory "you" statements.

Here are a few of the "I" statements: "I'm frustrated," "My feelings are hurt," "I feel anxious," and "I'm getting upset." And here are a few of the "you" statements: "You are frustrating me," "You are hurting my feelings," "You are making me feel anxious," and "You are upsetting me." Which set of statements do you think participants responded to more negatively? Exactly. The accusatory "you" messages. That's a no-brainer. This part of the study merely demonstrated the obvious.

In addition to being evenly divided between "I" statements and accusatory "you" statements, the sixteen statements also differed in a second way. Half were expressions of distress, and half were expressions of anger. Here are a few of the expressions of distress: "I'm frustrated," "My feelings are hurt," "I feel anxious," and "I'm getting upset." And here are a few of the expressions of anger: "I'm pissed off," "I'm angry," "I'm getting mad," and "I am feeling resentful."

Which set of statements do you think subjects responded to more negatively? Right. The anger statements. Interestingly, accusatory statements of distress, such as "You're hurting my feelings," had the same impact as "I" statements of anger, such as "I'm getting angry." Expressions of distress "softened" the impact of "you" statements, while expressions of anger increased the negative impact of "I" statements. Of course, the statements that evoked the most anger and antagonism were accusatory expressions of anger; for example, "You piss me off."

12.10. A Broad View of Verbal Aggression

So, just to be clear, it's generally the case that expressing anger is likely to evoke an antagonistic reaction no matter how the anger is expressed, whether as an "I" statement or as a "you" statement. "I" statements that convey anger and hostility are aggressive, and anger expressed in any way has a negative impact. In fact, any verbal message that conveys anger, hostility, or disrespect is aggressive. The same is true of any statement that attempts to impose a person's views on someone else.

12.11. Aggressive "I" Statements

Beyond "I" statements of anger, Dr. Kubany and his colleagues have identified three other categories of "I" statements that are aggressive and have a negative impact because they stir up anger and antagonism: aggressed-upon statements, masked aggression, and scorn or character assassination. Let's take a closer look at each of these.

12.12. Aggressed-Upon Statements

Aggressed-upon "I" statements convey that the person addressed has caused harm to the speaker, and as such, they imply an accusation. Here are some examples: "I'm getting screwed," "I've been duped," "I'm being taken advantage of," and "I'm being used." In research on the social impact of different kinds of "I" statements, aggressed-upon statements had approximately the same negative impact as "I" statements of anger (Kubany, 1995). Both types of statements evoked more anger and antagonism than assertive messages of distress.

12.13. Masked Aggression

In masked aggression, statements start with an "I" but end with a "you." It's like this: Imagine yourself talking to a friend who says, "I just went to an assertiveness workshop and learned about the importance of communicating with 'I' messages. Well, I just want to tell you how I feel and what I think. I feel that you're codependent and in denial. And I think you're a hypocrite." Does this sound assertive? Of course not. In fact, these really aren't "I" messages at all, are they? They're actually critical and aggressive "you" statements only thinly veiled by an introductory "I" phrase.

In research on the impact of various types of "I" messages, masked aggression evoked much more anger and antagonism than aggressed-upon statements and even "I" anger statements. Masked aggression statements are the wolves in sheep's clothing of "I" statements.

12.14. Scorn or Character Assassination

The final type of aggressive "I" statement is scorn or character assassination. This category of "I" statement attacks the fundamental character or very core of the person at which it's directed. Imagine that someone says to you, "I resent you," "I don't trust you," "I don't care about you," "I don't respect you," or "I hate you." Would you be likely to do or want to do what that person wants you to do? Almost certainly not! Scorn statements evoke anger and antagonism at levels on par with masked aggression.

12.15. How to Respond to Verbal Aggression

When someone talks to you in a verbally aggressive way, I strongly recommend that you focus your response on the aggressive *style* of the message, rather than getting into a conversation about the content of the aggressive message. Here's an example: Let's say someone says to you, "You don't know what you're talking about." The subject matter of this message is whether you know what you're talking about. In situations like this, don't get into a discussion regarding the accuracy of the accusation. Instead, convey in some way that the person is talking to you in a disrespectful way and that you don't deserve to be spoken to that way. For example, you might say, "That's not a very nice thing to say" or "I don't deserve to be talked to that way." Or you might say, "Just because you say I don't know what I'm talking about doesn't mean I don't know what I'm talking about." The latter response conveys that a person saying something is not evidence for what they say, which will often put an end to conversation on the topic.

Responding to the style of verbal aggression rather than the content draws attention to the behavior of the aggressor and away from the person who is the target of the aggression. I'll illustrate with an example of a situation in which a person is publicly criticized or treated disrespectfully by a person in authority. People often feel humiliated in such situations.

Janice, a fourth-grade teacher, was in a meeting chaired by the vice-principal. The topic was promotions. The vice-principal said to Janice, "You're too immature and unmotivated to be promoted to vice-principal." Janice replied, "Mr. Smith, that's not a very nice thing to say. And just because you say that I'm too immature and unmotivated doesn't mean it's true." If Janice had defensively said that she was mature and motivated, this might have given the vice-principal an opportunity to build his case with more verbally aggressive remarks. After the meeting, several of Janice's fellow teachers complimented her on how well she handled the vice-principal's remarks. They also agreed unanimously that Janice didn't deserve to be talked to that way, and that the vice-principal's remarks were inappropriate and unprofessional.

12.16. How to Respond to Aggressive Questions

Aggressive questions are a subtle form of verbal aggression that most people have difficulty handling in an effective way. Here are a few examples of aggressive questions: "Why are you so defensive?" "Why are you in such a bitchy mood?" "Why are you so hypersensitive?" "Why are you angry?" "Why are you such a wimp?"

Typically, people respond to aggressive questions in a way that is either defensive or aggressive. Defensive reactions, such as "I'm not being hypersensitive," simply invite further aggression; for example, "Oh yes you are!" And aggressive responses to aggressive questions, such as "You should talk," usually trigger more verbal aggression and escalate the conflict.

Responding effectively to aggressive questions is actually quite easy once you learn how to do it. Let's look at this using the question "Why are you so selfish?" First, let's examine the message that the aggressive question conveys. If someone asks you why you're so selfish, doesn't it imply that they've already concluded that you're selfish, and now they just want you to agree with them? When you look at it this way, you can see that aggressive questions are nothing more than accusatory "you" messages in disguise and conveyed indirectly.

Keeping in mind the recommendation to focus on the disrespectful style of aggressive messages, rather than their content, what might you say if someone says to you, "You are so manipulative!" Right. You might say, "That's not a nice thing to say," "I don't deserve to be talked to that way," or "Your saying I'm manipulative doesn't mean I am manipulative." So what might you say if someone asks you, "Why are you so manipulative?" You can respond exactly the same way as if they had directly accused you of being manipulative. For example, you might say, "That's not a nice thing to say," "I don't deserve to be talked to that way," or "Your suggestion that I'm manipulative doesn't mean that I'm manipulative."

12.17. How to Respond to Aggressive or Disrespectful Comments by Family Members or Others Who Mean Well

Friends and family members of battered women, as well as many health professionals, are unaware that post-traumatic stress can be long lasting and may not dissipate with the passage of time. In their impatience to see a battered woman get back to so-called normal once she's safely out of an abusive relationship, people who mean well can actually make matters worse by the ways they try to help.

For example, people close to a battered woman often urge her to get over it with a variety of "you" messages, as if recovery from PTSD is a simple matter of choice. Take a minute to reflect on whether anyone who cares about you has ever made statements like these: "Just put it behind you and move on with your life," "You need to stop feeling sorry for yourself," or "Do you enjoy being upset all the time?" When this happens, assertively respond by explaining that such remarks aren't helpful, despite the person's good intentions. You might say something like "I know you mean well, but it doesn't help for you to say that."

12.18. The Importance of Not Tolerating Disrespect

There's some good news and some bad news about the way that other people talk to you. The bad news is that you can't control the words that come out of other people's mouths. You can't stop people from speaking in aggressive and disrespectful ways. The good news is that you can control your exposure to the words spoken by other people. You can end the conversation or leave the situation, or if the problem is ongoing, you can end your relationship with someone who persists in treating you with disrespect.

If someone says two or three unkind things to you and you respond assertively, it's a good idea to advise the person that you'll end the conversation if he or she continues talking to you in a disrespectful way. Let's take a look at an interaction illustrating persistent aggression and how you might respond. If the person says, "You're too needy," respond by saying something like "That's not a nice thing to say, and your calling me needy doesn't mean I am needy."

If the person goes on to say, "You're being defensive because you're needy," respond by saying, "I am not going to stay in this conversation if you continue to talk to me that way."

If the person persists and says something like "Your problem is that you're too closed minded," simply say "Excuse me" or "I've got to go." Then say good-bye and walk away.

12.19. Practicing Assertive Ways of Responding to Verbal Aggression

Let's practice responding to aggressive statements in the recommended ways. First, I want you to select and say aggressive statements from the first part of this handout [handout 12.1]. I'll respond with statements along the lines of those shown in the second half of the handout. Do the role-playing exercise for three or four different statements. Now I'll say aggressive statements from the first half of the handout, and you respond with some of the statements suggested in the second half. Do the role-playing exercise, choosing different aggressive statements than the client had chosen.

This type of role-playing exercise allows you to practice new assertiveness skills. It's helped many women feel less anxious when spoken to in aggressive ways. It has also increased their skill and confidence in responding assertively to verbally aggressive comments. If you'd like more practice, ask a friend or family member to do this with you.

12.20. The Effectiveness of Responding to the Style of Verbal Aggression

Many clients have reported that responding to the style of other people's verbally aggressive remarks enabled them to take control of conflictual interactions that in the past would have escalated or left them feeling distressed, cheapened, or depressed. For these women, saying things like "That's not a nice thing to say," "I don't deserve to be talked to that way," or "Your saying that doesn't mean it's true" has derailed the other person's attack or left the person speechless.

These types of statements don't provide ammunition for an escalation of verbal aggression. They really do work in terms of influencing other people's verbal behavior and, as a result, have helped many clients become more empowered. If you incorporate these strategies for responding to verbal aggression into your repertoire, you'll find that they work for you, too, and they'll contribute to your empowerment.

12.21. The Importance of Avoiding Verbal Aggression

So far, I've focused on helping you identify verbal aggression and learn how to respond assertively to it. However, we know that many people tend to become aggressive when engaged in conflict with people who are being aggressive. For example, there is experimental evidence that wives of abusive men get as angry as their partners during marital arguments (Jacobson et al., 1994). Hostility does indeed beget hostility.

This makes it important that you think about what you want to accomplish whenever you address conflict with anyone. If you just want to get the other person upset—and sometimes people do intentionally say hurtful things out of anger—you may choose to express anger and make hostile and aggressive statements. However, if you want to influence the other person to do something or stop doing something, you're unlikely to accomplish this objective with verbal aggression. Instead, you'll alienate the other person and invite counteraggression.

12.22. Assertive Communication Basics

Let's discuss some of the basics of assertive communication. Learning to use these techniques will increase the likelihood that you'll get your interpersonal wants and needs satisfied and also increase the chances that you'll influence other people in a positive way.

By expressing feelings, wants, or opinions in ways that respect the rights and opinions of others, the focus is on you rather than on the person you want to influence. You'll be owning your feelings, wants, and opinions, rather than attributing negative intentions or qualities to the other person. Communicating assertively doesn't guarantee that the person will do what you want. However, it does increase the chances that the person will respond in a positive way. In addition, communicating assertively is unlikely to escalate conflict or fuel the other person's hostility. I'll focus on three specific techniques: refusing requests or saying no, assertive ways of expressing your feelings and wants, and assertive escalation.

12.23. Refusing Requests or Saying No

It is always your right to say no. If you have a hard time saying no to people, you probably have problems in all areas of assertiveness. Refusing requests requires only a minimal response, yet many women have a hard time turning other people down, even when requests are extremely unreasonable. Do you ever have trouble refusing requests or saying no? Under what circumstances do you have a hard time with this?

There are at least two reasons why many battered women have difficulty refusing requests from other people: because they don't want to hurt people's feelings, and because they don't want to appear rude or selfish. Have you ever had trouble saying no because you didn't want to hurt a person's feelings? A closer examination often reveals that hurting other people's feelings isn't the primary problem. The real problem is that many battered women are afraid other people will get upset or angry if they don't comply. Plus, they don't want to be perceived as the direct cause of anyone's negative feelings. I'll illustrate this point with a story about Alma.

Alma, who was extremely unassertive, was in therapy. On one occasion, Alma told her therapist that a friend asked her to go to the beach and she didn't want to go. However, she agreed to go because she didn't want to hurt her friend's feelings. Her therapist then asked, "Well, how was the beach?" to which Alma replied, "Oh, I didn't go." She said that when she next saw her friend, she was going to make up an excuse about why she didn't show up and apologize profusely.

This was clearly a situation where hurting someone's feelings was not the issue. Certainly, Alma's friend was far more hurt and upset because Alma didn't show up at the beach than she would have been if Alma had simply said, "I can't make it today." But Alma was afraid to say something she thought would be directly followed by anger directed at her. She avoided this in the immediate moment by saying she would go to the beach, but this was only a short-term solution. In the end, her friend was much more angry. Alma's short-term relief came at considerable cost to her relationship with her friend.

How about you? In situations where you didn't say no because you didn't want to hurt other people's feelings, might the real issue have been that you were afraid the other person would get upset or angry with you if you said no?

A second reason many battered women have trouble saying no is because they think doing so would be rude or selfish, and this causes them to feel guilty. Have you had trouble saying no because you thought it would be rude or selfish? Now consider those occasions when you did put your own needs first and said no. Did you actually feel guilty when you did this?

How you choose to spend your time is up you. No one else has a right to spend time with you or dictate how you spend your time unless you give your time freely. You have no obligation to spend time doing what someone else wants you to do, and you aren't violating anyone's rights by turning down requests for the use of your time. Saying no to something you don't want to do is a form of self-advocacy. Doing something for someone else at your own expense means you put that person's needs ahead of your own. If you don't put yourself first, who will? Does this make sense?

It's in your best interest to be able to say no without making excuses or giving reasons. This is important because people who put their wants ahead of yours will try to talk you out of your decision to say no. If you give reasons for saying no, they'll attack or argue with those reasons to try to get you to change your mind. Has anyone ever done this to you and gotten you to say yes when you initially said no or wanted to say no? Clients almost always say yes. Briefly describe what happened.

12.24. Turning Down a Request for a Date

Now let's take a look at some specific situations where you might want to say no. If you think about these and practice them in advance, you have a better chance of being successful at saying no when these situations actually arise. Let's say that someone asks you out on a date but you don't want to go. You might say something like "That's nice of you to ask, but I can't make it." If the person asks you why you won't go or tries to get you to change your mind, repeat or paraphrase your initial response. For example, you might say, "Again, I can't make it. But thanks anyway." If the person persists, escalate your response to something like this: "I am not available to go out with you, and I have to go. Good-bye." Then hang up the phone or say "Excuse me" and walk away.

12.25. Turning Down Requests from Friends and Family

Many battered women find it hard to stick to their guns and say no to friends or family. Although these people mean well and are often motivated by love or concern, it's still inappropriate for them to try to talk you out of your reasons for saying no. You can handle these situations just like you would a request for a date. Rather than fearing a negative outcome, remember that the person cares about you and hope for the best.

A client named Bernice assumed the worst would happen if she just said "I can't make it" to her mother. She thought her mother would get mad and stop talking to her. Two weeks later, when her mother asked Bernice to do something with her, Bernice summoned up her courage and said, "I can't make it this weekend, Mom." Nothing dramatic happened. Her mother simply said "Okay," and accepted what Bernice had said. At her next therapy session, Bernice expressed amazement and said, "Wow! I feel so empowered."

12.26. Turning Down Requests That You Buy Something

Dealing with telemarketers and other salespeople provides an excellent opportunity to practice your assertiveness skills. Because you don't know these people and have absolutely no relationship with them or obligation to them, you may find it easier to say no to them. In these situations, keep the interaction very brief. On the telephone, as soon as you realize it's a sales call, you might say something like "I'm not interested, but have a nice day. Good-bye" or "I'm not interested in buying anything. I don't want to take any of your valuable time. Good-bye" or "I don't have time for this call. Good-bye." Some people might think this last response borders on being rude. However, if you know that you're eventually going to say no, you're wasting not only your own time, but also the salesperson's time by staying on the phone.

12.27. Refusing to Talk About Something

Some battered women think that if someone asks them about something, they have to tell the other person about it. This is simply untrue. What is in your mind belongs to you, and you have no obligation whatsoever to talk about any topic or tell a person anything. To these sorts of requests, you might respond with something like "I'd prefer not to talk about that. Could we please change the subject?" This also goes back to saying no without giving reasons why. Remember, your reasons for whatever you want to do or don't want to do are your property. You have no obligation to disclose your reasons if you'd rather not.

12.28. Saying No After You Said Yes

Sometimes people agree to requests to do something and subsequently regret saying yes. This can happen for many reasons: The situation or your feelings may change, or upon closer consideration you may realize that there are other things you need to do or would rather do. As we discussed before, you always have the right to change your mind, especially in light of new information.

For example, let's say you agreed to help someone out on the weekend but later realize that if you help the other person out, you won't have time to do something you wanted to do. In this type of situation, you can contact the other person and explain directly and concisely, saying something like "I know I said I would help you out, but I didn't realize how much I have to do. I won't be able to help you after all." Or you might say, "I won't be able to make it after all. I have some other things to do."

12.29. Communicating Feelings

To get your needs and wants satisfied, tell people how you feel and what you want. Other people can't read your mind and won't know how you feel or what you want unless you tell them. Unless you want to escalate conflict (which is seldom productive), communicate negative feelings as distress rather than as anger. Distress often evokes empathy and an inclination to nurture or help, whereas anger evokes hostility and antagonism. Here are a few recommended ways of communicating distress: "My feelings are hurt," "I'm upset," "I'm frustrated," "I'm disappointed," or "I'm feeling sad."

12.30. Making Requests and Communicating Wishes

Communicate your wishes directly and specifically, with "I would appreciate" language. Here are some examples: "I would appreciate it if we could go to a movie that I'd like tonight," "I would appreciate it if you don't call after 8 p.m. on weeknights," "I'd be grateful if you'd give me a ride," "I'd like it if you wouldn't borrow my belongings without my permission," or "I'd appreciate it if you'd keep your voice down."

Communicating your wants in this way conveys that the other person has the power to please you. Communicating in this way or in similar ways increases the probability the other person will do what you wish, especially if the other person wants to please you. However, it's extremely important that you be explicit about what you want.

Several phrases similar to "I would appreciate" can also be used to communicate your wishes in ways that convey to others that they have the opportunity to do something that would give you pleasure: "It would really please me if," "You'd make my day if you would," "It would really make me happy if you would," "You'd be doing me a big favor if," or "I'd be grateful if."

Again, it's important to be direct and explicit. Many people express their desires and make requests indirectly in the form of questions, such as "Would you like to go to a movie tonight?" One of the pitfalls of this approach is that it's much easier to say no to questions than to a direct statement of wants. Plus, questions are often misinterpreted or misunderstood. Another issue is that many people in distressed relationships falsely assume that their partner knows what their specific wants are.

Here's an example that illustrates how direct requests can be more influential than indirect requests, asked as questions: A woman lived a couple hundred miles from her family. She wanted her boyfriend to accompany her on a long weekend visit to her family and asked him if he'd like to go. He answered that the last time he went they argued the whole time, so he didn't think it was a good idea. She lamented the outcome to her therapist, who suggested that she approach her boyfriend again, this time with an assertive request, such as "I know we didn't have a very good time on our last visit to my family, but it would mean a lot to me if you'd join me this time. I'd like you to come with me." At her next therapy appointment, she happily reported that when she approached her boyfriend that way, he immediately agreed to go with her. She said it was a valuable lesson about how the way she expressed herself could influence the outcome of situations.

12.31. Assertive Escalation

Asking someone to do something, or to stop doing something, doesn't guarantee that your request will be granted. This circumstance may sometimes call for a technique known as assertive escalation, especially in situations where the other person continues to be disrespectful of your rights. Assertive escalation involves either a more forceful request or telling the other person what you're going to do if he or she doesn't grant your request. This "if ... then" strategy can be phrased in a couple of different ways: "If you don't ... , then I'll have no choice but to ..." or, "If you won't ... , I'm going to ..."

I gave you an example of assertive escalation earlier, when we talked about responding to the style of verbal aggression, rather than the content. I suggested that when people persist in being verbally aggressive, you can let them know that if they don't stop, then you'll end the conversation. It might be a bit harsh or abrasive to say this in response to the first verbally aggressive remark. However, if you respond, "I don't deserve to be talked to this way," and the person persists in being verbally aggressive, outlining the consequences is a very appropriate way of dealing with the situation.

Let's look at a hypothetical situation in which you're having a disagreement and you ask the other person to lower his voice. If he doesn't comply, you might say, "If you won't lower your voice, I'm going to end this conversation." If the other person continues to speak in a loud voice, you would follow through and end the conversation. It would probably be excessive to say you're going to end the conversation as soon as the other person raises his voice, but it's an appropriate and assertive course of action if he refuses to honor your reasonable request.

It's very important that you follow through on what you say you're going to do. If you say you're going to end a conversation if the person persists in being aggressive and you follow through, you'll build credibility.

12.32. Assertive Escalation in the Workplace

Assertive escalation can be an influential tool for dealing with interpersonal conflict in the workplace. Let's say you're having an ongoing, unresolved conflict with a coworker. It would be important to resolve it if the conflict is a source of chronic stress. After all, sometimes people actually quit their jobs because of workplace conflict. Other times, they may go directly to their supervisor without first telling the person with whom they are in conflict. Unfortunately, this tactic almost always alienates the coworker and may do irreparable harm to the relationship.

Assertive escalation is a better approach. Try saying something like this to your coworker: "As I told you before, I'd really like to work this out at our level—just between the two of us. But if we can't work it out, I'll have no choice but to go to my supervisor." Threatening to go to a supervisor at the first sign of conflict would be somewhat abrasive and might aggravate the conflict. However, if your coworker shows no willingness to resolve the conflict, giving him or her an option of avoiding going to a supervisor would be appropriate and professional.

People don't like it when others go over their head. Would you want a coworker you were having a conflict with to go over your head and complain to your supervisor? On the other hand, if the person said that he or she was going to go to your supervisor if the two of you couldn't work it out, wouldn't that increase your motivation to work on the problem?

Sexual harassment and other types of harassment in the workplace often call for assertive escalation. Unassertive women often say little or nothing when they hear sexually inappropriate remarks. Unfortunately, there's some evidence to suggest that passivity may unintentionally invite continued harassment, and that it may even be a precursor to victimization or revictimization (Rosen & Martin, 2000).

If someone at work makes a sexually offensive remark that isn't clearly malicious or intentional, you may wish to overlook the first occurrence as an anomaly—something that's unlikely to occur again. Or you may choose to respond with a low-level assertive response, such as "I would appreciate your not using that kind of language" or "That remark was offensive. I certainly hope you never say anything like that again." However, when it comes to unmistakable and intentional sexual harassment, the best policy is zero tolerance. If the first remark is grossly inappropriate or offensive, use assertive escalation right from the start. For example, you might say something like "That's sexual harassment, and I won't tolerate it. If you ever say or do something like that again, I'll have no choice but to report it immediately. I mean it." This sort of response may also be called for if you were previously harassed and have already made your wants or requests known.

12.33. Assertive Escalation in Intimate Relationships

You can also utilize assertive escalation to promote your best interest in an intimate relationship. For example, let's say you want to do something you think your boyfriend wouldn't want to do, like go to a certain concert. You could just tell him that you're planning to go to the concert with a friend because you know he doesn't like that type of music. However, this might invite a response like "How do you know what I like?" Instead, try asking your boyfriend to go with you first. Then, if he says, "You know I don't like that kind of music," you can say, "I understand. But if you don't want to go with me, I'm going anyway. I'll ask a friend to join me." If he says, "You would go without me?" you can say, "I'd prefer to go with you, but I'd rather go with a friend than go alone or not go at all."

Here's an example of assertive escalation in a dating situation: Clara was having trouble getting her needs met with her boyfriend. He wasn't abusive, but he was quite selfish and self-centered. After she learned about assertiveness in therapy, Clara and her boyfriend went out for pizza. He wanted pepperoni, and because Clara didn't like pepperoni, she asked if they could order the pizza with the pepperoni on one side. Her boyfriend replied, "What's the big deal? You can just pick it off." To which Clara replied, "You're right. It wouldn't be a big deal to pick the pepperoni off. But it also wouldn't be a big deal to have all of the pepperoni on one side of the pizza. I'd like to order it that way, and if that isn't possible, I think I'll go home." Clara and her boyfriend ended up enjoying their pizza with all of the pepperoni on one side.

In a later session, we're going to look at how you can identify potential abusers. At that time, one thing I'll recommend is that you tell any potential boyfriend early on that you don't plan on having sex with a guy until you know him really well. Then, when he subsequently brings up the subject of sex, you can say something like "I would really appreciate it if you wouldn't bring up the subject of sex. If or when I'm ready to have sex with you, I'll let you know." If he continues to bring up the subject or put pressure on you to have sex, the situation calls for assertive escalation. For example, you might say, "I told you before that I'm not interested in getting intimate and that I'll let you know if I decide that I am. Please respect my rights and stop pressuring me. If you don't stop, I'll have no choice but to stop seeing you. I'm not kidding."

12.34. Summary of the Keys to Assertive Communication

Now I'd like to summarize several keys to influential communication: First, respond to the *style* of verbal aggression; don't get into a conversation about the subject matter the other person has raised. Second, don't tolerate disrespect, and if disrespect persists, remove yourself from the situation. Third, avoid using verbal aggression yourself. Fourth, make sure you know what you want to accomplish before you communicate. Fifth, communicate negative feelings as distress, not as anger. Sixth, be able to say no without giving reasons why. Seventh, communicate your wants and needs directly, specifically, and clearly. And eighth, use assertive escalation if the situation warrants it.

12.35. Additional Important Benefits of Becoming Assertive

There's one more important benefit of becoming assertive that we haven't discussed. Research indicates that people tend to avoid activities and situations they think they can't cope with but readily undertake challenges they think they can handle (Ozer & Bandura, 1990). Consistent with this research, there's evidence that assertive women interpret potentially stressful social situations as challenging, whereas unassertive women interpret the same kinds of situations as threatening (Tomaka et al., 1999). Practicing and applying the assertiveness skills you've learned here will increase your self-confidence in social situations and may directly decrease your level of stress and symptoms of PTSD.

Tell me what you've learned from our work on assertiveness ... What are some of the situations you face where you might start using these skills?

CONCLUDING REMARKS

Completing the assertiveness module helps almost all clients become less intimidated by potentially stressful conflicts. At this point, most believe they are better prepared for managing verbal aggression from others and more well equipped to express their feelings and wishes effectively. Although the techniques recommended for responding to the style of verbally aggressive comments are relatively simple and straightforward, we believe they make a positive impact and go a long way toward reducing conflict. The assertiveness skills clients learned in this module may be helpful when implementing the strategies for identifying potential abusers and managing unwanted contacts with former abusers—topics addressed in later modules.

Handout I2.1: Assertive Behavior, Aggressive Behavior, and How to Take the High Road

Assertive behavior is expressing feelings, wants, or opinions in ways that respect the rights and opinions of others. Assertive speech usually involves "I" language, but in certain contexts, "I" language can be aggressive, communicating hostility or disrespect.

Aggressive behavior is expressing feelings, wants, or opinions in ways that violate or disrespect the rights or opinions of others. It includes violation of your rights by physically forceful behavior but also occurs when others put you down or attempt to force or impose their desires or even just their opinions on you. Aggressive behavior is disrespectful, violates ethics of social communication, and influences people negatively. Almost all "you" statements with negative content are aggressive—not assertive.

TYPES OF AGGRESSIVE OR DISRESPECTFUL REMARKS AND EXAMPLES

"You" Statements

Accusatory "You" Statements

■ You're immature [lazy, codependent, rude, selfish, crazy, manipulative, lying, in denial, and so on].

■ You don't know what you're talking about.

■ You're just like your mother [sister, grandmother, and so on].

■ You're making me angry.

Orders (with the implied subject "you")

■ Shut up.

■ Keep quiet.

■ Go away.

Shoulds (which represent others trying to impose their will on you)

■ You should [do something or feel a certain way].

■ You shouldn't [do something or feel a certain way].

- You're supposed to [do something or feel a certain way].

Types of "I" Statements That Are Aggressive

"I" Statements of Anger

- I'm pissed off.

- I'm angry.

- I'm getting mad.

- I feel resentful.

Aggressed-upon "I" Statements

- I'm getting screwed.

- I'm getting a raw deal.

"I" Statements of Masked Aggression

- I feel that you are narrow-minded.

- I think you're selfish.

- I think you're a liar.

- I feel that you're insensitive.

"I" Statements of Scorn or Total Disrespect

- I resent you.

- I don't trust you.

- I don't care about you.

- I don't respect you.

- I hate you.

Aggressive Questions

■ Why are you being defensive [selfish, so needy, such a wimp, in such a bitchy mood]?

ASSERTIVE WAYS OF RESPONDING TO DISRESPECTFUL AGGRESSIVE COMMENTS

Effectively dealing with aggressive words requires that you respond to the aggressive *style* of the communication and disregard its content. Being defensive or attacking back isn't a good strategy. For example, if someone says you're stupid, you might respond with the statement "That's an unkind thing to say." This focuses on the fact that something unkind was said, not on the subject matter. Similarly, the statement "Your saying I'm stupid doesn't mean I'm stupid" is neither defensive nor aggressive, so it won't get you sucked into an argument about whether or not you're stupid. In addition, you could say, "It hurts my feelings." Here are some more examples of assertive responses to verbal aggression, followed by some examples that pertain to specific situations:

■ Your saying that I'm lazy [or whatever] doesn't mean it's true.

■ I don't deserve to be talked to that way.

■ That's not a nice thing to say.

■ That's a hurtful (or unkind, or nasty) thing to say.

■ I would appreciate it if you didn't talk to me that way.

■ If you're going to continue to talk to me that way, I'm going to end this conversation. (If the disrespect persists, say, "I have to go," "I'll talk to you later," or "Good-bye.")

■ I would appreciate it if you could say that in a nicer way.

■ Could you please say that in another way?

■ If you never say that again, I'll be better off and you and I will have a better relationship.

■ I know you mean well, but it doesn't help for you to say that.

Saying No

Don't give reasons or excuses why you don't want to do whatever the person wants you to do. Reasons and excuses just provide fuel to the person to try to talk you out of your decision. Remember: Your reasons for whatever you want to do (or don't want to do) are *your property*, and you have no obligation to disclose those reasons if you don't want to.

- I'm not interested. Have a nice day. (Then hang up, close the door, or keep walking.)

- I'm not interested. I don't want to take up any of your valuable time.

- I won't be able to make it. Thanks for asking.

- Sorry, I can't make it. (This is useful when someone asks you to do something you don't want to do, like go on a date.)

- If the person persists, you may wish to repeat yourself once; for example, Again, thanks for asking, but I won't be able to make it.

- If the person is pushy and tries to get you to disclose your reasons, you may wish to say something like "Personal reasons. I'd rather not go into it. I have to go now."

- I'm not going to change my mind. I have nothing to talk to you about. Please stop calling me. I have to go now. Good-bye.

Assertive Requests

Assertive requests communicate *directly* that you want something and say what it is that you want:

- I would appreciate it if you would keep the noise down.

- I'd appreciate it if you wouldn't smoke in my room.

- It would really please me if you would do me a favor.

- I'd appreciate it if you wouldn't borrow my belongings without my permission.

- It would make me happy if we could go to a movie that I like.

Assertive Escalation and Demanding Respect

This strategy involves establishing consequences. You must clearly state what you'd like to happen and be clear about how you will respond if the person doesn't agree to your request:

- If you don't stop putting me down, I'm going to have to end this conversation.

- If you won't go with me, I'll go with a friend. I'd rather go with you, but if you don't want to, I'll go with someone else.

■ I told you before that I'm not interested in getting intimate. Please respect my rights and stop pressuring me. If you don't stop, I'll have no choice but to stop seeing you. I mean it!

■ If you don't stop bothering me, I'll have no choice but to call the probation officer and tell them you violated the restraining order [tell the manager, end our relationship, and so on].

Managing Mistrust

For obvious reasons, many battered women have difficulty with trust, and particularly with trusting men. In order to survive, it may have been healthy and adaptive for a woman to develop an increased level of mistrust, but once she is safely out of the abusive relationship it is no longer helpful. More importantly, many battered women mistrust based on emotional reasoning rather than facts and logic, and this can interfere with healthy functioning. This module is often an eye-opener for clients as they learn that trusting their "female intuition" isn't the best way to make decisions about trust.

Some clients resist giving up emotional reasoning in making decisions about trust. In these cases, it's important to help them examine the evidence supporting the thought they labeled as a feeling. Some clients resist giving up emotional reasoning because their emotions are so strong and real. In all cases, encourage clients to pay attention to their feelings, but only as a signal to search for evidence rather than as a cue to leave or get away.

OBJECTIVES

■ For the client to understand that there's a tendency to overestimate the likelihood that traumatic events are going to happen again, and that emotional reasoning is the reason why this happens

■ For the client to understand that mistrust is not a pure emotion, and that a gut feeling that someone can't be trusted is not evidence that this is true

■ For the client to realize that feeling mistrustful, like feeling unsafe, is not a pure emotion and often involves emotional reasoning

■ For the client to use gut feelings only as a signal to search for evidence as to whether someone can or cannot be trusted and whether it would be in her best interest to avoid that person

MATERIALS

■ None

HOMEWORK

■ Listen to session audio-recordings.

■ Continue to monitor and record negative self-talk.

■ Practice PMR while listening to the PMR recording, twice a day.

■ Do a body scan and over-tense and relax muscles when experiencing stress.

PROCEDURES CHECKLIST

1. _____ Introduction to mistrust

2. _____ Trauma survivors' tendency to overestimate the probability that similar bad things will happen again

3. _____ Some good news and bad news about abusive men

4. _____ Acting on gut feelings

5. _____ The meaning of mistrust (referring to handout 9.1)

6. _____ Understanding that gut feelings aren't evidence

7. _____ Using feelings as a signal to search for evidence

8. _____ Understanding that gut feelings in and of themselves do not reflect evidence

DETAILED PROCEDURES FOR MODULE 13

13.1. Introduction to Mistrust

Now we're going to explore the issue of mistrust and how you can manage it. Many women with a history of abuse or victimization have problems with trust—of people in general and especially in regard to men. This is understandable, because these women were often abused, exploited, and victimized by men who were supposed to love and protect them, not betray them. If experience taught you that you can't trust your father, stepfather, boyfriend, or husband, why would you trust a man who's a perfect stranger?

13.2. The Tendency to Overestimate the Probability That Similar Bad Things Will Happen Again

When really bad things happen to people, afterward they tend to overestimate the likelihood that similar bad events could happen again. I'll give you a few examples to illustrate.

People who have been in an accident on the freeway think freeways are more dangerous than other people do, and they think driving on the freeway is more dangerous than it really is. Imagine the following scenario involving a woman who had a bad accident on the freeway. As she drives up the ramp onto the freeway, she already feels a little anxious. Then she notices the traffic and the speed of the cars. Her anxiety increases, she doesn't "feel safe," and she concludes that an accident is likely. Can you see what's happening here? The woman is engaging in emotional reasoning. She's falsely using her anxiety as evidence of how likely she is to have another accident.

Similarly, many people with a fear of flying think that airplanes are far more dangerous than the facts indicate. Based on their fear, they may choose to drive somewhere instead of flying. However, an examination of the facts would reveal that driving actually is more dangerous than flying—by some counts, more than ten times as dangerous. A related example has to do with the two snipers who went on a killing rampage on the East Coast of the United States in 2002. For a while afterward, many people wouldn't let their children go out and play after school for fear that they would become sniper victims. This was in spite of news reports that the chances of dying on the freeway were much greater than those of being killed by a sniper.

Do you remember the story I told you about a woman who was traumatized when she saw an elephant trample his trainer at the circus? Going to the circus again became unthinkable to this woman, and now she even considers zoos unsafe and refuses to take her children to the zoo. Obviously zoos aren't inherently dangerous; they are popular destinations for families with young children. This woman is using her fear as evidence that zoos aren't safe, and basing her decisions on that fear. Again, this is emotional reasoning.

13.3. Some Good News and Bad News About Abusive Men

Let's bring the discussion back to the issue at hand: managing your mistrust of people, and particularly of men. There's some good news and some bad news about abusive men. The bad news is that there are far too many abusive men out there. The good news is that there probably aren't nearly as many abusive men out there as most battered women think there are.

There is reason to believe that a small minority of men do the majority of abusing. For example, many child molesters have molested many children, and many rapists have raped more than one woman. The same is true of batterers: Most of them have abused more than one intimate partner. In addition, predatory men, who often have sociopathic traits, know how to identify vulnerable women. This makes it seem like there are more abusive men out there than there really are—especially to women who have been abused by more than one intimate partner. Unfortunately, this is all too common. In one study of 162 battered women, about half of the women had been physically hurt by more than one intimate partner (Kubany et al., 2003; Kubany, Hill, et al., 2004).

13.4. Acting on Gut Feelings

Some formerly battered women are ambivalent about getting involved in an intimate relationship with a man again. Although they may be attracted to men, they're also on guard and mistrustful around men—often especially so around men they find attractive. The thought process involved is something like "If I like him, he has a greater ability to hurt me." This complex set of thoughts and feelings may lead to uncertainty, which can create anxiety and heighten mistrust as a result. When these trust issues come up, many formerly battered women refer to their gut feelings, hunches, female intuition, or even a "sixth sense" and use these feelings as evidence that it's in their best interest to leave or avoid contact with the person.

13.5. The Meaning of Mistrust

Let's examine the meaning of mistrust. What is the relatively pure emotion you experience when you sense that you can't trust a man? Stated another way, when you've been in situations in which you didn't trust someone, what is the relatively pure emotion you were experiencing at the time? If the client has trouble remembering what the relatively pure negative emotions are, refer her to table 1 of handout 9.1.

Right. Anxiety or fear. And what were your thoughts? What thoughts were going through your mind as you were experiencing this anxiety or fear? Right. Thoughts that you were in some kind of danger or would be if you continued to hang around this person. Thoughts that the person had the potential to harm you in some way—perhaps physically, or perhaps psychologically or emotionally.

13.6. Understanding That Gut Feelings Aren't Evidence

Mistrust isn't a pure emotion. It's a hybrid emotional experience—a combination of one of the relatively pure emotions, such as anxiety, and the thought that you might not be safe or that the person you don't trust has the potential to harm you in some way. In fact, "feeling mistrustful" is just the same thing as "feeling unsafe." Both reflect emotional reasoning, where feelings are mistakenly assumed to be evidence that you aren't safe or that the other person can't be trusted. In and of itself, the anxiety or fear you feel when you have gut feelings that you aren't safe is not evidence that you're actually in danger.

After the terrorist attack on the World Trade Center on September 11, 2001, thousands of Americans didn't feel safe flying on commercial airlines, as witnessed by the precipitous drop in air travel after 9/11. Ironically, air travel was probably safer than ever in the aftermath of 9/11, and how safe air travel is can only be determined by an objective analysis of the evidence available.

13.7. Using Feelings as a Signal to Search for Evidence

I'm not suggesting that you disregard your gut feelings. Instead, I want you to use these feelings as a signal to search for information about the validity of your conclusions. If you "feel" you can't trust someone, that's your cue to look for evidence as to whether this is a safe person to be around. Your feelings may reflect your conditioning—past experiences that taught you to mistrust certain types of people. In this case, it may not relate to the person at all. Alternatively, you may be perceiving information that indicates there actually is something to worry about, but the information hasn't come into your full, conscious awareness yet.

Use your gut feelings as a signal to scan the situation for genuine evidence that you aren't safe or can't trust the person. Look for factual clues that may indicate this is the case. We'll take an in-depth look at some clues to look for a little later. For now, here are a few examples: Is a guy standing unusually close, especially if you don't know him very well? Is he asking personal questions that you would rather not answer and pressing you for an answer? Is he trying to get you to do something you don't want to do? Is he putting you down in some way, even subtly, or trying to impose his values on you? Is he making sexual remarks or trying to rush you into a relationship? Is he being excessively flattering? Is he bragging about himself or making big promises?

Or is he just the same race as your abuser or someone who raped you? Is it just that he's in the military or wearing some kind of uniform and your abuser was in the military? Or does he maybe have the same haircut or some personal mannerism that reminds you of your abuser? Is it just that he's talking in a loud voice? Or is it just that he's a man? All of these things are nothing more than harmless reminders, like the light our mouse Millie learned to fear in the shuttle box.

If you can't identify any evidence that someone can't be trusted, don't leave or escape the situation merely to get short-term relief. Hang around for a while. The only way to get over anxiety about nondangerous cues is to allow yourself to experience these cues. Label the anxiety you feel as "inconvenient anxiety" that you'd like to get over, and stay with the person for a while. This certainly doesn't mean you need to go out with the guy. You'll probably want to gather a lot more evidence before you do that. But if you stay in the situation, you'll gradually overcome your anxiety about these nondangerous cues, and you'll actually become a better observer.

13.8. Understanding That Gut Feelings in and of Themselves Do Not Reflect Evidence

Because I don't want to leave you with the impression that you should ignore your gut feelings, I'll conclude this discussion of mistrust with a couple of examples illustrating how gut feelings can sometimes reflect perceived evidence that a person hasn't become fully conscious of. The first is about Marsha. When her therapist asked her to describe a man she had recently met, Marsha said he was overbearing. When her therapist probed as to what she meant by "overbearing," Marsha replied that she didn't know, she just had a gut feeling that she couldn't trust him. Her therapist asked what the man had done that gave Marsha that feeling, to which she again replied that she didn't know, she just had a gut feeling. Her therapist said, "Try hard. Go back and analyze what happened that suggested he couldn't be trusted." Finally they made some progress. Marsha reported that even though she had just met this man, he wouldn't stop staring at her and that he stood too close to her, making her feel uncomfortable. After thinking a bit longer, she realized that he had also asked her some questions that were very personal, especially considering that she had just met him.

Here's another example: Louise had a hard time accepting the view that gut feelings aren't evidence. She said that everyone had always told her to go with her initial gut reactions, and she believed this was the best advice. Her therapist asked her to describe a situation where she relied solely on gut feelings to decide what to do, and Louise shared a recent incident where she dropped her son off at his father's house. His father, Louise's ex-boyfriend, had abused Louise when they lived together. Louise said that she had a weird feeling that it wouldn't be a good idea to hang around and visit with her ex-boyfriend about their son, so she left almost immediately.

Louise's therapist then asked her to describe exactly what happened. Louise said that when she arrived at her ex-boyfriend's house, she got out of her car and walked toward the carport, where he was working on his car. Louise said, "I got about ten feet from the carport, and the whole place smelled like a brewery." Louise's therapist then asked her, "Did he ever abuse you when he was drinking?" to which Louise replied, "That's the only time he was abusive—when he drank." Can you see that there was actually evidence in this situation to suggest that Louise was in danger and that her ex-boyfriend couldn't be trusted?

What did you get out of this discussion of mistrust?

CONCLUDING REMARKS

Becoming better at managing mistrust by looking for evidence takes practice. Some clients make faster progress than others in being able to use their gut feelings as a signal to search for evidence rather than as a basis for concluding whether a person is trustworthy. For those who make slower progress, encourage them to be on the lookout for gut feelings and, whenever possible, to use this as a cue to search for evidence before drawing conclusions. This will help the skills taught in this module become second nature. The next module, on identifying potential abusers, will give the client additional tools for determining who is trustworthy.

Identifying Potential Abusers

Most clients eagerly look forward to this module because they aren't confident about their ability to identify an intimate partner who is likely to become abusive before they become emotionally invested in the relationship. Learning about red flags, or signs that a potential intimate partner is likely to become abusive, also allows formerly battered women to resolve issues related to trust by giving them specific qualities to look for—and avoid—in potential romantic partners. The approach here is particularly empowering because the therapist also offers the client strategies for eliciting these behaviors. Rather than waiting for these characteristics to spontaneously present themselves, the client can take charge of the situation. If only all young women were offered this sort of education early on, perhaps many abusive relationships could be avoided altogether.

OBJECTIVES

- To teach the client about twenty red flags, or warning signs, that someone has the potential to become abusive

- To teach the client what she can actively do early in a relationship to identify someone who is likely to become abusive

- To increase the client's confidence that she can identify potential abusers before she becomes emotionally involved, thereby preventing the possibility of being victimized by another intimate partner

MATERIALS

- Red Flags That Indicate Someone May Have the Potential to Become Abusive (handout 14.1)

HOMEWORK

- Listen to session audio-recordings.

- Continue to monitor and record negative self-talk.

- Practice PMR while listening to the PMR recording, twice a day.

- Do a body scan and over-tense and relax muscles when experiencing stress.

- Read and complete chapter 15 in *Healing the Trauma of Domestic Violence* (optional).

PROCEDURES CHECKLIST

1. _____ Introduction to identifying potential abusers

2. _____ Red flags that someone has the potential to be abusive

3. _____ Red flag 1: Possessiveness

4. _____ Red flag 2: Jealousy

5. _____ Red flag 3: Dislike of your family or friends

6. _____ Red flag 4: In a hurry to get romantically involved

7. _____ Red flag 5: Lying

8. _____ Red flag 6: Secrecy

9. _____ Red flag 7: Imposition of his opinions or beliefs

10. _____ Red flag 8: Belittling your opinions or beliefs

11. _____ Red flag 9: A bad temper

12.   _____ Red flag 10: Physical aggression with others

13.   _____ Red flag 11: Verbal mistreatment of others

14.   _____ Red flag 12: Blaming others for his problems or mistakes

15.   _____ Red flag 13: "Playful" use of force during sex

16.   _____ Red flag 14: A regular or past heavy user of alcohol or drugs

17.   _____ Red flag 15: A reputation as a womanizer

18.   _____ Red flag 16: Unreliability

19.   _____ Red flag 17: Acting differently when the two of you are alone than when you're with others

20.   _____ Red flag 18: Invasion of your privacy

21.   _____ Red flag 19: Cruelty to animals or children

22.   _____ Red flag 20: Charm or charisma

23.   _____ Signs exhibited by your abusive partner before he abused you (handout 14.1, an in-session questionnaire)

24.   _____ Identifying potential abusers during the early stages of a relationship

25.   _____ Identifying a skill deficit common among abusers (the inability to resolve conflict in a mutually respectful way)

26.   _____ Why provoking conflict early in a relationship isn't dangerous

27.   _____ Ways of provoking conflict #1: Disagreeing and being selfish

28.   _____ Ways of provoking conflict #2: Refusing to be rushed into a relationship

29.   _____ Ways of provoking conflict #3: Postponing intimacy and issuing an ultimatum on the discussion of sex

30.   _____ Ways of provoking conflict #4: Telling him you're going to continue dating other people

31.   _____ Ways of provoking conflict #5: Insisting on reliability

32. _____ Ways of provoking conflict #6: Programming in an unexplained refusal to get together

33. _____ Ways of provoking conflict #7: Finding out about his prior relationships

34. _____ Ways of provoking conflict #8: Checking out his background

---

DETAILED PROCEDURES FOR MODULE 14

14.1. Introduction to Identifying Potential Abusers

Many formerly battered women are still attracted to men but are reluctant to become involved in new romantic relationships because they aren't confident that they'll be able to identify someone who is likely to become abusive. To help ensure that doesn't happen to you, the next major topic we'll cover is how to identify potentially abusive men long before you become emotionally involved or invested in a romantic relationship. If you know how to identify someone with the potential to be abusive, it's likely that you'll be less wary of men, more comfortable spending time with men, and maybe more open to the idea of getting romantically involved again at some point.

14.2. Red Flags That Someone Has the Potential to Be Abusive

The developers of cognitive trauma therapy have identified twenty red flags, or early warning signs, that someone has the potential to become an abusive intimate partner. I'll briefly describe and discuss each of these signs, and then we'll talk about strategies you can use to intentionally elicit these behaviors. Most of us are on our best behavior when we first get involved in a relationship. Putting these techniques to use will ensure that you don't have to wait for this "honeymoon" phase to end before these qualities emerge.

14.3. Red Flag 1: Possessiveness

Potentially abusive or predatory men tend to be very possessive or over-controlling, sometimes causing their partners to believe they are owned, like a piece of property. He may want to keep you all to himself and be overly controlling about how and where you spend your time. He may want to do everything with just the two of you. He may want you to quit doing other activities that don't involve him.

He may even want you to reduce the amount of time you spend with your family or close friends. Possessiveness can also be exhibited by an insistence that you account for all of your time or whereabouts. He may frequently check in to be sure you're where you're supposed to be.

Sometimes women initially perceive possessiveness as flattery. For example, getting several phone calls a day may be interpreted as strong attraction. You may think "Gee, he really likes me." But think about it: Repeated phone calls, even if the calls are supposedly loving, can border on stalking. By calling you repeatedly or persuading you to repeatedly call him, he's keeping track of your activities or where you are. In the early "honeymoon" stages of a relationship, he might say something like "Gee, honey, I called you at three o'clock and couldn't reach you. I missed you. Where were you?"

14.4. Red Flag 2: Jealousy

Jealousy is a huge red flag. If a potential boyfriend is even slightly jealous, don't get involved with him. Jealous men are insecure, tend to be very possessive and controlling, and have a high potential to become abusive.

14.5. Red Flag 3: Dislike of Your Family or Friends

Does he find fault with or otherwise bad-mouth your friends or family? If he does, this is a red flag. Dislike of family or friends often results in a woman seeing less and less of family and friends and sometimes even cutting ties completely. In fact, this sign and the two other signs we've identified thus far—possessiveness and jealousy—result in a woman becoming socially isolated and vulnerable to abuse.

14.6. Red Flag 4: In a Hurry to Get Romantically Involved

Abusive men typically try to sweep women off their feet and rush them into romantic relationships. Similarly, early on in the relationship abusive men often try to get commitments from women not to go out with anyone else. They rush women into sexual relationships, into moving in with them, and into marriage. For example, one client had four abusive husbands, and in each case they were married within two months of having met. Rushing a woman into a relationship is akin to stalking or obsessively checking up on her. If a guy is spending a great deal of time with a woman, he always knows where she is and is more assured that she isn't spending time with other men.

14.7. Red Flag 5: Lying

Lying is another huge red flag. If you catch him in even the smallest lie, drop him like a hot potato. Predatory men are pathological liars and even lie when there is no reason to do so. For example, consider the following interaction: A woman asks her new boyfriend, "Why did you say you weren't at the shopping mall yesterday?" and he responds, "Because I wasn't there." When she says, "But my sister saw you there!" he replies, "Well, your sister is nuts."

14.8. Red Flag 6: Secrecy

Is he secretive about his activities or whereabouts? Are there large gaps of his time that you can't account for? And are there certain things he doesn't want to talk about, such as his prior intimate relationships? Does he talk on the phone with people who remain anonymous? Sometimes this can signify that he's involved in some illegal activity, such as using or dealing drugs. Some women don't find out until well into a relationship with an abusive man that he was using or dealing drugs.

14.9. Red Flag 7: Imposition of His Opinions or Beliefs

Does he try to impose his opinions or worldview on you? Abusive men are opinionated, often with traditional beliefs about gender roles, favoring the dominance and authority of men in relationships with women.

14.10. Red Flag 8: Belittling Your Opinions or Beliefs

Related to imposing his opinions, does he belittle your opinions in even subtle ways? In this case, he might say things like "You are so naive," "You really don't know what you're talking about," or "Where have you been for the last twenty years?"

14.11. Red Flag 9: A Bad Temper

Many abusive men are explosively angry. Does he have a bad temper? This is an issue even if most of the time he seems to be so happy-go-lucky or mellow.

14.12. Red Flag 10: Physical Aggression with Others

Have you seen him being physically aggressive with someone else, or even heard stories about him doing this? Abusive men who are violent outside the relationship as well as with their girlfriends or wives are, as a group, the most violent in intimate relationships (Holtzworth-Munroe & Stuart, 1994).

14.13. Red Flag 11: Verbal Mistreatment of Others

If a potential boyfriend is being nice to you but you see or hear him being verbally abusive to someone else, such as an employee or relative, this would be a cause for concern. If he acts this way with other people, it's likely he will also act this way with you.

14.14. Red Flag 12: Blaming Others for His Problems or Mistakes

Abusive men tend to blame others—the boss, you, people they do business with—for their own mistakes or problems of their own making. If something goes wrong, it's always somebody else's fault.

14.15. Red Flag 13: "Playful" Use of Force During Sex

Some abusive men get unduly rough during sex in the name of "fun." Does he throw you down? Does he hold you down against your will during sex?

14.16. Red Flag 14: A Regular or Past Heavy User of Alcohol or Drugs

Many men with a history of heavy alcohol or drug abuse are sociopathic (Morgenstern, Langenbucher, Labouvie, & Miller, 1997), with inclinations to become abusive with their intimate partners. For example, in two studies at a residential substance abuse program, 90 percent of the women residents had been physically hurt by an intimate partner, and almost all of them had been abused by a partner who had a problem with alcohol or drugs (Tremayne & Kubany, 1998). About the only place more risky than a bar for meeting a batterer is an Alcoholics Anonymous or Narcotics Anonymous meeting.

14.17. Red Flag 15: A Reputation as a Womanizer

If a potential boyfriend has a reputation as a womanizer or if you know he has cheated on someone in the past, be very wary. If he's been married before, ask him if he wore a wedding ring. Many abusive men don't wear wedding rings because they don't want women they flirt with and try to get sexually involved with to know that they're married.

14.18. Red Flag 16: Unreliability

Many abusive men are irresponsible and extraordinarily unreliable. Does he call you when he says he's going to call you? Does he pick you up when he says he's going to pick you up? Does he do what he says he's going to do when he says he's going to do it?

14.19. Red Flag 17: Acting Differently When the Two of You Are Alone

What if a guy is sweet and loving toward you when the two of you are alone but is somewhat aloof or standoffish when you're with other people, especially your girlfriends or other women? What might this behavior pattern signify? Right. He may not want other women to know that he's taken. If other women know he's going out with you or is seriously involved with you, they'll become upset and offended if he starts hitting on them. In one woman's case, many of her husband's friends didn't even know that she and her husband were married!

Alternatively, some abusers are sweet and nice when the two of you are with other people, and rude and mean when you're alone. When no one else is around to observe, they may be more likely to let down the act and show their true nature.

14.20. Red Flag 18: Invasion of Your Privacy

Many abusive men have no qualms about invading the privacy of their girl-friends and wives, and they may even accuse their partner of making a big deal over nothing when they do. Does he open your mail or your e-mail? Does he check your phone messages? Does he look through your purse? Does he go through your closet or look through your dresser drawers?

14.21. Red Flag 19: Cruelty to Animals or Children

Does he mistreat animals? It has been estimated that approximately half of male batterers mistreat or even torture family pets (Ascione, 2000). Does he expect children to do things that are far beyond their ability? Does he ever tease children until they cry?

14.22. Red Flag 20: Charm or Charisma

Many predatory men can be extraordinarily charming, witty, and fun to be with. They can also appear to be very empathic or understanding about a woman's past problems, and some can even cry on demand. Charm or charisma is by no means a certain sign that a guy is going to become abusive, but as a group, abusive men are probably far more charming than men who aren't going to abuse their girlfriends or wives. One of the reasons may be because they have no trouble giving women compliments that are exaggerations or lies. Be suspicious if a man is extremely complimentary, for example, if he tells you how absolutely wonderful you are before he really knows you.

14.23. Signs Exhibited by Your Abusive Partner Before He Abused You

Give the client handout 14.1, Red Flags That Indicate Someone May Have the Potential to Become Abusive. **On this checklist, place check marks next to the red flags or signs exhibited by your abusive partner before he became abusive with you.** Once the client has completed the questionnaire, ask, **Would you have gotten intimate and emotionally involved with him if you had been aware of these red flags before you became emotionally involved?**

14.24. Identifying Potential Abusers During the Early Stages of a Relationship

Many formerly battered women are particularly anxious about their ability to tell whether a guy could become abusive. Early in relationships, people don't know each other that well and they're usually on their best behavior—even guys who may become abusive later on. Many of my clients have said things like "My husband was a really nice guy when I first met him. And look what he turned out to be." To help you with this concern, I'll teach you a few strategies you can use early in a relationship to tell whether a guy is a potential abuser.

14.25. Identifying a Skill Deficit Common Among Abusers

Sociopathic, controlling men, who are likely to become abusive, have a certain deficit in their communication skills—something they can't do and have no interest whatsoever in getting better at or learning how to do. It will be important for you to identify this skill deficit so you can break off a relationship with a potentially abusive guy before you get emotionally involved. Do you have any idea what this deficit is?

The skill is the ability to resolve conflict in a mutually respectful way. If the client doesn't come up with an answer along these lines, offer some hints: **It is often exhibited during couples counseling that isn't working. It's the most common problem in dysfunctional relationships. It's not sex, finances, free time, or disagreements about child rearing. It's a communication skill deficit that manifests itself when there is conflict. Your abusive partner probably had this skill deficit. What do you think this deficit might be?** Pause to allow the client to think and answer.

Well, let me ask you this: Did your abusive partner want to resolve conflict in a mutually respectful way? Did he want to learn how to resolve conflict in a mutually respectful way? No. Abusive men are selfish and controlling and want to force their will on their girlfriends and wives. They lack the ability and desire to resolve conflict in a mutually respectful way.

Abusive men can be extremely charming and come off like great guys when things are going their way. However, they're ultimately very self-centered and controlling and will react negatively when others don't let them have their way. You can use this trait to your advantage. Provoking conflict with abusive men will trigger their tendencies to become overly controlling and verbally abusive. Their true colors are very likely to reveal themselves in response to conflict.

Now that you know what this deficit is, you can use a variety of strategies to determine whether someone has the potential to be abusive. How can you find out whether a guy is unable and unwilling to resolve conflict in a mutually respectful way? What would you need to do? Right. You can provoke conflict. As one client said, "Yeah. Piss him off!"

Intentionally provoking conflict is the last thing that would occur to most battered women when they first start therapy. Most of them have learned to habitually avoid conflict because it reminds them of the abuse. Also, when they were in an abusive relationship it may have been dangerous to get mad or disagree, because when they did talk back or stand up for their rights, the abuse got worse.

14.26. Why Provoking Conflict Early in a Relationship Isn't Dangerous

It's important for you to know that it isn't dangerous to provoke conflict early in a relationship. An abusive man knows that a woman won't go out with him anymore if he becomes physically or even verbally abusive before she's emotionally involved or invested in the relationship. Most women don't become emotionally invested in or committed to a relationship before there is sexual intimacy, and sometimes not until they've become pregnant, started living with a guy, or gotten married.

And in a parallel way, abusive men rarely abuse a woman before they have had sex, at the earliest, or before she is pregnant or they've moved in together, or on or soon after their wedding day. You would be surprised at how many battered women are first abused on their wedding day or shortly thereafter. When did your partner first abuse you?

14.27. Disagreeing and Being Selfish

Disagree and be "selfish" early on in the relationship. Argue your viewpoint when it differs from his and disagree when your opinions are different than his—

about politics, sports, the activities you do together, whatever. Insist on getting your needs and wishes met in the relationship and insist on engaging in activities that you enjoy, not just those he enjoys. Don't be so nice that you're willing to do anything he wants to do. For example, you might say, "We've gone to two movies that you wanted to see and haven't gone to any that appeal to me. This Sunday, I would like us to go to a movie I'm interested in."

If you say something like this on the second or third date and he responds with something like "What are you, a feminist?" you can say, "Nice knowing you. Goodbye." This approach allows you to see his true character before he hits you and before you become emotionally involved—before you become dependent on him and he can get away with it.

Many battered women find it a foreign concept to make a fuss over little things. But that is exactly what I suggest you do. For example, one client said she didn't have a single argument with her abusive boyfriend until the day he hit her and broke her jaw. Her therapist probed for examples of earlier conflict. The woman recalled that she didn't like his cologne, so she bought him another kind but he wouldn't wear it. She said she didn't pursue the issue because she didn't want to jeopardize the relationship over such a little thing. Her therapist responded, "You mean his cologne means more to him than you do? You're darn right you make a fuss about such a little thing! Find out what kind of guy he is early on."

Back when we discussed assertiveness, I gave you an example of a woman who made a big deal about her boyfriend's objection to ordering a pizza with all of the pepperoni, which she didn't like, on one side of the pizza. He wanted her to pick the pepperoni off of her pieces. She provoked conflict by telling him she wanted to go home if they didn't order the pizza with all of the pepperoni on one side.

If the client has children, make the following suggestion: If you're dating someone new, you might insist that the children come along every other time you get together. Many abusive men won't like this because they would prefer that just the two of you get together.

One client narrowly avoided getting involved with an abuser when she inadvertently and unintentionally provoked conflict on their second date. They were driving to a restaurant when he saw something out of the corner of his eye and said, "Don't turn around." What do you think she did? Right. She turned around. In response, the guy verbally went off, hurling obscenities and insults at her. She asked him to take her home, and she never went out with him again. This story also illustrates why the typical abusive man consciously tries not to be abusive before a woman is emotionally involved. He knows she'll stop seeing him if he acts this way before she really cares about him.

Some potential abusers won't even call back for a second date if they perceive you to be the type of woman who wants equal standing in a relationship. In response to this observation, one woman said, "I guess that's a compliment."

14.28. Refusing to Be Rushed into a Relationship

As we discussed, one of the red flags is when a man is in a hurry to get romantically involved. Go slow in the early stages of a relationship. I recommend that you refuse to get together more than once a week for the first several months of a relationship. Don't allow him to rush you or pressure you to get together more frequently. Abusive men are usually impatient. Most will probably break off the relationship if a woman remains assertive about her interests and needs and only sees him once a week or less—especially if there's no sex involved, which brings us to the next strategy for provoking conflict.

14.29. Postponing Sexual Intimacy and Issuing an Ultimatum on the Discussion of Sex

On your first date with a guy, I suggest you tell him up front that you have zero tolerance for abuse. For example, you might say something like "I have no idea whether you and I have any future together, but I want to tell you something. I've been in an abusive relationship, and I want you to know that I'll never be in an abusive relationship again. I don't want to get into details about what happened. However, I do want you to know that if you ever think about getting physical with me, the first time will be the last time. I will end the relationship right then and there. I also want you to know that if you ever start verbally abusing me—for example, swearing at me or calling me dirty names—you'll be inviting me to call it quits."

I recommend that you also tell him you're planning to postpone sexual intimacy. For example, you might say, "I've been stung in the past, so I'm not going to get intimate with anyone until I know him really, really well. I just want to tell you that up front so that you won't have any false expectations." If he asks, "How long is that going to take?" tell him something like "I don't have any idea." If he's only interested in sex, your decision to postpone it will be a good indirect way to provoke conflict. If he generally enjoys your company, he'll stick around and not keep pressuring you for sex.

If a guy persists in pressuring you for sex, tell him you want him to stop bringing up the topic, and then say something like "If and when I'm ready to have sex with you, I'll let you know." If he persists, tell him that if he won't change the subject, you're going to end the conversation or go home. Then, if he brings up the subject again, follow through by ending the conversation or going home. Also tell him that you won't continue dating someone who continues to pressure you for sex. You might say, "If you want to continue dating me, you're going to have to stop talking about sex." If he keeps bringing up sex, I suggest that you terminate the relationship.

14.30. Telling Him You're Going to Continue Dating Other People

When you start going out with a guy, tell him that you're going to continue to date other people, and that you'll never date only one person until you are in love and have been intimate. Then, after you've gone out with him for a while, I recommend you program in a date or night out with someone else, even if it's just a male friend you aren't interested in romantically.

14.31. Insisting on Reliability

On the first or second date, I recommend that you tell a potential boyfriend that reliability is important to you. For example, you might say, "Do you want to know what I'm looking for in a guy? I'm looking for someone I can count on—someone who's reliable. I'm looking for someone who calls me when he says he's going to and picks me up when he says he's going to—someone who does what he says he's going to do when he says he's going to do it."

Then, if he doesn't follow through on something, remind him of what you're looking for. You might tell him, "I won't continue to go out with someone I can't count on," and perhaps postpone your next date for at least a week. For example, you might say, "I can't make it next Saturday. How about a week from Saturday?"

14.32. Programming in an Unexplained Refusal to Get Together

After you've been going out with a guy on a regular basis, program in a refusal to get together. For example, if he asks you out next week, tell him, "I can't make it next week. How about the following week?" Don't offer an explanation. If he asks you why you can't make it, simply repeat that you can't make it. If he continues to pressure you for a reason, tell him you want to change the subject. If he still persists, ask him if he wants to go out with you in two weeks, because if he continues to ask why you can't go out with him next week, you aren't going to go out with him in two weeks, either.

14.33. Finding Out About His Prior Relationships

What is something you want to know about him? It would be worthwhile to know something about his previous relationships. For example, how many girlfriends or wives has he had? What did they argue or disagree about? How did they resolve their differences? What differences didn't they resolve? And why did they break up?

Abusive men will be threatened by this line of questioning and may go on the offensive. For example, they may get angry or accuse you of being insecure. In response, you might say, "That's not a nice thing to say" or "You don't have to tell me, but if you don't, I'm not going to go out with you again." In the latter case, he may accuse you of being a hypocrite because you won't tell him about your abuse history. If he does this, tell him that these are two different subjects. If he doesn't want to date you anymore because you're not willing to talk about your past, that's his right and his choice. You're simply telling him the conditions under which you're willing to continue to see him.

14.34. Checking Out His Background

In the workplace, employers check out job applicants' references before they make important hiring decisions. It's just good business to do this. Making a romantic commitment to a man has far greater implications for a woman's well-being than hiring a key employee for her business. For example, you can always fire an employee who doesn't work out, but it's much more complicated to get out of a bad relationship. Therefore, if you get to the point where you're considering having sex with a guy, moving in with him, or getting married, I recommend that you check out his background.

I recommend that you tell your boyfriend that you want to speak to his ex-girlfriends or ex-wife and ask for their phone numbers. If he gets upset, say something like "This doesn't have anything to do with you. I intended to do this before we ever met. You can be flattered that I would even consider a serious relationship with you. If you don't have anything to hide, you don't have anything to worry about." If the guy breaks off the relationship over this issue, you can be certain he has something to hide.

In some states, it's possible to do a search of a person's criminal record. It's also relatively easy to find information about a person, including any criminal history, by searching on one of the many online personal information sites. If a boyfriend has a criminal record that you didn't know about, he's a bad bet for a good relationship.

Has our discussion of how to identify potential abusers been helpful? Are you more confident about being able to identify potentially abusive men? What else did you get out of this session?

CONCLUDING REMARKS

At the completion of this module, clients always express confidence that they now have the skills to identify an intimate partner who is likely to become abusive—*before* they become emotionally involved. Many clients also say they plan to look for red flags and to provoke conflict in any new relationship. In addition, occasionally a client will indicate that what she learned in this module has helped her become more open to the idea of getting involved in a new intimate relationship.

Handout 14.1: Red Flags That Indicate Someone May Have the Potential to Become Abusive

Client Initials: _____   Date: _____

On this checklist, place check marks next to the red flags, or warning signs, exhibited by your partner before he became abusive with you.

1.   _____ Possessiveness

2.   _____ Jealousy

3.   _____ Dislike of your family or friends

4.   _____ In a hurry to get romantically involved

5.   _____ Lying

6.   _____ Secrecy

7.   _____ Imposition of his opinions or beliefs

8.   _____ Belittling your opinions or beliefs

9.   _____ A bad temper

10.   _____ Physical aggression with others

11.   _____ Verbal mistreatment of others

12.   _____ Blaming others for his problems or mistakes

13.   _____ "Playful" use of force during sex

14.   _____ A regular or past heavy user of alcohol or drugs

15.   _____ A reputation as a womanizer

16.   _____ Unreliability

17.   _____ Invasion of your privacy

18.   _____ Acts differently when the two of you are alone than when you're with others

19.   _____ Cruelty to animals or children

20.   _____ Charm or charisma

Would you have gotten intimate or emotionally involved with this person if you had been aware of these signs in advance? _____

Managing Unwanted or Stressful Contacts with Former Abusers

Many abusive ex-partners continue to harass or verbally abuse their ex-wives and ex-girlfriends even after the relationship is over. For this reason, it is important for battered women to have a plan in place for managing ex-partners' attempts to manipulate and control them—and to practice implementing that plan. This module informs clients about the best ways to manage unwanted contacts and then leads them through role-playing scenarios to practice these new skills. Clients often find this module empowering and even fun as they learn specific ways to be assertive when faced with their ex-partner.

OBJECTIVES

- To help the client understand the importance of keeping contact brief

- To develop a plan for what to say and to understand the importance of closely adhering to that plan

- To help the client increase her skill in responding effectively to telephone and face-to-face contacts with former abusive partners

MATERIALS

- None

HOMEWORK

- Listen to session audio-recordings.

- Continue to monitor and record negative self-talk.

- Practice PMR while listening to the PMR recording, twice a day.

- Do a body scan and over-tense and relax muscles when experiencing stress.

- Read and complete chapter 13 in *Healing the Trauma of Domestic Violence* (optional).

PROCEDURES CHECKLIST

1. ____ Introduction to managing unwanted contact

2. ____ Guidelines for assertive management of contacts with former partners

3. ____ Face-to-face contact

4. ____ Telephone contact

5. ____ When contact is necessary because of the children

6. ____ Role-playing conversations with an ex-partner

7. ____ Role-playing phone calls

8. ____ Creating a script for unanticipated face-to-face encounters

DETAILED PROCEDURES FOR MODULE 15

15.1. Introduction to Managing Unwanted Contacts

The prospect of running into or receiving phone calls from abusive ex-partners is a source of considerable anxiety and even dread for many formerly battered women. What would you say if—out of the blue—your abusive ex-partner came up to you or called you on the phone? Many women say things like "I don't know," "I don't think we'll be in contact," "I'd freeze," "I'd panic," "It depends on what he said," or "I'll deal with it if or when it happens."

If your relationship is over and you have no intention of reconciling, it is in your best interest to go ahead and come up with a plan for dealing with any future contact, even if it seems unlikely. In the event that the two of you are in contact, say the same thing no matter what your ex-partner says—that the relationship is over and there's nothing to talk about because your decision is final. Any further discussion would be pointless or a waste of time.

Most batterers are extremely manipulative, however, and will use a variety of strategies to influence their ex-wives or ex-girlfriends to change their minds about ending the relationship, or other things. If one strategy doesn't work, they'll try something else. For example, an abusive man may become extremely complimentary when he's trying to convince his ex to come back. If that doesn't work, he may say he can't live without her. If that doesn't work, he may try to lay a guilt trip on her. And if all else fails, he may fall back on raising his voice or becoming verbally abusive.

15.2. Guidelines for Assertive Management of Contacts with Former Partners

Fortunately, there are some straightforward general guidelines for assertive management of unwanted contact that can help you manage these situations. Following these guidelines will help you to remain calm and in control both in person and on the phone. There are four main things to keep in mind: First, carefully plan and rehearse exactly what you're going to say, even if it's unlikely that you will see or be contacted by your ex-partner, and then say nothing more than you plan to say. Second, keep the interaction as brief as possible. We're talking about a matter of seconds here, not minutes. Third, speak softly, slowly, and in a matter-of-fact way. If the contact is face-to-face, look him straight in the eye. And finally, stay with your script. Say the same things no matter what he says and no matter why he says he's contacting you.

In certain respects, this is a continuation of something we've already worked on: assertiveness. Remember, how you spend your time belongs solely to you. Your ex has no right to your time. The bottom line is to not tolerate disrespect and to keep any unwanted contact extremely brief.

15.3. Face-to-Face Contact

If your ex-partner approaches you in person, I recommend that you say something like this: "Our relationship is over. There is nothing to discuss. Please excuse me," and then walk away. If your ex continues to follow you and talk to you, you may choose to say something like "If you don't leave me alone, I will have no choice but to …," and then outline the consequence, such as calling a manager or security guard, screaming, or letting the police know he violated the restraining order.

269

15.4. Telephone Contact

If your ex contacts you by phone, handle the situation similarly. For example, you might say, "Our relationship is over and there's nothing to discuss. Please don't call me again. I have to go. Good-bye," and then hang up. Again, speak slowly, in a matter-of-fact way, and without raising your voice.

Sometimes ex-partners keep calling back anyway. If this happens, the next time he calls try saying something like "I have nothing more to say. Please don't call me anymore. If you call again and I hear your voice, I'm going to hang up without saying anything." I recommend that you answer all subsequent calls in an upbeat or cheery voice and then softly hang up if you hear your ex-partner's voice on the phone.

15.5. When Contact Is Necessary Because of the Children

This section only applies to women with children, and only to those whose abuser has joint custody, visitation rights, or other involvement with the children. If this isn't the case for a particular client, skip to section 15.6. **For some battered women, it's necessary to have regular or continuing contact with an abusive ex-partner because of child visitation rights or joint custody. Ex-partners often use these occasions, which are usually phone contacts, to dish out verbal abuse. They may take the opportunity to be accusatory, say cruel things, or try to degrade the woman, saying things like "You're too needy," "You're crazy," or "You're a bad mother." Under such circumstances, I advise you to tell your ex something like this: "You have a relationship with the children, but you don't have a relationship with me. If you bring up anything other than something important about the children, I'm going to say good-bye. And if you criticize me or put me down, I'm also going to say good-bye." If calls are primarily for the purpose of speaking to the children, don't say anything beyond "Hello." Then call to your child and say, "Your father's on the phone."**

15.6. Role-Playing Conversations with an Ex-Partner

If your anxiety is high when you speak with your ex-partner, your ability to function may be seriously impaired. This is particularly problematic if you don't have a plan of action. In that case, you may freeze or act impulsively in ways that aren't in your best interest.

Let's simulate some conversations with your ex-partner with a role-playing exercise. First, we'll work on telephone interactions, then we'll do face-to-face interactions. Initially, I'll play the role of you and you'll play the role of your ex. Then, we'll reverse roles.

15.7. Role-Playing Phone Calls

The phone interaction starts with the therapist saying "Ring, ring," picking up an imaginary phone, and saying "Hello." Then the client says what she thinks her ex-partner might say. The therapist responds as recommended above. After role-playing this way for a while, the therapist and client switch roles, with the client playing herself and the therapist playing the role of her ex-partner. This exercise allows the client to practice what she's going to say if and when she has contact with a former abuser. It also usually lowers the client's anxiety about the prospect of contact with her ex. Here's an example from the first round, where the therapist is playing the role of the client, and the client is playing her ex-partner, Jack. The series below reflects three steps: (1) following the script; (2) assertive escalation (stating the consequences if he calls back again); and (3) following through by simply hanging up. **In this role-play, when the phone rings you say, "It's Jack."**

Step 1

Therapist:	**"Ring, ring, ring! Hello!"** Speak in a cheery voice, but also as softly, calmly, and unemotionally as possible.
Client:	"It's Jack."
Therapist:	**"Hello, Jack. Jack, I want you to know that the relationship is over, and I'm not going to change my mind. Please don't call me anymore. I have to go now. Good-bye."** Hang up the phone very softly—this time and every time he calls.

Step 2

Therapist:	**"Ring, ring, ring! Hello!"** Again, speak in a cheery voice.
Client:	"It's Jack."
Therapist:	**"Jack, I told you that it's over and asked you not to call again. If you call again and I hear your voice, I'm just going to hang up. Please don't call. Good-bye."**

Step 3

Therapist:	**"Ring, ring, ring! Hello!"** Again, speak in a cheery voice.
Client:	"It's Jack."
Therpist:	Hang up the phone very softly. If you hang it up softly enough, he won't know whether you've hung up and he may continue to talk into an empty receiver. This will be a bigger inconvenience for your ex than for you. He'll have to redial your number, and all you have to do is say hello and then hang up.

It's extremely important that you follow through completely on this step of hanging up without saying anything. Batterers can be very creative in coming up with things to talk about to tempt, seduce, or intimidate you into staying on the line and getting involved in a conversation.

One woman's ex repeatedly called her at work. Each time he called, she just hung up after hearing his voice. Finally she decided the line had to be available for business callers and told her manager. The next time her ex called, the manager answered and loudly said, "Who is this?" Her ex was so flustered that he gave his name. Shortly thereafter he finally agreed to the divorce she'd been requesting.

15.8. Creating a Script for Unanticipated Face-to-Face Encounters

Now let's talk about what you would do if you ran into your partner at a public place, like the supermarket. How do you think you'd react? It's extremely important that you have a plan for what you'll say and what you'll do, even if it's highly unlikely that you'll see him. You can take an approach similar to that outlined for phone calls.

As before, this example uses the name Jack, but it's best to supply the name of the client's ex. Speak as softly, calmly, and unemotionally as possible. For example, you might say, "Hi, Jack. Our relationship is over and I have nothing to say to you. Please excuse me." Then turn around and walk away. If he follows and continues to talk to you, reiterate what you said: "The relationship is over, and I'm not going to change my mind. Good-bye, Jack. Good luck." If he still continues to follow you, say, "If you don't leave me alone, I'll have no choice but to ..." and then outline the consequences, such as calling a manager or security guard, screaming, or letting the court know that he violated the restraining order.

Again, if you've decided that the relationship is over, there's nothing to talk about no matter what your ex says. For example, if he tries to get you to change your mind or disputes your reasons for ending the relationship, there's still nothing to talk about because you've made your decision. Any further discussion would be pointless or a waste of time. As a result, your brief script of what you'll say will be appropriate no matter what he says.

Was this training on managing unwanted or stressful contacts useful for you? What did you get out of this discussion of managing unwanted contacts? If you'd like more practice, ask a friend or relative to do some similar role-playing exercises with you.

CONCLUDING REMARKS

This module is an excellent conclusion to the earlier work on assertiveness training. Interacting with a former abuser is one of the most challenging interactions for a formerly abused woman. Her success in role-playing the interaction and then following her plan when actually dealing with a former abuser will be very empowering. It also calls upon many of the other lessons she's learned in the course of cognitive trauma therapy, such as overcoming learned helplessness and challenging guiding fictions. If a client has difficulty with the role-playing exercise or expresses concern that she won't be able to follow through in a real interaction with her ex, encourage her to continue the role-playing exercise with friends or family members.

Managing Anger

Managing anger is the first of the optional modules. This module is ordinarily conducted if the client continues to express anger, at least occasionally, in the course of therapy. Ideally, handout 1.3, on letting go of anger, is given to the client at the end of the session just prior to beginning the anger module so she can complete it as homework and bring it to the session on anger. But if this isn't done, the client can complete the worksheet during the session. This homework is initially assigned at the first session because, for at least some clients, completing this handout serves to dissipate anger. Clients with ongoing anger issues are to complete it a second time before this session.

OBJECTIVES

■ For the client to see that getting or staying angry isn't in her best interest and only causes emotional pain for her—while not causing pain to her abuser

■ For the client to realize that most anger is a secondary reaction to a more fundamental emotion, such as fear or frustration

■ For the client to understand that letting go of anger involves a conscious decision to stop ruminating about an injustice or stop retaliating against the perceived source of one's anger

■ For the client to learn that chronic anger is often associated with poor health and a variety of medical conditions

MATERIALS

- Is Anger Worth the Hangover? Strategies for Letting Go (a fresh copy of handout 1.3; given as a homework assignment at the previous session)

HOMEWORK

- Listen to session audio-recordings.

- Continue to monitor and record negative self-talk.

- Practice PMR while listening to the PMR recording, twice a day.

- Do a body scan and over-tense and relax muscles when experiencing stress.

- Read and complete chapter 3 in *Healing the Trauma of Domestic Violence* (optional).

PROCEDURES CHECKLIST

1. _____ Introduction to anger, a hybrid emotion

2. _____ Discussion of whether anger is ever helpful or beneficial

3. _____ Explaining that most anger is a secondary emotional experience

4. _____ Chronic anger and health

5. _____ Homework review (handout 1.3, Is Anger Worth the Hangover?)

6. _____ Elaborating on item 2 on the handout

7. _____ Elaborating on item 5 on the handout

8. _____ Elaborating on item 6 on the handout

9. _____ Concluding thoughts on the exercise

10. _____ Explaining that anger offers relief from more painful emotions

11. _____ Angry feelings aren't evidence for angry conclusions

12. _____ Examples illustrating that an absence of anger can help ward off PTSD

DETAILED PROCEDURES FOR MODULE 16

16.1. Introduction to Anger, a Hybrid Emotion

Now we're going to address the issue of anger. Anger is the flip side of guilt. As we've discussed, guilt is an unpleasant feeling plus the belief that you should have thought, felt, or acted differently. Anger is an unpleasant feeling plus the belief that *someone else* should have thought, felt, or acted differently. By the way, do you hear all of those "shoulds"?

Both guilt and anger are hybrid emotions because both have a feeling part and a thinking part. In guilt, the finger is pointed at yourself, whereas in anger, it's pointed at someone else. I'll explain several ways in which anger generally isn't good for you, but for starters, consider that anger interferes with the ability to overcome PTSD—whether or not your anger is legitimate or justified. Even if you have every right to be angry, it's in your best interest to let go of your anger.

16.2. Discussion of Whether Anger Is Ever Healthy or Beneficial

Do you agree that anger isn't in your best interest—that you'd be better off if you could get rid of your anger or weren't angry anymore? How could your anger possibly benefit you in terms of promoting your long-term happiness? The point is not whether your anger is legitimate or justified. The target of your anger may very well deserve some kind of punishment. But to stop being angry is not letting someone off the hook. That person may still deserve punishment.

Some therapists and victim services providers believe that anger is a healthy and adaptive emotion for battered women who are safely out of an abusive relationship. Chronic abuse can leave some women so completely numb that they're unable to express any kind of negative feelings and continue to tolerate disrespect and violations of their rights. Feeling anger is a healthy response when it stirs a woman to get out of an abusive relationship. In addition, it is far better to express anger than to keep it bottled up inside, which almost always contributes to depression and low self-esteem. So, to a limited extent, anger may be viewed as a healthy, temporary bridge to self-empowerment, and to some extent, expressing it may offer relief from depression.

To overcome your PTSD, it is essential that you be able to experience unpleasant feelings and express dissatisfaction. If you can't get in touch with your negative feelings, you may be unwittingly allowing yourself to tolerate being treated with disrespect. However, it is very important for you to know that you don't have to express anger to express dissatisfaction or negative feelings.

16.3. Explaining That Anger Is a Secondary Emotional Experience

Most anger is a secondary emotional experience, in that it's usually a reaction to a more fundamental emotional experience, such as fear or frustration, that's associated with a problem. Anger can be viewed as a strategy for dealing with a more fundamental problem. Consider the following example: Jane is looking forward to a can of soda she's been keeping in the refrigerator. She goes to get it, but it's not there. Jane's initial reaction is frustration or disappointment—a form of distress, which is a fundamental or relatively pure emotion. Then Jane says, "Who the heck took my soda? That really pisses me off!"

When we discussed assertiveness, I emphasized the importance of expressing dissatisfaction in terms of *distress*, saying something like "I'm upset," "I'm frustrated," or "My feelings are hurt." This approach is more likely to direct the focus of your thoughts and the conversation toward the problem and how it can be solved than toward the person perceived to be the source of the problem. If your anger involves wants and needs that aren't being met, it's important to express this in a very direct and assertive but nonaggressive manner. We'll take a closer look at how to do this a little later on.

A major problem associated with expressing anger is that it typically escalates conflict and alienates the person who is the target of the anger (e.g., Kubany, Bauer, Richard, & Muraoka, 1995). Expressing anger is unlikely to influence the target of your anger in a positive way, and unlikely to lead to the outcome you desire.

16.4. Chronic Anger and Health

There's another reason why you may want to learn to let go of anger. In addition to perpetuating PTSD, chronic anger can also have negative effects on physical health. For example, as a group, Vietnam veterans with PTSD are known to be very angry and cynical, and they also have far more medical problems than Vietnam veterans without PTSD. If you let go of your anger, you'll probably live longer because the chronic personality pattern known as cynical hostility is a risk factor for a variety of medical problems and premature death (Friedman, 1992).

16.5. Homework Review

The following script uses the client's completed homework, handout 1.3, Is Anger Worth the Hangover? If the client hasn't completed the handout, ask her to answer the questions off the top of her head as you proceed through the following script. In that case, ask the client to read each question aloud and then respond to it. In either case, pause to elaborate on the questions indicated in the script below.

I'd like to do an exercise with you using the handout Is Anger Worth the Hangover? The statements in this exercise challenge the ways you may have been thinking about anger in the past and provide tips or strategies for breaking the anger habit. The ideas it conveys make sense and appeal to most women and typically increase their motivation to let go of their anger. Even if you rarely experience anger, this exercise may increase your understanding of why anger is often toxic, and not just for battered women.

How did this exercise go for you? What did you get out of it? Let's go through it together. I'd like you to read the statements out loud. Then read your answers, and expand or elaborate on your answers if you wish. I may have some comments, too.

16.6. Elaborating on Item 2

For item 2, give a couple of examples: During the O. J. Simpson murder trial, did you ever see Ron Goldman's sister or father being interviewed on TV? Both of them were so angry and suffering so much. It was as if the anger were eating away at them like some acid. Research has shown that rape victims who were more angry exhibited less fear and facial expressions of distress during prolonged exposure but benefited less from the therapy than victims who were less angry (Foa et al., 1995). Ultimately, their anger stood in the way of their recovery.

16.7. Elaborating on Item 5

For item 5, elaborate along these lines: If you aren't planning to do anything to change the situation or to correct an injustice, anger is a waste of your time. Are you going to get involved in a campaign to eliminate some injustice or see to it that the perpetrator is punished? Even if you do, is it in your best interest to proceed by filing a lawsuit or pressing charges? It's important to realize that you might not win. For example, the lawsuit might not be successful or the defendant might be found not guilty. Is pursuing a righteous cause worth your time and energy even if you don't win? If not, it may be a waste of your time and energy to devote it to being angry.

A woman pressed charges of abuse of a household member against an ex-boyfriend. She became extremely angry because he kept getting postponements to appear in court on the charges. Her therapist challenged her to examine whether it was worth all of her efforts and frustrations, knowing that the case might be drawn out indefinitely and that in the end he might not even be convicted. The woman said it was worth pursuing regardless of the outcome. Her therapist then encouraged her not to become upset if there were further postponements or if her ex-boyfriend was found not guilty. A cause may be worth pursuing for its own sake, but anger won't be good for you in any case, and it won't advance your cause.

16.8. Elaborating on Item 6

For item 6, provide some examples: **I'll give you some examples that illustrate how letting go of anger involves a conscious decision. There was a segment on the TV news show Dateline about a physician who was studying how the brain functions by working with patients who had severe brain injuries. Many times, certain parts of the brain will take over functions previously performed by parts of the brain that have been destroyed. However, one patient had a part of his brain destroyed that wasn't compensated for by other parts of his brain. His problem was that he had a very short memory. He could only remember the last minute of recent events. For example, if he was introduced to someone and the person left for more than a minute and then came back, he couldn't remember that he had previously met the person. The doctor said that this patient had absolutely no anger because anger requires an image or a memory with a running commentary or rumination. This person had no memories, so he was unable to ruminate or obsess on them. This underscores how choosing not to ruminate about past injustices can help with letting go of anger.**

Optional example of solution-oriented attitude: In spite of this man's handicap, he found a way to do something he'd always enjoyed: telling and hearing jokes. Given his memory problem, you may wonder how he could do this. He had a notebook that said "Jokes" on the cover. The cover reminded him to tell jokes he had written in the notebook, and when someone else told him a new joke, he would write it in his notebook immediately.

Here's another example: For years, a woman wanted nothing more than to have a career in research. Finally she got a job that was just what she had been looking for. After six months, however, she wanted nothing more than to get away from someone at work whom she disliked immensely. Around this time, this woman took a vacation to visit her brother in northern California. They enjoyed bicycling together and were biking along a beautiful stretch of coastline on a cloudless day, and she was having a great time except for occasional intrusive thoughts about how this person at work had treated her maliciously and unfairly. Whenever she started ruminating about this person, she started getting herself worked up and stopped having fun. All of a sudden, she said to herself, "You are the last person on this planet I would invite on my vacation. Stop! Get out!"

She made a conscious decision to immediately distract herself and think about something else if negative thoughts, images, or memories started to creep into her mind or if she started ruminating about this person. She stopped the rumination, and the associated distress, anytime she realized what she was doing, and as a result, she was able to enjoy the rest of her vacation.

Years ago, a therapist had a disagreement with her supervisor late on Friday afternoon, and the conflict wasn't resolved when she left for the day. The soonest it could be resolved was when she went back to work on Monday. She said that she kept obsessing about what had happened and it was interfering with her ability to concentrate and to complete some important work she needed to finish by the end of the weekend. So she decided to use a behavior modification technique called thought stopping.

One of the most common thought-stopping techniques involves imagining yourself looking at a large stop sign or yelling "Stop!" at the top of your lungs and then shifting to a positive image, such as lying on the beach or taking a bubble bath. The therapist tried yelling "Stop!" to herself and then shifting to a positive image, but it wasn't working. She just wasn't able to get the unresolved incident out of her mind, and the time she was spending thinking about it wasn't solving anything. So she decided to punish the rumination by imagining herself doing something she disliked doing every time she started thinking about the conflict with her supervisor.

She lived in a third-floor condominium with no elevator and no washer or dryer, so she imagined herself doing her laundry. First she imagined herself putting her dirty clothes in a hamper. Then she imagined herself taking the hamper down to her car and driving to the laundromat. Next she imagined herself putting the clothes into a washer, then taking them out and putting them in a dryer, and then folding them. After imagining herself doing her laundry about five times, the ruminations started decreasing, and within a few hours she was able to concentrate on what she needed to do. She also made a deal with herself that she would spend fifteen minutes on Sunday night talking with a colleague about the best way to address the disagreement with her supervisor.

16.9. Concluding Thoughts on the Exercise

Do you agree that anger isn't in your best interest—that you would be better off if you could get rid of your anger? Getting the client to acknowledge that she would be better off letting go of anger is important because many clients think their anger is a legitimate emotion (for example, "He deserves my anger") and that they would be letting the person off the hook if they stopped being angry. If this is the case, the client isn't sufficiently motivated to learn how to stop being angry.

16.10. Explaining That Anger Offers Relief from More Painful Emotions

Anger may help to perpetuate PTSD because it provides relief from more painful emotions, such as fear or the sadness associated with acceptance of some loss. For example, hostile ruminations about wanting your abuser to suffer may be less painful than reexperiencing the fear associated with your victimization or the grief associated with the loss of your hopes and dreams for the relationship.

16.11. Angry Feelings Aren't Evidence for Angry Conclusions

The intensity of your feelings is not evidence for angry conclusions. For example, one veteran got up and shouted, "My father and brother have no redeeming qualities.

They're totally untrustworthy!" His therapist gently pointed out that his raised voice wasn't evidence that his father and brother couldn't be trusted. When talking about someone you're angry at, try not to use emotionally charged words and phrases, such as "maniac," "personality of a serial killer," "pig," "bastard," or "evil," whether or not the person is responsible for the injustice or whatever is causing your anger. Using emotionally charged words usually provides fuel for your anger, and as we've discussed, your anger ultimately has a greater negative impact on you than it does on the object of your anger.

16.12. Examples Illustrating That an Absence of Anger Can Ward Off PTSD

Here's some examples of people who had legitimate reasons to be extremely angry, but weren't. And although they had experienced terrible traumas, they also didn't have PTSD. If nothing else, these examples illustrate that trauma survivors without anger (and without guilt) have greater peace of mind and fewer symptoms than people who are angry. Consider the founder of Mothers Against Drunk Driving, Candy Lightner, whose daughter was killed by a drunk driver. If you ever saw her on TV, you could see that she wasn't angry. This just goes to show that you can believe in and pursue a just cause to undo some wrong without anger.

Another example is a woman who was molested by her father from early childhood until she finally left home at age twenty-six. She was referred for cognitive trauma therapy because of a nurse's knowledge of her long history of abuse. Amazingly, this woman had no PTSD symptoms and no depression. Also she had absolutely no anger toward her father—and no guilt. When she heard that her father was dying, she met with him, confronted him about the abuse, and forgave him.

Or consider a professional basketball player who saw his sister get brutally assaulted when he was eight and she was fifteen. His sister subsequently got into drugs, and influenced a younger sister to start using drugs, too. Both contracted HIV and both subsequently died from AIDS. The police caught the perpetrator of the assault, and he was sent to prison. At one point, the brother was planning to exact revenge on the perpetrator when he was released from prison. However, by the time the perpetrator was released, the brother had a change of heart. He had let go of his anger and concluded that nothing would be gained by exacting revenge.

Can you see how these people benefited by not getting stuck in anger? Does this seem worthwhile to you? What else did you get out of this discussion of anger?

CONCLUDING REMARKS

With most women, it is relatively easy to get them to acknowledge that getting angry is not in their best interest and that they would be better off if they had little or no anger. In addition, few women have problems due to acting on their anger, in that few women have problems associated with being verbally or physically aggressive.

Personality Characteristics
of Abusive Partners

This module is particularly important if the client's comments in the course of therapy suggest that her abusive partner clearly exhibited psychopathic or sociopathic tendencies. It is also indicated if the client took an inordinate amount of responsibility for making the relationship work or blamed herself for "choosing" an abusive partner. For a variety of reasons, many battered women with PTSD believe they chose their abusive ex-partner. Furthermore, they often think they have some kind of deficit in picking nonabusive partners, as many have had more than one abusive relationship. Friends, family, and unenlightened therapists may contribute to a woman's belief that she has poor skills in choosing good partners.

In this module, clients learn that they don't have a deficit in choosing a good partner and come to see that their partners chose them. Clients are almost always relieved to learn that their past experiences, which have left them mentally, emotionally, and socially wounded, make them an attractive prospect for abusive men, who are skilled at preying on vulnerable women. Clients learn about the characteristics of antisocial personality disorder (ASPD), which helps them understand that their relationship and the abuse they endured was more about their abuser than about themselves.

Ideally, handout 17.1, Characteristics of Abusive Partners, is given to the client at the end of the session just prior to beginning this module so the client can complete it as homework and bring it to the session on personality characteristics of abusive partners. If this isn't done, the client can complete the worksheet during the session.

OBJECTIVES

- To help the client realize that no woman would intentionally choose to be in an abusive relationship and that in most cases it is predatory men who do the choosing

- To help the client become aware of past experiences that may make a woman vulnerable to being seduced into an abusive relationship

- To familiarize the client with research suggesting that partners who are abusive are much more likely to exhibit characteristics of antisocial personality disorder

- To help the client realize that many batterers are probably incapable of having a healthy intimate relationship with anyone, and that their relationship may have been doomed from the start

MATERIALS

- Characteristics of Abusive Partners questionnaire (handout 17.1; given as a homework assignment at the previous session)

HOMEWORK

- Listen to session audio-recordings.

- Continue to monitor and record negative self-talk.

- Practice PMR while listening to the PMR recording, twice a day.

- Do a body scan and over-tense and relax muscles when experiencing stress.

PROCEDURES CHECKLIST

1. _____ Introduction and explanation that many battered women think they have bad judgment in their choice of romantic partners

2. _____ Estimates of the prevalence of antisocial personality disorder among men

3. _____ Explanation that predatory men usually do the choosing

4. ____ The problem with niceness

5. ____ Traits associated with niceness that may be risk factors for abuse

6. ____ Features of antisocial personality disorder

7. ____ Interpreting the client's responses to the Characteristics of Abusive Partners questionnaire (handout 17.1; assigned at previous session)

8. ____ Total disregard for the feelings of others

9. ____ The take-home message

DETAILED PROCEDURES FOR MODULE 17

17.1. Introduction and Explanation That Many Battered Women Think They Have Bad Judgment About Romantic Partners

When they start therapy, many battered women think they have bad judgment in their choice of romantic partners. For example, I've heard women say things like "Why do I pick that kind of man?" or "What is it that attracts me to this type of man?" Have you ever asked yourself such a question? For many battered women, this problem is compounded by supposedly well-meaning family, friends, and therapists who ask similar questions, like "Why do you choose these kinds of guys?" Has anyone ever asked you a question like this?

Whether well-intended or not, such questions blame the victim and are totally misguided. As we discuss this issue, you'll learn that you and other battered women didn't want, pick, or choose to be with an abusive man, either consciously or subconsciously. No one wants to suffer, and it is just plain wrong to suggest that any woman would choose to suffer or be in an abusive relationship.

17.2. Estimates of the Prevalence of Antisocial Personality Disorder Among Men

As of 2007, more than 250 battered women suffering from PTSD related to partner abuse had been treated with cognitive trauma therapy, the approach I'm using with you. Based on these women's accounts, almost all of their abusive partners could be characterized as psychopathic or sociopathic (Kubany et al., 2003; Kubany, Hill, et al., 2004). These men had many characteristics of antisocial personality disorder as defined by the American Psychiatric Association (1994).

What do you think the prevalence of antisocial personality disorder is among men in the general population? In other words, what percentage of men can be characterized as having psychopathic or antisocial personalities? The estimates made by battered women and victim services providers are typically quite high—rarely less than 25 to 30 percent, and many battered women think that most men have antisocial personalities. However, according to published research, the prevalence of antisocial personality disorder among men is only about 3 percent (Robins et al., 1984). Are you surprised?

Many of my clients have found this statistic hard to believe, especially in light of their own trauma history. For example, half of the women in the studies of cognitive trauma therapy had been physically hurt by more than one intimate partner, and most had been physically or sexually abused while growing up (Kubany et al., 2003; Kubany, Hill, et al., 2004).

17.3. Explanation That Predatory Men Usually Do the Choosing

So what do we conclude from all of this? Are we to conclude that, because the great majority of battered women undergoing cognitive trauma therapy are in relationships with sociopathic men, these women look for, find, and intentionally choose the 3 percent of men who have antisocial personalities as their boyfriends and husbands? Absolutely not.

Unfortunately, it appears that sociopathic men know how to identify women who are vulnerable to being battered, and that they are skillful in engaging them in relationships. These men seek out women who exhibit characteristics associated with vulnerability, much as lions prey on injured zebras.

17.4. The Problem with Niceness

So what are these characteristics that indicate a woman may be vulnerable to being seduced into an abusive relationship by means of deceit and manipulation? One of the hallmark signs that a woman may be vulnerable to interpersonal victimization is a personal quality I wouldn't want to change. It also happens to be one of the reasons why women who have been abused are enjoyable clients to work with. What do you think this personal quality might be? Right. Being nice. How often have you been told that you're nice?

Some women say, "Yeah, too nice." In fact, formerly battered women are some of the nicest people I've ever met. However, niceness is correlated with several other traits that indicate vulnerability to revictimization, explaining why predatory men seek out women who are nice.

17.5. Traits Associated with Niceness That May Be Risk Factors for Abuse

Many women who are very nice have prior histories of physical, sexual, or emotional abuse and are overly concerned with avoiding disapproval. In their efforts to avoid conflict, they are often passive and unassertive. They may have a hard time saying no or standing up for their rights in other ways, and they may allow themselves to be treated with an inordinate amount of disrespect. In addition, many very nice women accept an excessive amount of responsibility when things go wrong and are easily made to feel guilty, which also makes them inclined to go along with the wishes of other people. Do any of these characteristics sound familiar to you?

Predatory men gravitate toward women with these qualities. One study investigated factors associated with revictimization in a sample of women who had all been sexually abused as children (Classen, Field, Koopman, Nevill-Manning, & Spiegel, 2001). The study found that women who were sexually abused in the preceding six months had more difficulty being assertive and were overly responsible and overly nurturing. The researchers concluded that these women tend to place the needs of others before their own needs and thus have a hard time saying no. They also suggested that these women may have lower self-esteem or that they may be afraid of the consequences of saying no.

This sounds like a description of battered women with PTSD, who often have spent a large part of their lives taking care of other people at their own expense, who are easily made to feel guilty, which can be used to influence them, and who have deficits in sorely needed self-advocacy and assertiveness skills.

17.6. Features of ASPD

The essential feature of antisocial personality disorder is a pervasive, long-standing pattern of disregard for and violation of the rights of others. To receive a diagnosis of antisocial personality disorder, a person must have a history of violating the rights of others beginning in childhood or adolescence and exhibit three or more of the following seven antisocial characteristics: repeatedly performing acts that are grounds for arrest; repeatedly lying, using aliases, or conning others for pleasure or profit; impulsivity or failure to plan ahead; repeated physical fights or assaults; reckless disregard for the safety of oneself or others; irresponsibility in regard to work or finances; and lack of remorse (American Psychiatric Association, 1994).

17.7. Interpreting the Client's Responses to the Characteristics of Abusive Partners Questionnaire

The homework I gave you last time, the Characteristics of Abusive Partners questionnaire, assesses these characteristics. Your answers can help us determine whether antisocial personality disorder was an issue with your ex. The first question looks into whether your ex-partner started violating the rights of others in childhood or early adolescence. Did your ex-partner start violating the rights of others before his fifteenth birthday? If the client says she doesn't know, explain that this isn't unusual: That's okay. Many women can't answer this question because they don't know much if anything about their abusive partner's childhood history.

Now let's examine the degree to which your abusive partner exhibited the seven antisocial characteristics I listed a few minutes ago. These are assessed by items 2 through 8 on the questionnaire. For each of these items, consider the antisocial characteristic present if you indicated that your partner exhibited the characteristic at least occasionally. Among questions 2 through 8, how many did you answer with "occasionally"? How many of the seven questions did you answer with "often" or "almost always"? The more often your abusive partner exhibited these traits, or the more outrageous, flagrant, or harmful his acts were, the more likely it is that he has an antisocial personality and would meet diagnostic criteria for antisocial personality disorder.

Optional: You may ask the client to read her responses.

To put your responses on this questionnaire into perspective, let me tell you about the results when forty-three women at a battered women's shelter filled out the questionnaire (Kubany et al., 2003). Only fifteen of forty-three women (34 percent) knew enough about their partner's childhood history to answer whether or not he violated the rights of others prior to age fifteen. However, fourteen of the fifteen women who did answer this question indicated that their partner violated the rights of others at least "often" before age fifteen.

Thirty-eight of the forty-three women (88 percent) reported that their partners exhibited at least three of the seven antisocial characteristics, suggesting that their partners had antisocial personalities. The average number of antisocial characteristics exhibited was five.

That same study also asked twenty-five women who were friends or relatives of the forty-three women at the shelter to fill out the questionnaire. None of these women had ever been abused by an intimate partner. Among these twenty-five women, only one had a partner who exhibited at least three antisocial characteristics—that's just 4 percent, compared to the 88 percent among the battered women. And twenty-three of the women had partners who exhibited no antisocial personality disorder characteristics at all. Based on the women's rating, this study suggests that the personality characteristics of men who batter are radically different from those of men who don't.

17.8. Total Disregard for the Feelings of Others

In their work with battered women, the developers of cognitive trauma therapy have noted time and again the total disregard that many abusive partners have for the feelings of others. Regardless of what they may say, many batterers, and possibly most of them, genuinely do not care or feel bad if other people, including their wives and girlfriends, suffer. The other side of the coin is that many battered women simply cannot comprehend that abusive men are so utterly lacking in empathy. They often say things like "When is he going to realize that what he's doing is wrong?" or "When is he going to see the error of his ways?" The best response would certainly be "Don't hold your breath."

You would have to appreciate this observation that many batterers "just don't care" in order to comprehend or make "sense" out of the behavior of the man in the following story: One night, a woman returned home to find her twenty-two-month-old daughter motionless in bed. An ambulance was called, and the girl was taken to a medical center, where she was pronounced dead. Her husband (the girl's stepfather) was suspected of killing the girl and was subsequently charged with the murder. The woman testified that after she and her then husband returned home, he made a bizarre request. She said that he asked her if she wanted to have sex, and told her that it would make her forget about what had happened.

This man was so sociopathic that not only was he not upset by having murdered his stepdaughter, he couldn't even appreciate why his wife was so upset. This is certainly an extreme example, but it may help explain how many batterers can so callously and atrociously violate the rights of the girlfriends and wives they claim to love.

17.9. The Take-Home Message

There are two really important things that I hope you learned from this discussion of the personality traits of abusive men: that you've never been attracted to abusive men, and that if your partner had an antisocial personality, your relationship was doomed from the start. Let's review each of those points just a bit.

When you first met your abusive partner, he was likable or charming. The man you were attracted to wasn't abusive, and you never would have chosen to get involved with him if you knew he was abusive. Rather, your abuser chose you, and using deceit and manipulation, he won you over. You never would have even gone out with him if you had known what he was really like. If a colleague, or anyone else, asks me what attracts women to men who batter, I may answer, "Is an injured zebra looking for lions, or does a lion know how to identify injured zebras?" This is how predation works: In the grasslands of Africa, lions run through large herds of zebras, ignoring all of them until they detect a zebra who's acting differently or vulnerable. These are the zebras the lions target as easy prey.

Now let's review what it means if your partner had an antisocial personality. Put simply, men with antisocial personalities are incapable of having a healthy and lasting intimate relationship with anyone on the planet. Because of this, your relationship was doomed when you first met. There's no way you could be responsible for the failure of your relationship, because you never had the power or capability to make it successful. Consider this: What if your responses on the Characteristics of Abusive Partners questionnaire were about you rather than about your ex-partner? If that were the case, do you think you would be capable of having a healthy and lasting relationship with a guy?

What did you learn from this discussion of the characteristics of abusive partners and antisocial personality disorder?

CONCLUDING REMARKS

For many clients, it's a huge relief to learn that they aren't doomed to always choose bad partners. Upon learning that the abuse was more about their partner than about themselves, some clients cry. If this happens, encourage the client to let it all out, and gently reiterate that the abuse was not about her to help maximize her relief.

Handout 17.1: Characteristics of Abusive Partners

Client Initials: _____   Date: _____

Please answer the questions below in relation to a current or former intimate partner who was physically or emotionally abusive toward you. Unless otherwise indicated, respond based on whether he has ever exhibited the behavior, whether in the past or at present. If you need more space, you may use an extra sheet of blank paper.

1. **Has he disregarded and violated the rights of others?**

   Never   Seldom   Occasionally   Often   Almost   Don't know
                                                                always

   If at least seldom: Did he start disregarding the rights of others before his fifteenth birthday? (Examples include aggression toward people and animals, destruction of property, deceitfulness or theft, or serious violation of rules.)

   Never   Seldom   Occasionally   Often   Almost   Don't know
                                                                always

   If at least seldom: Please describe specific examples in which he disregarded and violated the rights of others before his fifteenth birthday.

   _____

   _____

   _____

   _____

2. **Has he done things that are grounds for arrest, whether he was arrested or not?** (Examples include illegal drug use, theft, or assault of anyone, including family members.)

   Never   Seldom   Occasionally   Often   Almost   Don't know
                                                                always

   If at least seldom: Please describe specific examples of things he did that would be grounds for arrest.

   _____

   _____

   _____

   _____

If you didn't describe acts where he threatened to kill you, seriously harm you, or physically hurt you, or made you engage in sexual behavior against your will, please describe examples of this kind of behavior.

_____

_____

_____

_____

3. **Has he been deceitful, as indicated by lying, use of aliases, or conning others for personal profit or pleasure?**

Never   Seldom   Occasionally   Often   Almost always   Don't know

If at least seldom: Please describe specific examples of lying, use of aliases, or conning others for personal profit or pleasure.

_____

_____

_____

_____

4. **Is he impulsive or does he fail to plan ahead?** (For example, does he do things on the spur of the moment without consideration of the consequences to himself or others?)

Never   Seldom   Occasionally   Often   Almost always   Don't know

If at least seldom: Please describe specific examples of his impulsiveness or failure to plan ahead.

_____

_____

_____

_____

5. **Is he irritable and aggressive, as indicated by physical fights or assaults?** (This includes beating you or your children.)

Never   Seldom   Occasionally   Often   Almost always   Don't know

If at least seldom: Please describe specific examples of physical fights or assaults.

_____

_____

_____

_____

6. **Has he displayed a reckless disregard for his own safety or the safety of others?** (Examples include drunk driving, repeatedly speeding, multiple accidents, or neglect of a child that puts the child in danger.)

Never   Seldom   Occasionally   Often   Almost always   Don't know

If at least seldom: Please describe specific examples of ways he displayed a reckless disregard for his own safety or the safety of others.

_____

_____

_____

_____

7. **Is he or was he consistently irresponsible, as indicated by failure to maintain consistent employment or honor financial obligations?** (Examples include repeated absences from work not explained by illness, extended unemployment even when jobs were available, defaulting on debts, or failing to provide child support.)

Never   Seldom   Occasionally   Often   Almost always   Don't know

If at least seldom: Please describe specific examples of his failure to maintain consistent work behavior or honor financial obligations.

_____

_____

_____

_____

8. **Has he displayed a lack of remorse, as indicated by being indifferent to or rationalizing having hurt, mistreated, or stolen from another?** (Examples include blaming the victim, minimizing the consequences of his actions, or failure to make amends.)

| Never | Seldom | Occasionally | Often | Almost always | Don't know |

If at least seldom: Please describe specific examples of his being indifferent to or rationalizing having hurt, mistreated, or stolen from another.

_____

_____

_____

_____

Countering Ideas of Denial and Codependence

This module is for clients who have referred to themselves as being codependent or in denial or have been labeled by someone else (for example, a therapist, friend, or relative) as being codependent or in denial. Many battered women come to therapy believing they are codependent and that they stayed in the abusive relationship as long as they did because they were in denial. In this module, clients learn that the terms "codependent" and "denial" are useless and explain nothing about their behavior. In fact, these terms may be damaging, as they imply blame for the continued abuse and only serve to maintain low self-esteem, a poor self-image, and unassertive behavior. Clients regularly experience relief upon learning that there are simpler and more logical explanations for their behavior that aren't laden with blame. This module also offers the opportunity to reinforce previous education about hindsight bias and assertive communication.

OBJECTIVES

- To teach the client that denial and codependence are neither relevant nor meaningful in CTT

- To teach the client that denial and codependence are nothing more than summary labels for certain behaviors and do not explain why a person behaves as she does

MATERIALS

- Denial: A Tautological Concept That Doesn't Explain Anything (handout 18.1)

HOMEWORK

- Listen to session audio-recordings.

- Continue to monitor and record negative self-talk.

- Practice PMR while listening to the PMR recording, twice a day.

- Do a body scan and over-tense and relax muscles when experiencing stress.

PROCEDURES CHECKLIST

1. _____ Introduction to the concepts of denial and codependence

2. _____ What it means to say that someone is in denial

3. _____ Denial—a defense mechanism from Freudian psychology

4. _____ Two levels of perception

5. _____ The law of parsimony

6. _____ The simplest explanation of beliefs about denial

7. _____ Codependence—a loosely defined pop psychology concept

8. _____ The distinction between medical and psychological diagnoses

9. _____ The circular logic involved in the concept of denial

10. _____ The circular logic involved in the concept of codependence

11. _____ Responding to being labeled as codependent or in denial

12. _____ Why denial doesn't apply to batterers

DETAILED PROCEDURES FOR MODULE 18

18.1. Introduction to Denial and Codependence

Has anyone, yourself included, ever said that you were codependent or in denial? Many therapists view their battered women clients as codependent or in denial, and many of those clients agree. If someone referred to you as being codependent or in denial, how would you feel? Probably not very good. These terms are somewhat demeaning, suggesting that there is something wrong with the person. As you'll learn, the terms "codependence" and "denial" don't apply to you. There are simpler and more straightforward ways of explaining or understanding the behaviors involved in these two so-called personality traits.

18.2. What It Means to Say Someone Is in Denial

First, let's talk about denial. If a formerly battered woman said, "When I was in an abusive relationship with my ex-husband, I was in denial," What would it mean? Do you think it might mean that, at some level, she thought she knew that she was being mistreated and that it was in her best interest to leave the relationship, but she stayed anyway? Yes. It means she knew the situation called for corrective action, but she couldn't accept this knowledge, so she unconsciously or subconsciously denied or disregarded it. Or maybe it means that she kidded herself, made excuses, rationalized, or told herself that the knowledge she possessed—that her husband wasn't going to change, for example—wasn't correct.

18.3. Denial—A Defense Mechanism from Freudian Psychology

Denial, a psychiatric concept that has filtered down into widespread popular use, was first introduced by Sigmund Freud, the famous Austrian psychoanalyst who had a profound influence on Western psychological thought in the twentieth century. According to Freud, denial is one of several defense mechanisms that protect us from unacceptable unconscious and instinctual impulses while allowing partial gratification of these impulses.

Freud had a very morbid view of human nature and believed that all human beings are fundamentally motivated by life instincts, which are unconscious urges for sexual expression and aggression, and death instincts, or unconscious urges for self-destruction. These instincts are constantly striving for release. Based on this line of thought, some early psychoanalytic thinkers used masochism, or the unconscious desire to be mistreated, to explain why many women remain in relationships with abusive partners (e.g., Snell, Rosenwald, & Robey, 1964). Do you think you have an unconscious desire to be mistreated? Of course not! Who would want to be mistreated?

Applying Freud's concept of denial, a woman could deny that she was battered, thereby allowing her to stay in the relationship and suffer as a partial gratification of her death instinct. Unfortunately, some therapists still buy into this line of thought and actually tell women things like "Subconsciously, you want to be revictimized."

18.4. Two Levels of Perception

For denial to be a valid psychiatric phenomenon requires that people perceive reality at two different levels or in two different ways, with no direct communication between the two. An example is the notion that the conscious mind doesn't know what the unconscious mind is thinking. In the 1950s, some psychologists tried to demonstrate that this was indeed the case, that people defend themselves against unacceptable unconscious impulses by dividing their perception in this way. But in the end, results of this research didn't support the notion that we operate with relatively independent dual levels of perception (Mischel, 1986).

18.5. The Law of Parsimony

The developers of cognitive trauma therapy believe it's best to use clinical practices that have been shown or proven to work, and that the simplest explanation for clinical observations is usually the correct one. In the philosophy of science, the law of parsimony stipulates that scientists seek the simplest level of explanation that can account for or explain all of the data, and not go to a more complex level if a simpler explanation will do the job. When you look at denial from this standpoint, it's clear that it involves an overly complex explanation for why battered women remain in abusive relationships.

18.6. A Simple Explanation of Beliefs About Denial

Now I'll offer you a parsimonious explanation for why many mental health professionals and many formerly battered women falsely conclude that the women were in denial when they stayed in abusive relationships. This explanation goes back to our discussion of guilt. A very important reason why many formerly battered women think they were in denial is that they're remembering themselves knowing things they didn't actually learn until later. The culprit here is hindsight bias: These women are allowing knowledge they acquired after finally leaving an abusive relationship to filter back into their memory of what they think they knew before they left. Back when they were still enduring the relationship, they really did think their partner would change and things would improve.

18.7. Codependence—A Loosely Defined Pop Psychology Concept

The concept of codependence didn't originate in mainstream psychology. In fact, it isn't mentioned in most textbooks on abnormal psychology, and it isn't identified as a personality disorder in the standard diagnostic manual used in the United States. The concept of codependence was originally developed to help account for the dysfunctional patterns of interpersonal behavior among family members of alcoholics or drug addicts.

Many behavioral scientists view codependence as a pop psychology term, and it certainly has been popularized in many unscholarly self-help books for women. In truth, codependence is a loosely described phenomenon at best, and as such is unhelpful.

Still, in order to dispel the myths surrounding codependence, it's important to understand how the term is usually used. Women characterized as being codependent have been described as enabling their partner by taking responsibility for his problems and even supporting his addictive habits by drinking or using drugs with him. They're also seen as making excuses for their partner or shielding him from the consequences of his actions. They've been described as being very unassertive, failing to advocate for their own wants and needs, and taking an excessive degree of responsibility for the relationship. Some of these observations may also apply to many battered women, but in the context of cognitive trauma therapy, people are never referred to as codependent, either in session or anywhere else. I encourage you to not use this confusing and potentially harmful term to describe yourself or anyone else.

18.8. The Distinction Between Medical and Psychological Diagnoses

With diseases and medical problems, diagnostic labels typically say something about the underlying cause of the problem and also have implications for treatment. For example, to say that someone has a cold is a summary label for a collection of symptoms, such as fever, chest congestion, and green phlegm. The label suggests an underlying cause, such as a bacterial infection, and as such, points to a course of treatment: antibiotics.

This model doesn't apply to psychological or psychiatric problems. Terms like "codependence" and "denial" say nothing about the causes of the behavior to which they refer, nor do they suggest a solution or course of treatment. For the most part, psychological labels and psychiatric diagnoses are little more than a form of shorthand for a collection of observed behaviors.

18.9. The Circular Logic Involved in the Concept of Denial

Let's take a closer look at the term "denial" and what it really means. Consider the following conversation between two people talking about a battered woman: The first person says, "She's in denial," to which the other person responds, "How can you tell?" The first person answers, "She's staying in an abusive relationship, and yet she says she's not a battered woman." When the second person asks, "Why is she staying, and why is she saying she's not battered?" the first person responds, "I already told you. It's because she's in denial."

What we have here is a tautology, or circular logic. Denial is defined as "staying and saying she isn't battered," and staying and saying she isn't battered is taken as evidence or proof of denial. The label "in denial" isn't an explanation. In that hypothetical conversation, the first person hasn't offered any evidence that the hypothesized trait of denial is the cause of this woman staying in the relationship. **This illustration depicts that circular logic.** Give the client handout 18.1, Denial: A Tautological Concept That Doesn't Explain Anything.

18.10. The Circular Logic Involved in the Concept of Codependence

Like denial, the label "codependence" is based on circular logic. To say that a woman is codependent because she's unassertive with her boyfriend and thinks she's responsible for changing him is nothing more than a tautology. There is nothing in this statement to suggest that some underlying or unconscious need to be codependent causes her to be unassertive or to believe that she's responsible for changing her partner.

Sometimes the catchier or more esoteric a new "diagnostic" label is, the more likely it is that people will believe it really does explain why something happens. The term "codependent" is an example; it's very catchy. Another example is the label "hyperkinesis." Would you be more likely to believe that your son has a disorder if a doctor or psychiatrist says he has hyperkinesis than if you're told he's hyperactive? Why should that be? In fact, hyperkinesis and hyperactivity are synonymous. In Greek, hyper means "excessive," and kinesis means "movement."

18.11. Responding to Being Labeled Codependent or in Denial

From now on, if anyone ever calls you codependent or says you're in denial, call upon your assertive communication skills. These labels are unhelpful and even disrespectful. I advise you to respond with something like "That's not a nice thing to say. And just because you say I'm codependent doesn't mean it's true. I would appreciate your not saying that again."

18.12. Why Denial Doesn't Apply to Batterers

Many therapists and counselors of battered women have lost count of the times that clients have said that their partner blamed them for the abuse, and that their partner really believed it. At first glance, this may seem to suggest that the batterers were in denial. When a client says something like this, I usually tell her that her partner was probably in denial only to the extent that he was consciously refusing to admit something he knew to be true. Batterers lie because they don't want to change their behavior. There is no unconscious denial here.

What did you learn from this discussion of codependence and denial?

CONCLUDING REMARKS

Clients are never upset after this module. In fact, they're usually relieved and happy to learn that codependence and denial are confusing, often harmful, labels that don't apply to them.

Handout 18.1: Denial: A Tautological Concept That Doesn't Explain Anything

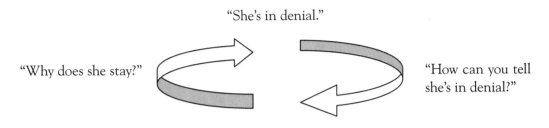

"She's in denial."

"Why does she stay?"

"How can you tell she's in denial?"

"She was abused and she stays."

Making Important Decisions

This module is for clients who have been contemplating but haven't yet made some important decision (for example, whether to get serious in a new relationship, whether to go back to school or get a job, or whether to press charges or file a lawsuit against a former partner). It will also be useful for clients who have displayed difficulty with decision making in the course of their therapy. In this module, clients are introduced to a method of decision making based not on what will make them feel better in the short term, but on an intellectual or logical analysis of the likely short-term and long-term positive and negative consequences of each contemplated course of action. Regardless of what they finally choose to do, if clients go through this kind of analysis they are less likely to be caught off guard by the implications their decisions have on their lives.

OBJECTIVES

■ For the client to learn that poor decisions are often based on immediate short-term benefits, whereas the benefits of better decisions often occur later but are more lasting

■ For the client to learn several guidelines for making decisions that promote her best interest

■ For the client to learn a method for making important decisions based on logic, reason, and rational thinking

■ For the client to utilize the recommended method for making decisions to analyze the potential positive and negative consequences of all of the options she considers

MATERIALS

- Positive and Negative Consequences of Leaving or Staying in an Abusive Relationship (handout 19.1)

- Worksheet for Making Important Decisions (handout 19.2)

HOMEWORK

- Listen to session audio-recordings.

- Continue to monitor and record negative self-talk.

- Practice PMR while listening to the PMR recording, twice a day.

- Do a body scan and over-tense and relax muscles when experiencing stress.

- Utilize the recommended decision-making method for analyzing the short-term and long-term positive and negative consequences of an important decision (optional).

PROCEDURES CHECKLIST

1. _____ Introduction to decision making

2. _____ Short-term gratification versus long-term benefits

3. _____ The importance of postponing important decisions until you're calm and rational

4. _____ Guidelines for making decisions that promote a person's best interest

5. _____ Taking your time

6. _____ Using stress management skills

7. _____ Avoiding emotional reasoning

8. _____ A method for making important decisions based on logic, reason, and rational thinking

9. _____ Identifying the decision and the options

10. _____ Listing the positive and negative consequences of each course of action

11. _____ Reviewing the evidence

12. _____ Homework: Utilize the recommended decision-making method for a current decision

---

DETAILED PROCEDURES FOR MODULE 19

19.1. Introduction to Decision Making

Decisions that have long-term adverse personal consequences may be one of the most preventable causes of suffering. For example, decisions driven by "should" or "supposed to" beliefs are often made blindly, without consideration of the long-term negative consequences to oneself. When making decisions, I encourage you to think in terms of what course of action is most likely to promote your long-term happiness or quality of life. What good things and what bad things are likely to happen if you choose one option? What good things and what bad things are likely to happen if you choose an alternative?

When faced with difficult choices, how have you made important decisions in the past? What kinds of criteria or guidelines have you used for deciding what to do? If the client says she doesn't know, reassure her by saying something like: **It's understandable that you aren't sure how you make your decisions, and it's not unusual. Many battered women have made important decisions based on "supposed to" beliefs or impulsively, based on a desire to get relief from negative feelings as quickly as possible.**

19.2. Short-Term Gratification vs. Long-Term Benefits

I'd like to help you start making decisions that are in your best interest, so I'm going to teach you a method for making important decisions that involves an intellectual analysis of the likely positive and negative consequences for each con-templated course of action. But before we get into the specifics of this method, let's discuss some background issues. Some people don't realize that anytime a person chooses to do anything, it's a decision. Even a choice to do nothing about a situation is a decision.

Many poorer choices provide immediate gratification, meaning they have short-term positive consequences. Better decisions, on the other hand, those that promote a person's best interest, are often characterized by delayed gratification. It's human nature—and animal nature—to seek immediate gratification. You may recall that we talked about this a while back, and I asked you whether a three-year-old child would rather have a small candy bar today or a large candy bar tomorrow. Of course the child would choose to have the small candy bar today. People have to learn to tolerate delayed gratification, for example, to save rather than to spend right now. It's not something that comes naturally, and none of us are ever completely successful in learning how to do this.

Frequently, the immediate gratification associated with poorer choices isn't an increase in pleasure. Rather, it's often relief from some kind of emotional pain, like relief from guilt or some other negative emotional state, such as anxiety. The costs or negative consequences of poorer choices are usually delayed or only emerge in the long term. However, these negative consequences are often substantial.

Compared to poorer choices, better choices are often associated with relatively few or only minor short-term benefits. Most of the positive consequences associated with better decisions are long-term, but they're often substantial and long lasting. These benefits often include increased personal happiness or enhanced quality of life. Compared to poorer choices, most of the negative consequences associated with better decisions are temporary or relatively short-lived.

Give the client handout 19.1, Positive and Negative Consequences of Leaving or Staying in an Abusive Relationship. This handout summarizes some of the common positive and negative consequences associated with the choice to leave an abusive partner or stay with him. The abbreviations ST and LT stand for short-term and long-term, respectively. This decision-making analysis may help explain why many battered women stay in abusive relationships or reconcile with an abusive partner shortly after leaving him.

First, take a look at the second half of the table. As you'll see, the benefits or positive consequences associated with staying are primarily short-term, and most of them provide considerable relief reinforcement. The costs or negative consequences of staying, on the other hand, are primarily delayed but substantial in magnitude. Now take a look at the top half of the table. As you can see, most of the negative consequences associated with leaving are relatively immediate but primarily short-term, whereas the positive consequences of leaving are for the most part long-term but substantial in magnitude. I believe that millions of women would have ended an abusive relationship sooner or would have been less likely to reconcile after leaving had they made their decisions on the basis of this type of analysis of likely consequences for each contemplated course of action, rather than on the basis of some "should" or "supposed to" belief.

19.3. The Importance of Postponing Important Decisions Until You're Calm and Rational

As I mentioned when we discussed negative self-talk, decisions driven by a desire for relief from strong feelings, such as anxiety, fear, or anger, are often not in a person's best interest (Leith & Baumeister, 1996). Strong feelings interfere with your ability to think clearly, and decisions driven by moods aren't based on logic or rational thinking. When you're in a bad mood, you're likely to make choices based on what you think will make you feel better immediately or as soon as *possible*, rather than on a rational analysis of what's best for you in the long term. This is a form of emotional reasoning.

It's extremely important to avoid making important decisions when you're distraught, angry, or in any other state of extreme distress. Too much is at stake to make an impulsive decision that provides relief but isn't good for you in the long run. Ideally, you'd be as relaxed as possible when you finally make any important decision. This doesn't mean you'll be free of anxiety during the process of deciding what to do. Just thinking about making a decision that may have important implications for you and others can cause a great deal of anxiety. This is one reason why many battered women who "feel trapped" in an abusive relationship don't even like to entertain thoughts of leaving.

19.4. Guidelines for Making Decisions That Promote Your Best Interest

Achieving a state of calm when facing difficult choices is easier said than done. And ultimately, a state of calmness may not be the most important objective to achieve in making the best decision. What is most important is that your final decision be based on logic, and that you reach the same conclusion no matter how you feel. In other words, what's most important is that you get to the point where you can figure out what course of action is most likely to be associated with long-term positive outcomes—whether you feel anxious, scared, angry, or relaxed.

In addition to the decision-making process I'll outline shortly, there are three important guidelines that will help you make decisions that are in your best interest. The first is taking your time to decide. The second is using your stress management skills while involved in the decision-making process. And the third is making certain that you aren't engaging in emotional reasoning. Let's take a closer look at each of these.

19.5. Taking Your Time

Don't rush into important decisions. Oftentimes, hasty decisions aren't clearly thought out. Take the phrase "sleep on it" literally. Even when you think you've decided what you're going to do, wait several days to see if your reasoning about what to do changes.

19.6. Using Stress Management Skills

If thinking about making a difficult or important decision causes you to feel anxious or upset, use the stress management skills you've learned here. Whenever you're thinking about or planning what to do and you feel yourself becoming tense, take a few deep breaths, then do a body scan and release any muscular tension. This will help bring your overall tension level down to a manageable level. It may even be helpful to take a break and do the entire progressive muscle relaxation exercise, and then go back to thinking about what to do.

19.7. Avoiding Emotional Reasoning

Observe your mental life or stream of consciousness very carefully whenever you're thinking about what to do, and make certain that you aren't engaging in emotional reasoning while weighing the options. Do you remember the example I gave you about the woman who allowed the emotional based thought that she would be abandoning her husband to influence her decision to stay with him? This was clearly emotional reasoning. Her decision to stay offered short-term relief from potential guilt about leaving her husband, but an analysis of the facts clearly revealed that she would be better off if she left.

If you feel anxious while deciding what to do, you're more likely to engage in emotional reasoning than if you're relaxed. For example, if a woman feels anxious and unsafe at the thought of leaving her abusive partner, it's more likely that she'll conclude that leaving is too dangerous. However, anxiety at the thought of leaving has nothing to do with whether leaving is dangerous. By the same token, being relaxed at the thought of leaving isn't evidence that leaving isn't dangerous. Whether leaving would be relatively risky or not can only be determined on the basis of considering the facts and the evidence.

19.8. A Method for Making Important Decisions Based on Logic, Reason, and Rational Thinking

Now I'll teach you a method for making decisions that's based on an intellectual analysis of the likely pros and cons for each contemplated course of action. Give the client handout 19.2, Worksheet for Making Important Decisions. This worksheet will guide you through the process, which involves three steps: identifying the decision and the options you're considering, listing the positive and negative consequences for each option, and reviewing the evidence. I'll explain these steps in detail, then I'll ask you to complete this worksheet as a homework assignment, using an important decision that you currently face.

19.9. Identifying the Decision and the Options

The first step using this decision-making process is to think about a decision you are considering and write what you are considering at the top of the worksheet.

For example, you might write, "When to go back to school." Next, you would write down the options you're considering. For example, you might write "Go back to school now" as Contemplated Course of Action #1 and "Go back to school when my daughter has graduated from high school" as Contemplated Course of Action #2.

If you're considering more than two courses of action, make more copies of the second page of the worksheet for evaluating the pros and cons of each additional option you're considering.

19.10. Listing the Positive and Negative Consequences of Each Course of Action

The next step is to write down the likely positive consequences of the first course of action and use ST and LT to signify whether the consequence is short-term or long-term. Most short-term consequences are temporary, and most long-term consequences are likely to be long lasting but may not materialize for a month, or six months, or even a year after a decision is made and acted upon. However, these long-term consequences may last for years or even a lifetime. Sometimes a consequence is both short-term and long-term. In that case, write both ST and LT after that item.

Next, you'll list the potential negative consequences of the first course of action and indicate which are short-term, which are long-term, and which are both. Then you repeat that entire process for each additional course of action you're considering: listing the positive consequences and designating them as short-term or long-term, then listing the negative consequences and indicating whether they're short-term or long-term.

19.11. Reviewing the Evidence

After you've written down the likely positive and negative consequences associated with each contemplated course of action, and whether those consequences are short-term or long-term, the next step is to review what you've written. Then, at the bottom of the last page of the worksheet, you'll write down which course of action is most likely to promote your long-term best interest and quality of life. Next, you'll write down whether you've chosen to pursue the option that's most likely to be in your best interest, and if yes, when you plan to act on your decision. If you decide to go with an option that isn't in your best interest, you'd write down your reasons for making that choice. People don't always act in their best interest, even if they know which options are most likely to promote their well-being. For example, a person with a phobia about having dental work done may know full and well that going to the dentist is a very good idea yet still choose not to go. In this example, the person's behavior is controlled by the prospect of immediate and severe negative emotions associated with going to the dentist, even though the discomfort is short-term and the benefits are long-term.

19.12. Assigning Homework

For homework, I'd like you to go through this decision-making process using a decision you're currently faced with. Use the worksheet and go through all of the steps. What is a decision you have been considering or have been postponing? If the client doesn't come up with anything, offer her a few suggestions based on decisions commonly faced by formerly battered women: whether to switch jobs, whether to go back to school, whether to file a restraining order, whether to go to court for increased child support or changes in custody or visitation, or whether to move. Other possibilities include whether to sever her relationship with a verbally abusive relative, friend, or acquaintance; whether to address a long-standing dilemma like confronting someone who mistreated the client in the past; whether to maintain contact with a former partner who was abusive; or whether to stop accepting something of value from an ex-partner, especially if it's something he can arbitrarily withhold or use manipulatively, like using a car that belongs to him or using him as a babysitter.

We'll review your completed worksheet at the next session. Make a note to review the homework at the beginning of the next session. At that time, ask the client what she got out of the homework, then go through the items one by one and discuss her responses.

CONCLUDING REMARKS

This module provides clients considerable food for thought and often helps them realize that they are more in control of their future well-being than they previously thought. Clients almost always find this module to be valuable.

Handout 19.1: Positive and Negative Consequences of Leaving or Staying in an Abusive Relationship

Positive Consequences of Leaving	■ Increased self-esteem and decreased depression (LT) ■ Opportunities to pursue a career or go back to school (LT) ■ A stable home atmosphere for the children (LT) ■ Freedom to come and go as you please (LT) ■ Not having to account for your time, activities, or behavior (LT) ■ Opportunities to develop a healthy intimate relationship (LT)
Negative Consequences of Leaving	■ Invalidation of "supposed to" beliefs (ST) ■ Anxiety about an uncertain future (ST) ■ Missing your ex-partner (ST) ■ Poverty or lowered standard of living (ST and LT) ■ Breaking up the family (ST and LT) ■ The stigma of being divorced or a single mother (ST)

Positive Consequences of Staying	■ Relief from guilt, such as anticipatory guilt about abandoning your partner (ST) ■ Yet another honeymoon period of getting along (ST) ■ Financial security (ST and LT) ■ Validation of "supposed to" beliefs (ST and LT)
Negative Consequences of Staying	■ More abuse (LT) ■ Children reexposed to domestic violence (LT) ■ Guilt about not leaving (LT) ■ Resentment if your partner abuses you again (LT) ■ Lower self-esteem (LT) ■ Persistence of depression and PTSD (LT)

Handout 19.2: Worksheet for Making Important Decisions

Client Initials: _____   Date: _____

What decision are you considering? _____

_____

Contemplated course of action #1: _____

_____

Contemplated course of action #2: _____

_____

Course of Action #1

What are the likely positive outcomes or consequences of the first course of action? List them below. In addition, write "ST" next to each outcome if it's a short-term outcome and "LT" if it's a long-term outcome. Write "ST and LT" if the likely outcome is both short-term and long-term.

1. _____

2. _____

3. _____

4. _____

5. _____

6. _____

What are the likely negative outcomes or consequences associated with the first course of action? List them below, and designate them as "ST," "LT," or "ST and LT."

1. _____

2. _____

3. _____

4. _____

5. _____

6. _____

Course of Action #2

What are the likely positive outcomes or consequences of the second course of action? List them below, and designate them as "ST," "LT," or "ST and LT."

1. _____

2. _____

3. _____

4. _____

5. _____

6. _____

What are the likely negative outcomes or consequences associated with the second course of action? List them below, and designate them as "ST," "LT," or "ST and LT."

1. _____

2. _____

3. _____

4. _____

5. _____

6. _____

Based on your review of the likely consequences of each contemplated course of action, which is most likely to promote your long-term best interest?

_____

Have you decided to act on this course of action? Yes _____ No _____ If yes, when are you going to act?

_____

If you decided not to go with the course of action that's in your best interest, why did you make that decision?

_____

_____

_____

Implications and Consequences of Remaining in an Abusive Relationship

Although cognitive trauma therapy is primarily for clients who are permanently out of an abusive relationship, some battered women have mixed thoughts and feelings about whether to stay in or leave an abusive relationship. By the same token, some clients who have left may still contemplate reconciling with an abusive partner. This module is primarily for these women.

OBJECTIVES

- For the client to understand the likely negative outcomes associated with remaining in an abusive relationship

MATERIALS

- Evidence and Likelihood That Your Partner Will Change (handout 20.1)

HOMEWORK

- Listen to session audio-recordings.

- Continue to monitor and record negative self-talk.

■   Practice PMR while listening to the PMR recording, twice a day.

■   Do a body scan and over-tense and relax muscles when experiencing stress.

PROCEDURES CHECKLIST

1.   _____   Introduction to the consequences of remaining in an abusive relationship

2.   _____   Rafting metaphor for looking at the big picture

3.   _____   Long-term implication 1: Continued PTSD symptoms

4.   _____   Long-term implication 2: Long-term guilt

5.   _____   Long-term implication 3: Modeling an unhealthy relationship for the children

6.   _____   Long-term implication 4: An uneven playing field

7.   _____   Long-term implication 5: Ongoing risks associated with self-advocacy

8.   _____   Long-term implication 6: The unlikelihood that an abusive partner will change (using handout 20.1, an in-session questionnaire)

9.   _____   Long-term implication 7: Missing out on life

DETAILED PROCEDURES FOR MODULE 20

20.1. Introduction to the Consequences of Remaining in an Abusive Relationship

Try to personalize the scripts that follow to correspond with the client's situation. If she's still in an abusive relationship, use language related to staying in the relationship. If she has left but is considering reconciling, use language reflecting that situation. **You may still be trying to make your relationship with your abusive partner work. You may still be hoping that your partner will change. You may think that your children need their father and be willing to sacrifice your own personal needs for the benefit of the children. Whatever your reasons for considering staying or reconciling, it will be important for you to be aware of the possible long-term implications of staying with a partner who has been abusive. Knowledge is power, and the more you know, the** better equipped you'll be to make enlightened choices that promote your long-term best interest and personal happiness.

20.2. Rafting Metaphor for Looking at the Big Picture

Consider the following scenario: Let's say you're rafting down a river in a remote wilderness area and are approaching a fork in the river. Which way do you go, to the left or the right? To the left, the river is calm. To the right, there are some rapids. Left looks pretty good, right? But not so fast. Let's take an aerial view to see the big picture, or the long-term implications of going left or right. To the right, we see that the rapids subside and the river slows and widens. And to the left, we see that the calm waters are short-lived and lead to raging, hazardous rapids and a potentially deadly waterfall.

This is analogous to what you may face in deciding whether to stay in a relationship with a partner who's been abusive. If you stay or reconcile, the foreseeable, immediate future may be associated with a period of calm or relief, such as relief from guilt associated with thoughts of leaving. However, you may not be seeing the potential long-term consequences of staying in the relationship. To help you make the decision that's best for you, I'll give you an aerial or long-term view of what you can expect to encounter if you stay in a relationship with someone who's been abusive.

20.3. Continued PTSD Symptoms

Your PTSD is unlikely to go away if you remain in an abusive relationship, even if the abuse only occurs once in a while. Ongoing or intermittent occurrences or threats of verbal or physical abuse provide fuel for symptoms of PTSD. If you choose to stay in a relationship where there is potential for further abuse, your symptoms, particularly emotional detachment, numbing, and depression, are unlikely to go away, even if you're in therapy.

20.4. Long-Term Guilt

You may get some relief from guilt by staying with a partner who has been abusive. For example, if you consider leaving, you might experience guilt because of the thought that you'd be abandoning your partner or that you're failing in your responsibility to make the relationship work. Unfortunately, by staying you may be setting yourself up for long-term guilt in the future related to choosing to stay in the relationship.

Many women who are in abusive relationships experience guilt about what they perceive as provoking their partner or about not being able to get him to change. By contrast, the most common guilt issues by far among women who are no longer in an abusive relationship are guilt about not having left sooner and guilt about problems their children are having as a consequence of witnessing the abuse.

In a study of formerly battered women, the average period of time between the first and last incidents of physical abuse was almost six and a half years (Kubany, Hill, et al., 2004). Some of these women remained hopeful that their partners would change for many years before they finally realized it would never happen. In the end, most of them experienced significant guilt about not breaking off the relationship much earlier. If you stay with or reconcile with a partner who has been abusive, there's a good chance that you'll eventually end the relationship. And if or when you do, you may very well experience guilt about not having left sooner.

20.5. Modeling an Unhealthy Relationship for the Children

Again, try to personalize the following section as appropriate to the client. If she has a daughter, simply say, "Would you want your daughter to stay … ?" If she doesn't have a daughter, say, "If you had a daughter, would you want her to stay … ?" Do the same for references to a son. **Would you want your daughter to stay with an abusive boyfriend or husband? Of course not. And would you want your son to mistreat a woman the way your partner has mistreated you? Of course not.**

Modeling is a very important means of teaching children ways to behave as adults. What might your daughter be learning if you stay in a relationship with a man who continues to verbally or physically abuse you? Right. She's probably learning that men can get away with treating women this way. She might also be learning that, if she gets into an abusive relationship, she's supposed to tolerate or put up with the abuse too. After all, Mom did. And what if a daughter of yours gets involved with an abusive man and you advise her to break off the relationship and tell her that she deserves better. What might she be likely to say? It wouldn't be surprising—or even inaccurate—if she were to say, "Mom, you're a hypocrite. You're telling me to leave, but you didn't leave."

And what would your son be learning if you stay with a partner who continues to verbally or physically abuse you? Right. He might be learning that he can probably get away with treating his girlfriend or his wife this way. He may also be learning that it's okay to disrespect and violate the rights of his girlfriend or wife, and others, as well. He may be more likely to become a batterer himself if you tolerate the abuse and remain in the relationship.

20.6. An Uneven Playing Field

An example of an uneven playing field would be a soccer field that slopes downhill. Certainly the team defending the goal at the top of the slope would have an advantage over the team defending the goal at the bottom of the slope. In an analogous way, abusive men have an advantage over their partners when it comes to who will get their way when there's conflict in the relationship. Oftentimes all they have to do to get their way or get their partner to back down is raise their voice. A batterer's raised voice is a sign of impending danger to his partner, as it's often a sign that violence will follow.

Many battered women get to the point where they stop expressing their opinions or point of view or stop disagreeing altogether because when they did in the past, the situation often became much worse. At the very least, you may have found that you had to choose your words very carefully when there was conflict with your partner for fear that you might accidentally say something that would set him off. You didn't have the luxury of being able to say anything that came into your mind without potentially serious adverse consequences. Even if your partner hasn't been physically abusive for quite a while, you may be reluctant to stand up for your rights or argue your viewpoint because you get intimidated or fearful when your partner is surly or angry. If you stay with a partner who has been abusive, the bottom line is that you will never have an even chance of getting your needs met.

20.7. Ongoing Risks Associated with Self-Advocacy

The type of therapy we've been doing is primarily intended for women who were previously abused by an intimate partner but are now safely out of the relationship. Throughout your therapy, I have recommended that you advocate for getting your own wants and needs satisfied as a top priority, even if that seems selfish. I've also encouraged you to not tolerate disrespect. Although these are universal rights that everyone deserves to have, the unfortunate truth is that this kind of self-advocacy is potentially dangerous in an abusive relationship, where your partner has placed his wants above your own and where the dominant strategy for keeping the peace has been for you to avoid conflict. If you plan to stay with a partner who has been abusive, advocating for your own needs and wants as a top priority could put you at increased risk for future violence.

20.8. The Unlikelihood That an Abusive Partner Will Change

Many women in abusive relationships are reluctant to give up hope that their partner will change. For example, many clients have asked whether there's a chance their partner will change and become the type of guy he was early in the relationship. I usually respond, "Yes, he might, and you might also win the lottery—but it's highly unlikely."

Unfortunately, many batterers have strong antisocial or even psychopathic tendencies. Such tendencies are generally stable, long-standing personality traits, which seldom change. For example, self-centeredness and disregard for the feelings of others are personality patterns that are very resistant to change. In fact, treatment programs for batterers, including anger management programs, may be woefully ineffective overall, especially among the batterers that are the most abusive. One reason is because many batterers have little or no motivation to change.

If you joined an online dating service, would you take a chance on a guy who had a record or history like this with another woman, even if he had many desirable or apparently redeeming qualities? Consider this analogy: A young man with a dozen speeding violations and two DUI convictions might not get any more speeding tickets or drunken driving convictions. However, do you think an automobile insurance company would be willing to take the risk and issue this guy an insurance policy?

Give the client handout 20.1, Evidence and Likelihood That Your Partner Will Change. **Now I'd like you to fill out this brief questionnaire.** Once she's done so, ask the following question: **If your daughter were in a relationship with a person like this, would you want her to stay or leave?**

20.9. Missing Out on Life

Many battered women don't leave an abusive relationship until they have lost all hope, maybe after five, ten, twenty, or even thirty years. They'll hold on to that last glimmer of hope with a death grip. They may think they're playing it safe by waiting to see what happens before deciding whether to abandon the relationship. And sometimes these same women will lament that they lost the best years of their lives by staying in the relationship and tolerating years of mistreatment and disrespect.

It's important to realize that waiting to see what happens is a decision. It's an active choice. If you think your relationship with an abusive partner is probably going to end eventually, wouldn't it be better if it ends now than one year from now, or three years from now, or five years from now? If your relationship doesn't end until five years from now, don't you think you'd give almost anything to have those five years back? Five years when you're younger and more resilient so you could start fresh and possibly find a partner who will treat you with the dignity and respect you deserve? Don't let life pass you by.

By the way, and not that I advocate making decisions based on the best interest of your partner, but if you know your relationship is going to end eventually, you aren't doing him any favors by choosing to stay at this time. It prevents him from getting on with the rest of his life too. Plus, if you end the relationship now, maybe this will be a wake-up call for him to change the way he relates to his next partner. As we've discussed, it isn't likely, but it is a possibility.

What did you get out of this discussion of the implications and consequences of staying with an abusive partner?

CONCLUDING REMARKS

Clients almost always say that this was a useful or enlightening module. Because the information is presented without telling the client what to do, clients seldom respond defensively to the information provided, as they might if the therapist actively encouraged permanently breaking off a relationship with an abusive partner. While the information provided in this module may not immediately motivate a client to end her relationship with an abusive partner forever, in many cases it influences clients to be more cautious about rushing into an unconditional reconciliation with an abusive partner.

Handout 20.1: Evidence and Likelihood That Your Partner Will Change

Client Initials: _____   Date: _____

Please write your answers to the following questions:

How many times has your partner …

1.   Physically hurt you? _____

2.   Verbally abused, insulted, or humiliated you? _____

3.   Forced you to have unwanted sex? _____

4.   Threatened to hurt you? _____

5.   Threatened to kill you? _____

6.   Stalked you or repeatedly checked on your activities or whereabouts? _____

7.   Verbally or physically abused you in front of or within earshot of the children? _____

8.   Verbally or physically abused one or more of your children? _____

9.   Apologized but then abused you again? _____

10. Promised to change? _____

Knowing that abusive behavior is very resistant to change, and given that history is often the best predictor of whether or not an abusive partner will change, is it likely that your abusive partner will change?   Yes _____   No _____

Would you want a daughter of yours to be in a relationship with a partner like this?

_____

If your daughter were in a relationship with a person like this, would you want her to stay or leave?

_____

This handout is in the public domain. Readers may copy, distribute, or use as they see fit.

Self-Advocacy Strategies Revisited

At the end of the session prior to the final session, give the client another copy of handout 1.2, Empowering Yourself: Self-Advocacy Strategies, and ask her to complete it a second time as homework prior to the final session. The twenty-five statements in the self-advocacy strategies questionnaire are things Dr. Kubany found himself saying over and over again to his clients. Most clients with PTSD hadn't been living their lives in accordance with these strategies when they first came to therapy. Many had spent a large part of their lives taking care of and meeting the needs of other people and trying to avoid disapproval, anticipate problems, and do damage control. Having the client complete this assignment again at the end of therapy allows her to see how much she has learned, grown, and changed over the course of therapy. This is extremely empowering and worthy of celebration.

OBJECTIVES

■ For the client to review the twenty-five self-advocacy strategies and endorse them as guidelines for living her life

MATERIALS

■ Empowering Yourself: Self-Advocacy Strategies (handout 1.2), assigned as homework, for a second time, at the previous session

HOMEWORK

■ Listen to session audio-recordings.

- Continue to monitor and record negative self-talk, as needed.

- Practice PMR while listening to the PMR recording, as needed.

- Do a body scan and over-tense and relax muscles when experiencing stress, as needed.

PROCEDURES CHECKLIST

1. _____ Asking the client to read each set of statements and her answers on the self-advocacy strategies questionnaire (handout 1.2)

2. _____ After selected responses (usually the items with the biggest change since the beginning of therapy), reading the client's corresponding response from the first time she completed the questionnaire, as homework for module 1

3. _____ Concluding the session, and the therapy

DETAILED PROCEDURES FOR THE LAST MODULE

LM.1. Asking the Client to Read Her Completed Homework Assignment

How did this assignment go? Clients typically respond very positively, often acknowledging that they have made great strides in self-advocacy and empowerment since coming to therapy.

I'd like you to read each statement on the questionnaire, and after each, read your answer. Feel free to elaborate on your answers if you wish. I may comment on some of your answers, and I may read some of your previous responses, from when you first completed this questionnaire at the beginning of your therapy.

LM.2. Reading Some of the Client's Earlier Responses to Items with the Greatest Change

You may wish to read some of the client's previous responses to the questionnaire, particularly those that are in sharp contrast to her recent responses. Here's an example of a situation where reading the client's previous response is worthwhile and validating: After the first session, one client responded to the first question as follows: "I always put the needs of my husband and others ahead of mine, but I've often been unhappy in the end. When I try to do things for myself, I feel selfish, rude, and guilty." Here's how she responded at the end of therapy: "If I don't advocate for myself, who will? I like advocating for myself immensely. It makes me feel happier. I've changed! I like being number one! I don't feel guilty anymore, I feel good!"

LM.3. Concluding the Session, and the Therapy

After the client has read all twenty-five statements on the self-advocacy handout and her responses, conclude the session. **Since this is our last session, give me an overall evaluation of what you've learned throughout the sessions we've had together. Off of the top of your head, what was the single most valuable or useful aspect of this therapy experience?** The majority of clients say it was the guilt work. Other common responses are the assertiveness training, the emphasis on modifying negative self-talk, and the emphasis on self-advocacy.

I am happy to say you've now graduated! Give the client a healthy dose of praise for everything she's accomplished, and encourage her to do the same for herself. You may wish to schedule one additional session in about a month to wrap up any loose ends or to get some final closure. In our experience, clients seldom require additional sessions or come back to therapy with important unresolved issues.

CONCLUDING REMARKS

By the time they complete CTT, the great majority of women are free of PTSD. A great burden has been lifted, new possibilities exist, and these women are more confident than they were even before the abuse. Many of the things taught in this therapy, such as stress management, assertiveness training, monitoring negative self-talk, and learning to overcome guilt, would contribute to a better quality of life for any woman, whether or not she had PTSD.

References

Altonn, H. (1999, September 6). Abused women to share in new therapy project. *Honolulu Star-Bulletin*, pp. 1-2.

American Psychiatric Association. (1980). *Diagnostic and statistical manual of mental disorders* (3rd ed.). Washington, DC: Author.

American Psychiatric Association. (1994). *Diagnostic and statistical manual of mental disorders* (4th ed.). Washington, DC: Author.

American Psychiatric Association. (2000). *Diagnostic and statistical manual of mental disorders* (4th ed., text revision). Washington, DC: Author.

Ascione, F. R. (2000). *Safe haven for pets: Guidelines for programs sheltering pets for women who are battered.* Logan, UT: Author.

Beck, A. T., Rush, A., Shaw, B. F., & Emory, G. (1979). *Cognitive therapy of depression.* New York: Guilford Press.

Beck, A. T., Steer, R. A., & Garbin, M. G. (1988). Psychometric properties of the Beck Depression Inventory: Twenty-five years of evaluation. *Clinical Psychology Review, 8,* 77-100.

Berkowitz, L. (1984). The experience of anger as a parallel process in the display of impulsive "angry" aggression. In R. G. Geen & E. I. Donnerstein (Eds.), *Aggression: theoretical and empirical review* (Vol. 1, pp. 103-133). New York: Academic Press.

Blake, D. D., & Sonnenberg, R. T. (1998). Outcome research on behavioral and cognitive-behavioral treatments for trauma survivors. In V. M. Follette, J. Ruzek, & F. Abueg (Eds.), *Trauma in context* (pp. 15-47). New York: Guilford Press.

Christensen, A., & Jacobson, N. S. (1994). Who (or what) can do psychotherapy: The status and challenge of nonprofessional therapies. *Psychological Science, 5,* 8-14.

Classen, C., Field, N. P., Koopman, C., Nevill-Manning, K., & Spiegel, D. (2001). Interpersonal problems and their relationship to sexual revictimization in women sexually abused in childhood. *Journal of Interpersonal Violence, 16*, 495-509.

Council on Scientific Affairs, American Medical Association. (1992). Violence against women: Relevance for medical practitioners. *Journal of the American Medical Association, 267*, 3184-3189.

Douglas, M. A., & Strom, J. (1988). Cognitive therapy with battered women. *Journal of Rational-Emotive and Cognitive-Behavior Therapy, 6*, 3349.

Faust, D., & Zlotnick, C. (1995). Another dodo bird verdict? Revisiting the comparative effectiveness of professional and paraprofessional therapists. *Clinical Psychology and Psychotherapy, 2*, 157-167.

Fischhoff, B. (1975). Hindsight does not equal foresight: The effect of outcome knowledge on judgment under uncertainty. *Journal of Experimental Psychology: Human Perception and Performance, 1*, 288-299.

Foa, E. B., Ehlers, A., Clark, D. M., Tolin, D. F., & Orsillo, S. M. (1999). The Posttraumatic Cognitions Inventory (PTCI): Development and validation. *Psychological Assessment, 11*, 303-314.

Foa, E. B., & Meadows, E. A. (1997). Psychosocial treatments for posttraumatic stress disorder: A critical review. *Annual Review of Psychology, 48*, 449-480.

Foa, E. B., Riggs, D. S., Massie, E., & Yarczower, M. (1995). The impact of fear activation and anger on the efficacy of exposure treatment for posttraumatic stress disorder. *Behavior Therapy, 26*, 487-499.

Foa, E. B., & Rothbaum, B. O. (1998). *Treating the trauma of rape*. New York: Guilford Press.

Frazier, P. A., & Schauben, L. (1994). Causal attributions and recovery from rape and other stressful life events. *Journal of Social and Clinical Psychology, 13*, 1-14.

Frederiksen, L. W. (1975). Treatment of ruminative thinking by self-monitoring. *Journal of Behavior Therapy and Experimental Psychiatry, 6*, 258-259.

Friedman, H. S. (1992). *Hostility, coping, and health*. Washington, DC: American Psychological Association.

Goodman, M. S., & Fallon, B. C. (1995). *Pattern changing for abused women: An educational program*. Thousand Oaks, CA: Sage.

Hawkins, S. A., & Hastie, R. (1990). Hindsight: Biased judgments of past events after outcomes are known. *Psychological Bulletin, 107*, 311-327.

Heise, L., Ellsberg, M., & Gottemoeller, M. (1999, December). *Ending violence against women. Population Reports*, Series L, No. 11. Baltimore, MD: Johns Hopkins University School of Public Health, Population Information.

Holtzworth-Munroe, A., & Stuart, G. L. (1994). Typologies of male batterers: Three subtypes and the differences among them. *Psychological Bulletin, 116,* 476-497.

Jacobson, N. S., Gottman, J. M., Waltz, J., Rushe, R., Babcock, J., & Holtzworth-Munroe, A. (1994). Affect, verbal content, and psychophysiology in the arguments of couples with a violent husband. *Journal of Consulting and Clinical Psychology, 62,* 982-988.

Jehu, D. (1989). Mood disturbances among women clients sexually abused in childhood: Prevalence, etiology, treatment. *Journal of Interpersonal Violence, 4,* 164-184.

Kessler, R. C., Sonnega, A., Bromet, E., Hughes, M., & Nelson, C. B. (1995). Posttraumatic stress disorder in the National Comorbidity Survey. *Archives of General Psychiatry, 52,* 1048-1060.

Knox, D. (1971). *Marriage happiness.* Champaign, IL: Research Press.

Korotitsch, W. J., & Nelson-Gray, R. O. (1999). An overview of self-monitoring research in assessment and treatment. *Psychological Assessment, 11,* 415-425.

Kubany, E. S. (1994). A cognitive model of guilt typology in combat-related PTSD. *Journal of Traumatic Stress, 7,* 3-19.

Kubany, E. S. (1995, March). Social impact of five different kinds of "I" messages. Poster presented at the 75th Annual Western Psychological Association Convention, Los Angeles.

Kubany, E. S. (1996). *Cognitive therapy for trauma-related guilt.* Audiotape distributed by the National Center for PTSD, Palo Alto, CA.

Kubany, E. S. (1997a). Application of cognitive therapy for trauma-related guilt (CT-TRG) with a Vietnam veteran troubled by multiple sources of guilt. *Cognitive and Behavioral Practice, 3,* 213-244.

Kubany, E. S. (1997b). Thinking errors, faulty conclusions, and cognitive therapy for trauma-related guilt. *National Center for Post-Traumatic Stress Disorder Clinical Quarterly, 8,* 6-8.

Kubany, E. S. (1998). Cognitive therapy for trauma-related guilt. In V. Follette, J. Ruzek, & F. Abueg (Eds.), *Trauma in context* (pp. 124-161). New York: Guilford Press.

Kubany, E. S. (2000). *The Trauma-Related Anger Scale (TRAS).* Unpublished scale. Honolulu, HI: Author.

Kubany, E. S., Abueg, F. R., Kilauano, W., Manke, F. P., & Kaplan, A. (1997). Development and validation of the Sources of Trauma-Related Guilt Survey—War-Zone Version. *Journal of Traumatic Stress, 10,* 235-258.

Kubany, E. S., Abueg, F. R., Owens, J. A., Brennan, J. M., Kaplan, A., & Watson, S. (1995). Initial examination of a multidimensional model of trauma-related guilt: Applications to combat veterans and battered women. *Journal of Psychopathology and Behavioral Assessment, 17,* 353-376.

Kubany, E. S., Bauer, G. B., Richard, D. C., & Muraoka, M. Y. (1995). Impact of labeled anger and blame in intimate relationships. *Journal of Social and Clinical Psychology, 14,* 53-60.

Kubany, E. S., Haynes, S. N., Abueg, F. R., Manke, F. P., Brennan, J. M., & Stahura, C. (1996). Development and validation of the Trauma-Related Guilt Inventory (TRGI). *Psychological Assessment, 8,* 428-444.

Kubany, E. S., Haynes, S. N., Leisen, M. B., Owens, J. A., Kaplan, A., & Burns, K. (2000). Development and preliminary validation of the Traumatic Life Events Questionnaire. *Psychological Assessment, 12,* 210-224.

Kubany, E. S., Hill, E. E., & Owens, J. A. (2003). Cognitive trauma therapy for battered women with PTSD (CTT-BW): Preliminary findings. *Journal of Traumatic Stress, 16,* 81-91.

Kubany, E. S., Hill, E. E., Owens, J. A., Iannce-Spencer, C., McCaig, M. A., Tremayne, K., et al. (2004). Cognitive trauma therapy for battered women with PTSD (CTT-BW). *Journal of Consulting and Clinical Psychology, 72,* 3-18.

Kubany, E. S., Leisen, M. B., Kaplan, A. K., & Kelly, M. (2000). Validation of a brief measure of posttraumatic stress disorder: The Distressing Event Questionnaire (DEQ). *Psychological Assessment, 12,* 192-209.

Kubany, E. S., & Manke, F. P. (1995). Cognitive therapy for trauma-related guilt: Conceptual bases and treatment outlines. *Cognitive and Behavioral Practice, 2,* 27-61.

Kubany, E. S., McCaig, M. A., & Laconsay, J. R. (2004). *Healing the trauma of domestic violence: A workbook for women.* Oakland, CA: New Harbinger Publications.

Kubany, E. S., Richard, D. C., & Bauer, G. B. (1992). Impact of assertive and aggressive communication of distress and anger: A verbal component analysis. *Aggressive Behavior, 18,* 337-348.

Kubany, E. S., & Ralston, T. C. (2006). Treatment of trauma-related guilt and shame. In V. Follette & J. Ruzek (Eds.), *Cognitive behavioral therapies for trauma* (2nd ed., pp. 258-287). New York: Guilford.

Kubany, E. S., & Watson, S. B. (2002). Cognitive trauma therapy for formerly battered women with PTSD (CTT-BW): Conceptual bases and treatment outlines. *Cognitive and Behavioral Practice, 9,* 111-127.

Kubany, E. S., & Watson, S. B. (2003). Guilt: Elaboration of a multidimensional model. *The Psychological Record, 53,* 51-90.

Kubany, E. S., & Watson, S. B. (2007). *A fear-loss model of chronic PTSD that emphasizes the role of irrational beliefs and evaluative language.* Manuscript in preparation.

Kulka, R. A., Schlenger, W. E., Fairbank, J. A., Hough, R. L., Jordan, B. K., Marmar, C. R., et al. (1990). *Trauma and the Vietnam war generation: Report of the findings from the National Veterans Readjustment Study.* New York: Brunner/Mazel.

Leith, K. P., & Baumeister, R. F. (1996). Why do bad moods increase self-defeating behavior? Emotion, risk taking, and self-regulation. *Journal of Personality and Social Psychology, 71,* 1250-1267.

Miller, D., & Porter, C. (1983). Self-blame in victims of violence. *Journal of Social Issues, 39,* 139-152.

Mischel, W. (1986). *Introduction to personality: A new look.* New York: Holt, Rinehart and Winston.

Morgenstern, J., Langenbucher, J., Labouvie, E., & Miller, K. J. (1997). The comorbidity of alcoholism and personality in a clinical population: Prevalence rates and relation to alcohol typology behaviors. *Journal of Abnormal Psychology, 106,* 74-84.

Mow, S. (2000, August 9). New hope for battered women. *MidWeek,* p. 48.

Ozer, E. M., & Bandura, A. (1990). Mechanisms governing empowerment effects: A self-efficacy analysis. *Journal of Personality and Social Psychology, 58,* 472-486.

Peterson, C., & Seligman, M. E. P. (1983). Learned helplessness and victimization. *Journal of Social Issues, 2,* 103-116.

Pitman, R. K., Altman, B., Greenwald, E., Longpre, R. E., Macklin, M. L., Poiré, R. E., et al. (1991). Psychiatric complications during flooding therapy for posttraumatic stress disorder. *Journal of Clinical Psychiatry, 52,* 17-20.

Rando, T. A. (Ed.). (1986). *Parental loss of a child.* Champaign, IL: Research Press.

Resick, P. A. (1993). *Cognitive processing for rape victims.* Newbury Park: Sage.

Resick, P. A., Nishith, P., Weaver, T. L., Astin, M. C., & Feuer, C. A. (2002). A comparison of cognitive processing therapy with prolonged exposure for the treatment of posttraumatic stress disorder in female rape victims. *Journal of Consulting and Clinical Psychology, 70,* 867-879.

Resick, P. A., & Schnicke, M. (1992). Cognitive processing for sexual assault victims. *Journal of Consulting and Clinical Psychology, 60,* 748-756.

Robins, L. N., Helzer, J. E., Weissman, M. M., Orvschel, H., Gruenberg, E., Burke, J. D., et al. (1984). Lifetime prevalence of specific psychiatric disorders in three sites. *Archives of General Psychiatry, 41,* 942-949.

Rohrbaugh, M., Riccio, D. C., & Arthur, A. (1972). Paradoxical enhancement of conditioned suppression. *Behaviour Research and Therapy, 10,* 125-130.

Rosen, L. N., & Martin, L. (2000). Personality characteristics that increase vulnerability to sexual harassment among U.S. Army soldiers. *Military Medicine, 165,* 709-713.

Rosenberg, M. (1965). *Society and the adolescent self-image.* Princeton, NJ: Princeton University Press.

Rosenhan, D. L., & Seligman, M. E. P. (1989). *Abnormal psychology* (2nd ed.). New York: W. W. Norton and Company.

Rothbaum, B. O., Foa, E. B., Riggs, D. S., Murdock, T., & Walsh, W. (1992). A prospective examination of post-traumatic stress disorder in rape victims. *Journal of Traumatic Stress, 3,* 455-475.

Shalansky, C., Ericksen, J., & Henderson, A. (1999). Abused women and child custody: The ongoing exposure to abusive ex-partners. *Journal of Advanced Nursing, 29,* 416-426.

Snell, J. E., Rosenwald, R. J., & Robey, A. (1964). The wifebeater's wife. *Archives of General Psychiatry, 11,* 107-112.

Staats, A. W. (1972). Language behavior therapy: A derivative of social behaviorism. *Behavior Therapy, 3,* 165-192.

Staats, A. W. (1996). *Behavior and personality: Psychological behaviorism.* New York: Springer.

Street, A. E., Gibson, L. E., & Holohan, D. R. (2005). Impact of childhood traumatic events, trauma-related guilt, and avoidant coping strategies on PTSD symptoms in female survivors of domestic violence. *Journal of Traumatic Stress, 18,* 245-252.

Tjaden, P., & Thoennes, N. (2000, July). *Full report on the prevalence, incidence, and consequences of violence against women.* Publication No. NCJ83781. Washington, DC: U.S. Department of Justice, Bureau of Justice Statistics.

Tomaka, J., Palacios, R., Schneider, K. T., Colotla, M., Concha, J. B., & Herrald, M. M. (1999). Assertiveness predicts threat and challenge reactions to potential stress among women. *Journal of Personality and Social Psychology, 76,* 1008-1021.

Tremayne, K., & Kubany, E. S. (1998). Differential prevalence and impact of intimate partner abuse among women and men in a substance abuse program. Poster presented at the annual convention of the American Psychological Association in San Francisco.

Walker, L. (1994). *Abused women and survivor therapy: A practical guide for the psychotherapist.* Washington, DC: American Psychological Association.

Waltz, J., Babcock, J. C., Jacobson, N. S., & Gottman, J. M. (2000). Testing a typology of batterers. *Journal of Consulting and Clinical Psychology, 68,* 658-669.

Western Psychological Services. (2003a). *PTSD Screening and Diagnostic Scale (PSDS)* [formerly *Distressing Event Questionnaire (DEQ)*]. Beverly Hills, CA: Author.

Western Psychological Services. (2003b). *The Trauma-Related Guilt Inventory (TRGI).* Beverly Hills, CA: Author.

Western Psychological Services. (2003c). *The Traumatic Life Events Questionnaire (TLEQ).* Beverly Hills, CA: Author.

Williams, L. M. (1994). Recall of childhood trauma: A prospective study of women's memories of childhood sexual abuse. *Journal of Consulting and Clinical Psychology, 62,* 1167-1176.

Index

Edward S. Kubany, Ph.D., was employed for fourteen years as a research clinical psychologist with the Department of Veterans Affairs, National Center for PTSD, in Honolulu, Hawaii. Since 1990, he has specialized in the assessment and treatment of PTSD in his research and clinical practice. Kubany has more than twenty-five peer-reviewed publications, was principle investigator or co-principal investigator on four federal grants, and is first author of a self-help book for battered women, *Healing the Trauma of Domestic Violence.*

Tyler C. Ralston, Psy.D., served a post-doctoral fellowship at the Department of Veterans Affairs National Center for PTSD in Honolulu, Hawaii. In his clinical practice, he specializes in the treatment of PTSD and trauma-related guilt, working with formerly battered women, combat veterans, and other trauma survivors.

For more information, please visit www.treatingptsd.com.

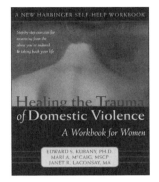
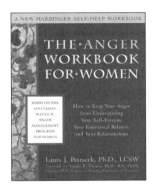